The Pez

The Manic Life of the Ultimate Promoter

Jennifer Wells

Macfarlane Walter & Ross
Toronto

Macfarlane Walter & Ross
37A Hazelton Avenue
Toronto, Canada
M5R 2E3

Canadian Cataloguing in Publication Data

Wells, Jennifer, 1955-
    The Pez: the manic life of the ultimate promoter

ISBN 0-921912-20-X

1. Pezim, Murray.   2. Vancouver Stock Exchange – Biography.   3. Promoters – British Columbia – Vancouver – Biography.   I. Title.

HX112.5.P49W45 1991   338'.04'092   C91-094617-5

Printed and bound in the United States of America

For Peter

Contents

CHAPTER 1

The Heat

M urray Pezim is floating in his swimming pool. It is mid-March, 1990, in Paradise Valley, Arizona. The temperature on this afternoon is slightly above eighty-five degrees. The pool temperature is a thick eighty-seven, which is just the way Pezim likes it. Muzak pipes through loudspeakers, floats out beyond the poolside portico, over the Pisces fountain and the Venus at the Bath statue, and fades into the Camelback mountain range beyond. The house is white, the sky is blue, the flowers are pink, and the day is hot.

Pezim's sixty-eight-year-old tanned body hangs heavily, belly down, on a plastic sunning raft. He is five foot ten and a half inches tall, perhaps 210 pounds, and has the flaccid breasts that older overweight men often have. He has a full head of hair, curly and short, black but greying. His eyes are brown, with spotted brown bags beneath them. Sun-induced moles are sprinkled across his back. His nose is comically large, slathered carelessly with moguls of sun lotion. Bubbles of air balloon his blue-and-pink checked bathing trunks up around his behind. Unbidden, Pezim lifts his head, squints into the sun, and says in the slightly lisping

1

way that he has, "Is this going to be an upbeat book or are you going to beat the crap out of me?"

I hadn't a clue. I simply wanted to spend some straight time with the guy. I wanted to get a fix on the private Pezim, to understand what kind of cosmic collision could produce a man so indiscriminate in his personal and public lives – a simple stock promoter who claims credit for finding the multibillion-dollar Hemlo gold field, a man with a knack for making and losing millions with viral speed, whose associates have included the football-player-cum-boxing-hopeful Mark Gastineau, the comedian Red Buttons, the securities dealmaker Peter Brown, a string of blonde babes, and every two-bit promoter who has worked the Vancouver Stock Exchange in the past two decades. What was this man made of? That was one of my first questions. When would he self-destruct? That would come later.

In the spring of 1990, Pezim was in the money. He had millions, at least on paper, and the kind of power that comes with that kind of money – which is to say, the fleeting kind. He was touting a gold play in northern British Columbia called Eskay Creek. In fact, Pezim had fifty penny-stock mining companies around Eskay Creek proper, what's known in the mining game as an area play. The previous summer, the Vancouver Stock Exchange had repeatedly hit record volumes because of Pezim's stable of companies. In one week alone $250 million worth of shares had been bought and sold. When the numbers were tallied at the end of 1989, the three most actively traded companies were Pezim's.

He should have been over the moon. The summer of 1990 was expected to be even more prosperous than the summer of 1989. There would be new stock issues. There would be the merciless flogging of the Eskay-play shares already listed on the exchange. There would be the non-stop cacophony of broker-barkers touting the new Pezim creations to their clients. Pezim

2

repeatedly exclaimed that Eskay was going to be bigger than! better than! richer than! Hemlo. It seemed so beautifully hyperbolic, so perfectly Pezim. Hemlo, in the northern Ontario bush, had turned into a multimillion-ounce gold property after its discovery in the summer of 1980. Could Eskay really top that?

Pezim said it could, but his promotional energies were waning. He was feeling persecuted. British Columbia's superintendent of brokers, the warden who watches over stock-market practices, was investigating possible infractions in the placement and pricing of shares and options in Calpine Resources and Prime Resources. Calpine had a fifty-percent interest in Eskay Creek itself and was, in turn, controlled by Prime, the holding company for Pezim's various mining interests. Prime itself, of which Pezim was chairman, was being probed for failing to report a twenty-three-day lapse in a private placement of Prime shares.

But even before this, things had started to sour. The previous October, the *Vancouver Sun* had revealed that Pezim had dumped $9 million worth of stock at the very same time he was stumping the shares all over Howe Street, which has always been synonymous with the Vancouver Stock Exchange even though the exchange moved from its headquarters on the street years ago. While Pezim's habit of selling while urging everyone else to buy has long been his practice, he didn't much like the way it looked in print. Pezim adores press coverage, as long as it is loving. He complained that nobody had bothered reporting the subsequent $4-million loss he suffered when his own brokers started making margin calls – that is, making him ante up the money he owed for Prime Resources stock. The *Sun* had also revealed that Pezim had been trading from a control position in a little company called Western Goldfields without meeting the proper disclosure requirements. By the spring of 1990, journalists were all over Pezim like ants on a stick of honey.

3

Pezim wanted the bad news to disappear. What was particularly worrisome was that he didn't know whether the SOB, as the superintendent of brokers is called in the Vancouver stock-market universe, had the gumption to lay charges. Nor could his lawyers determine whether the SOB had enough evidence to lay charges. The greatest unknown was the SOB himself, a thirty-seven-year-old one-time prosecuting attorney named Wade Nesmith who had risen to the job just five months earlier. Nesmith had the power to blow Murray Pezim's summer apart.

Pezim's personal life, too, was a mess. His wedding to twenty-seven-year-old Tammy Patrick, usually referred to in the press as "reformed cocaine addict Tammy Patrick," had fallen through. The Murray-Tammy show, of course, made good ink for print journalists and marvellous sound bites for television crews. In Vancouver, the locals' fascination with Pezim's love life far exceeds their interest in his business pursuits.

The public harassment and the private disappointment had pulled Pezim into a state of depression, which in turn propelled him to Phoenix. Every now and then he'd pop up to Vancouver, only to have the skies open and dump an uncharacteristic amount of snow. Pezim abhors the cold and snow – the entire winter season north of the thirty-third parallel. Nor did the weather help a persistent phlegmy chest cold that would throw him into uncontrollable coughing spasms. No sooner would Pezim land in Vancouver than he'd get on a plane and head right back down south. The sun. The pool. The heat.

Phoenix was meant to be an escape.

It is six a.m. on a Friday morning. The bungalow in Paradise Valley, a wealthy suburb of Phoenix, is quiet. Pezim rises from his king-size bed in the sparsely furnished master bedroom and moves to his enormous bathroom, spacious enough for an intimate cocktail gathering.

The tub, a twofer, sits under a yellow and green stained-glass skydome. Gold faucets, gold door handles, marble floors, marble sinks. He bathes. He shaves. He slides his feet into black patent-leather slippers with red corduroy tops. He dresses in his weekday "Valley of the Sun" attire: bathing suit and striped velours robe.

He slaps along the marble corridor, past the unlived-in living room, past the unused formal dining room, past the guest bathroom and on past the two guest bedrooms. One of the guest bedrooms is empty, save for a few Tammy togs in the closet. The other is occupied by Pezim's assistant, Harvey Gould, and his wife Dotty, who have already risen. Pezim always needs someone to do for him. Which is why Harvey and Dotty, lovely, gentle people, are here at Pezim's home, watching out for his health, running errands, waiting on him.

Pezim arrives in his enormous kitchen, a favourite spot. He gets the television going, always the Cable News Network, and half listens. The kitchen is decorated in soft pinks and greens. There are porcelain bunnies and a porcelain piggy on the breakfast table. A big porcelain bunny is wearing a bonnet with ribbons running through it. Whoever is responsible for the porcelain bunnies probably was not responsible for the guest bathroom, which is wallpapered in a black fabric with a moiré finish and has black lacquer cupboards and black handsoap by the basin. In the cupboard beneath the sink are a couple of mask-like half faces, made of leather. They used to hang here on the black wallpaper. Someone has removed them.

The entire house is decorated in the Mixed Wives Period. Marilyn, Pezim's second spouse, loves black and white. Not a little black and white. Black-and-white everything. When she lived in this house there wasn't anything anywhere that wasn't one colour or the other or a combination of the two. Marilyn drove a black Rolls-Royce, a gift to Murray from a stock buddy. She later replaced it with a white Corniche. Marilyn has since gone on to create another B&W palace. When Pezim's third wife, Susan, took over domestic affairs, she started replacing B&W with P&G. She was well on her way to eradicating B&W when the marriage ended.

There is little physical evidence of Tammy, the almost-fourth wife, though on a coffee table is a large tome entitled *The World Atlas of Archeology*. It is inscribed, "To Tammy, with love, Helen and Norman." Norman is Murray's brother. Helen is his wife.

Coffee in hand, Pezim slaps through the family room – past the wet bar, the leisure furniture, the entertainment centre, the huge built-in aquarium. His office is off the far end of this room. Just before he enters, he brushes past a wall with built-in bookcases, which are littered with photographs. Most are of Pezim with somebody famous. Henny Youngman. Gordie Howe. Foster Hewitt. Rocket Richard. There is a montage of an attractive young woman in her late twenties wearing a "The Pez says, go gold go" T-shirt. She looks lively and fun. She has written in one corner, "For Dad. With Love, Cheryl. XOX." Cheryl, a teacher and writer with a master's degree from Columbia University, is Pezim's eldest child, the first of three he had by Bernice, his first wife. There is also a university graduation picture of his son Michael, a surgeon at Vancouver General Hospital, and one of Pezim with his youngest child, Nanci, a graphic artist. These are his only children. The relationship between Pezim and each of his offspring has often been strained, sometimes nonexistent. There is also an empty heart-shaped porcelain frame, white with pink roses with green leaves, smashed and glued back together.

Pezim settles into a brown recliner in his office and waits for the Vancouver Stock Exchange to open at 6:30 a.m., 7:30 Arizona time. The patio doors, which open out to the pool, are behind him. On most days, Pezim spends seven hours in front of his computer-trading

6

monitor. He scrutinizes the size of the bids, the size of the offerings. He'll phone one broker or another and get the size all the way up and all the way down. He'll try to find the strength on the bid and the strength on the offer. Pezim loves trading. He trades stocks every single day that the market is open. When trading is slow he heads for the pool, bake and dip, bake and dip.

This morning the air is cool and Pezim has a hacking cough, so he keeps his robe wrapped tightly about him. He sips his coffee. His reading glasses are propped on his forehead. The television is on. Pezim wants to hear a weather report. He hopes it will be hot-hot today. He feels like a sick old man, which is pretty much the way he looks. He is trying to quit smoking. He says he hasn't had a cigarette in forty-eight hours. Dotty has placed gum and Lifesavers throughout the house. Pezim starts popping candy, which doesn't seem his style. Pezim's paternal grandfather smoked four packs of Lucky Strike a day, and he lived to ninety-six. Pezim would like to do the same.

Leaning back in his chair, the early-morning sun flooding through, Pezim spends a megasecond being reflective. He says he doesn't mind breaking his life open for a reporter. The rules of our relationship are simple. I can write anything I want provided I write the truth. Oh, and the women. I have to understand that he loves women, that he loves having them around.

Pezim's appearance, his slow, easy manner, lend a sense of slumber to the day. This is misleading. When the market opens, the fissures appear in minutes. He starts to snap at Harvey, whose large, affable, sunburnt face bobs above a desk facing Pezim's, to get him this guy, that guy, another guy on the phone. As if Pezim didn't have enough to worry about, what with the SOB and the media and his love life. Watching the early trades, he starts to suspect that maybe, just maybe, he's got a corporate battle on his hands.

The Vancouver mega-entrepreneur Jimmy Pattison, used-car

king of Canada and head of a private, multi-billion-dollar conglomerate, is accumulating shares in Calpine and Prime. Pattison has not reached the point in his buying – a ten-percent position, according to British Columbia's securities law – at which he must disclose his share position. Pezim knows that Pattison is acquiring shares, because Pezim has the right connections. Sometimes the connections trade information that, strictly speaking, they shouldn't.

In itself, having Pattison on the buy side is not bad news. He has a reputation for being a shrewd investor. Jimmy getting in on a stock lends a Jimmy sort of credibility to the enterprise. But Pezim doesn't like his timing.

Calpine and Prime are set to merge on April 2. When that happens, Corona Corp. of Toronto, controlled by the financier Ned Goodman, will have twenty-three percent of the stock. Ever since Hemlo, there have been short corporate links between Goodman and Pezim. Corona at one time was Pezim's company, and it had the first pieces of Hemlo. Then Goodman bought him out. The two have retained some semblance of a business-like relationship – though it is a relationship that often erupts in acrimony, public fights, and various attempts on the part of one to yank the chain of the other.

In 1987 Goodman, Pezim, and a couple of other associates created Prime Capital, the predecessor company to Prime Resources. The idea was to give Pezim a publicly traded Vancouver vehicle into which he could place the junior mining prospects he managed to snare. The dream was to find another Hemlo. In the penny-mining business, Pezim has incomparable contacts. Little people bring their little deals to him, and on occasion a little deal becomes a big deal. Corona, with control of Prime, could scoop up the most appealing assets and leave Pezim to continue his search for the next gold lode. Throughout this exercise, Pezim and Goodman have been keeping their distance. However, everyone knew that, if Prime came up with something really worthwhile, Pezim and Goodman would start fighting again.

Pezim needs to maintain his share strength so that he can hold his own against Goodman. When he is forced to walk away from a mining company under the Prime umbrella – which is inevitable with Goodman, who has more stock and plays in more powerful company – he wants to walk away wealthy. In the case of Calpine and Prime, Pezim and his longtime associate, Art Clemiss, will have fourteen percent of the merged company. When they throw in the interests of other companies in their control they say they will have twenty-one percent compared with Goodman's twenty-three percent. Pattison will have fifteen percent. Pattison is looking for profit – not ownership, not control. He will tender his stake to the highest bidder. All of this is virtually certain in mid-March.

Pezim knows that within a matter of weeks he will be out of Calpine and Prime. He needs to leave rich. He needs $2 million just to pay his tax bill. So when the stocks start to show considerable trading volume he starts to worry. Pezim doesn't want anyone to muck up the plan.

"Everyone's playing cute," he says of his supposed allies. "Everyone says, 'I'm going to stay out of the market and wait till it settles down.' Then they sneak around the corner and start buying it. Understand how big this ball game is. It may sound small. I'm here in my bathing suit and my robe. This is a big ball game. This prize is several billion dollars."

What Pezim can't figure is why L.O.M. Western Securities, the West Coast brokerage run by Peter Brown, a man whom Pezim considers a friend, is trading the stock in a big way. "They're bidding for it," he says. "Then they jump up as soon as some gets offered, then they pull it out of the way, then offer it to make it look weak."

Pezim wants to talk to Brown. Pezim wants to talk to Ned

Goodman. He wants to hear directly what everyone's playing at. Why is L.O.M. so busy? Why is Goodman doing nothing? No-one returns his calls. He heads to the pool for a quick fry on the chaise.

Marilyn Murray, who was once Marilyn Pezim and now uses her maiden name, appears from the house. She walks along the stone path beside the pool, past the fountain and the hot tub and the swimming pool. She is a beautiful woman of about fifty, wearing black pants, a black-and-white striped blouse, black shoes with black-and-white checked bows on the toes. Her jewellery is silver, her nails are red. Tucked under her arm is a blackish-grey poodle puppy, twelve weeks old, that has black-and-white bows in its hair. Marilyn's hair, black and bluntly cut, falls across one side of her face to just above her shoulders.

She lives not far from here, and has been divorced from Pezim for the better part of a decade. Pezim says he's friends with all his wives. I wonder if this has something to do with money. Susan, wife number three, has just phoned from Hawaii. Pezim has yet to pay Susan the $1 million cash that she is owed as part of her $3-million prenuptial agreement. Pezim and Susan were man and wife for six months. No sooner does Marilyn appear than so does Tammy Patrick, who parks her little red Corvette behind the Pezim house.

Pezim supports Tammy, pays Susan $12,000 a month, and pays his first wife, Bernice, $15,000 a month. He figures these three women cost him $400,000 per annum. Figures he's got room for a couple more. Marilyn is the only one who got a flat settlement: $1 million.

Tammy is fair-skinned, with blonde hair, an enormous toothy smile, and a smoky voice. She, too, is beautiful, but then, she is just twenty-seven years of age. She wears a massive emerald and diamond ring, which, given her T-shirt, blue jeans and bare feet, creates a rather charming effect. Tammy sits beside Marilyn.

They chat about Marilyn's recently departed Yorkshire terrier. Tammy asks if the replacement puppy is female. What a question.

"Yes, of course. I wouldn't have boys," says Marilyn. "Because they have drooling doofers."

"Noooo shit," replies Tammy, who has a West Highland terrier and a Shih Tzu. They are male and their doofers, one supposes, do drool. A quick look at Pezim's carpets will confirm this, says Marilyn, who picked out the large black and white harlequin rug, now stained, in the family room.

Tammy is on her way to a spiritual retreat high in the Mexican mountains with an equally blonde chum named Pearl Whalley. Tammy believes in the power of crystals. Pearl, who used to be Susan's best pal, is now Tammy's best pal. In fact, she helped line up Tammy and Murray because she thought Susan had turned into a shrew.

Meanwhile, Marilyn wants lunch. That's why Pezim invited her here. "Where's this wonderful lunch I came for?" she asks.

"You'll have to make it," says Pezim, making some vague reference to meatballs.

Marilyn leaves shortly thereafter, announcing that she's going to take her puppy home to its paper to pee as girl puppies do. Tammy heads for Mexico with Pearl. Pezim fingers a crystal on his desk. "Tammy goes in for all that crap with the Indians. They go up into the mountains at the weirdest time of night."

I forget to ask this curious man for his definition of weird.

Pezim never leaves business behind. It doesn't matter what he's talking about. It doesn't matter what he's doing. He's always thinking about the market. Despite Marilyn's chatter and Tammy's excursion, Pezim is preoccupied by Calpine and Prime.

As he starts to shovel into a large bowl of tomato-and-egg salad, he is joined by Art Clemiss and Clemiss's son-in-law, Mike

11

Reynolds, a broker with L.O.M. Western. They are in Phoenix for two reasons. One is to play a little golf at Tatum Ranch. (Reynolds says he ran into a rattlesnake on the eighteenth hole during his last visit.) Clemiss has a house in Phoenix. Has had for years, ever since his buddy Pezim bought one there.

The second reason for the visit is to check up on Pezim. Clemiss has been a companion and associate for twenty-five years, and the closest thing to an alter ego that Murray Pezim has. Clemiss listens to his troubles, be they real or imagined. Clemiss has also made millions out of Pezim's deals. He sells out smart. He doesn't go bust when Pezim's deals do, or, for that matter, when Pezim himself does. Described by the press as shrewd and reclusive, he seems soft-spoken and friendly. His thin, sandy-brown hair comes to a soft partial curl on the forehead of his cherubic face, heightening his Hardy Boy appearance. Clemiss spent his early years in the northern Ontario mining town of Timmins, then moved to Toronto during his teens. Pezim and Clemiss came together in Vancouver in the sixties when they were both working as brokers. A family man with two grown children, Clemiss seems eons removed from Pezim's flashy, flaky, often vulgar lifestyle. Though unpretentious, he wears a starburst diamond ring, which seems not in keeping with the rest of his appearance.

Pezim and Clemiss try to get a fix on Ned Goodman. Goodman is staying out of the market. He likes to buy his stock wholesale; they figure this is the reason he is not buying shares to defend against Pattison.

"He's taking a terrible gamble," says Pezim.

"Best thing that could happen to you and me," says Clemiss. "Until this came along he was in the driver's seat. He isn't any more."

Clemiss is calm, distanced, in control. Sitting in a tapestry chair, he places his fingers together at the tips, rolling them forward and back. He steps out to the patio and clips his nails. He appears unflappable.

Pezim, however, is starting to teeter. There's heavy buying in Calpine. "There should be all kinds of screaming and yelling going on. My opponent right now has gathered in 120 or 150,000 more shares and I'm sitting losing strength every day."

He is now desperate to talk to Goodman. Out of the blue, he hands me a business card given to him by the comedian Henny Youngman that says Coat of Arms. It has a picture of an overcoat with lots of arms. "I don't know what the hell is going on," he says.

I don't either, and the Youngman thing isn't funny.

Pezim explains why he's worried: "If what we say we expect is going to be the biggest, the richest and everything, one would think that if you expect that and you're telling the public that, you should own fifty-one percent. Right?"

He returns to his screen and sees that Peter Brown's L.O.M. Western has crossed 142,000 shares of Prime – that is, the firm is acting as broker for both the seller and the buyer. Pezim freaks. Usually, he knows where his stocks are and how much is available and who's in the market to buy and who's in the market to sell.

He phones John Ivany, the president of Prime, who is in his Vancouver office. "John, you know what I'm going to do, starting tomorrow? There's going to be a third competitor in the ring. I'm going to start a ball game starting tomorrow. . . .The problem is, I'm getting weaker every minute, OK? I'm fighting for myself. I've got a lot of money in this. I'm fighting for Art. He's got a lot of money in this. You know who's buying the stock. He's only inter-ested in the dollars. That's short-term dollars. He couldn't give a shit whether I'm Irish or Jewish or whatever. Give me the dough."

He hangs up. Pezim has been talking about Jimmy Pattison.

"Art, I gotta talk to you," says Pezim, who's getting increasingly balled up. The two head toward the kitchen. "I think

13

I control something," he says, plaintively. "I don't control nothing. I don't trust anybody."

Within minutes he's back in his recliner, getting back to the phones. "I got a queasy stomach. I know why I got one. This bothers the shit out of me, Art."

Peter Brown returns his call.

"Hi Pete, I'm sick. I'm bothered. . . . .Peter, the object of the exercise – I'm over twenty-one and I've got to protect myself. I've got to go buying in the market. I've got somebody who's going to come through for serious buying. That's not going to hurt you. That's the last thing I'd want. . . . .I'm worried that he'll sell to Ned. Peter, I can't gamble. . . . .I've been out of your way all the way through. I've known Jimmy for twenty-five years. He's a nice guy, he's my friend and everything. But also he's a businessman."

It is now clear that Pezim is the victim of a squeeze play. He needs partners, friends, and allies. They are not there for him. There are no serious pro-Pezim buyers. If Pattison is successful in building a substantial share position, the strength of Pezim's own stock holdings will diminish. If Pattison aligns with Goodman, Pezim is dust. It is not at all clear that even Clemiss would stick with him. Clemiss has dumped Pezim in the past.

"I wake up in the morning and I say I don't trust anybody," Pezim continues. "Peter, I can't. I can't leave myself out on the hook and suddenly become a minority shareholder and everything gone."

He gets off the phone. "He says, 'I can't swear 100 percent that Ned and Jimmy might not get together,'" Pezim tells Clemiss. "Jimmy's for money. You can't blame the guy. I tell you, I don't like it. Ah, fuck it, I don't like it, Art. I'm sick." Pezim has streaks of sun cream running across his forehead.

Clemiss attempts to introduce a note of calm. "It's a buck," he says simply. "It's a business deal."

"He has another 300 or 400 Calpine to buy," says Pezim of L.O.M.'s activities on Pattison's behalf. He means 300,000 or 400,000 shares. "Figures he'll be finished by Tuesday. He'd like me to wait until that's done. Then he's going into Prime."

Pezim has been told to stay clear. Pezim is worried that if he does so, he will be left powerless. He can't find Goodman. He's in a sweat.

He gets Harvey to phone one contact, then another. "I need you to buy a couple hundred Calpine. There's a buyer on the scene. What I'm concerned about is if Ned and this buyer on the scene get together and say 'Adios, amigo.' I think you could look to the end of July certainly getting a $15 equivalent on your stock." That would represent a doubling of the stock price. "Seriously, can you give it thought and help me for 50,000 or 100,000? I need help. Now."

It's too late. The market closes. Pezim's mood, which has swung from impassive to near hysteria, collapses. The monitors switch off and so too does Pezim. You can see it in his eyes. The stock ticker is his soul. The animation drains from his face. He looks dead.

Moments later, he is on the phone talking to Nell Dragovan, the promoter who was behind the early financing of Hemlo. Dragovan still keeps her offices at Prime headquarters in Vancouver. She is married to Chet Idziszek, Prime's chief geologist.

"The problem is this," explains Pezim to Dragovan very matter-of-factly and without any of the earlier upset. "Jimmy Pattison's going to own fifteen percent of the company by Tuesday. Did you know that? Well, you might as well know it. If he gets together with Ned, who's got twenty-three percent, then suddenly they get together and good-bye us. Out of a job. We're out of everything. Jimmy would have to declare it once the merger takes place. He's got to buy another 400 Calpine, another million out of Prime."

15

In a later meeting, we argue about the conversations I have been privy to. He wants to vet what I write. I refuse. He's worried about the way it will look. We agree that I will make it very clear that Pezim has had no conversations with the purchaser, that is, Jimmy Pattison. I believe this to be true. If I screw up Pezim says he'll tell the world that we slept together.

My understanding of the day's events is this: that Peter Brown's objective is to round up shares for Pattison with only the slightest of share-price fluctuations; that Brown wants Pezim to chill out; that Pezim has been shut out. Peter Brown in this instance does a beautiful job: Pezim tells me later that Brown gets Pattison his shares within a half point. What is masterly is the timing of Pattison's purchase.

Heading into the weekend, Pezim knows that the future looks less than promising. In the meantime, there are two long days to get through before the market reopens. Clemiss and Reynolds have left. The phones are silent.

Half an hour later, at three p.m., Ernie Gastineau appears at poolside. He is the father of Mark Gastineau, the one-time football star, who is on the roster at the moment for the B.C. Lions, which Pezim, inexplicably, owns. Mark Gastineau's chief claim to fame is that he was once married to Brigitte Neilsen, ex-wife of Sylvester Stallone and pseudo-actress.

Ernie finds it difficult to explain his role in the Pezim orbit. He makes oblique references to putting Pezim together with other dealmakers and taking a piece of the action for himself, which sounds very Wall Street. In more practical terms, what he does to put bread on the table is sell telephone service in the Phoenix area for American Telephone & Telegraph.

Ernie met Pezim by chance one day at the bar of the local Hyatt Regency. Pezim was dripping with blondes. Ernie was intrigued. Like legions of others, he started to leech off the Pezim excitement. On this afternoon, he is visiting Pezim to discuss an oil-and-gas deal of unspecified size and nature, but finds time to give me a capsule of his personal philosophy:

"Life is a funny thing, innit? You know what? Most people wait for life to come along. Listen, it's here. You know I've believed this all my life and I keep preaching to myself every day because, you know what, the more you practise what you preach the more you believe yourself. I think I'm the happiest and luckiest guy on the face of the earth. Happier than Murray. If you laid $100 million right there on that table and said, hey, take his place, I wouldn't do it. What's headaches to one, another person thrives on. His life is no more important to me than mine is to him. My deals are big too. The old boy pumping gas around here, his deals are big. Too many people believe in the size of the things as being important. Hey, at one time Murray was a butcher. I was a shoeshiner. God isn't going to love us for how much stock we sell or how many shoes we shine."

Gastineau stands stock still. Maybe he's stopping for breath. In bas-relief against the late afternoon sun, his fifty-three-year-old muscles bulging, his blonde hair nestling at his shoulders, in his blue jeans and pink-and-white striped T-shirt shrink-wrapped over his torso, Gastineau and the Arizona backdrop look like a colour-corrected picture postcard.

But Gastineau is dead wrong about one thing. How much stock Murray Pezim buys or sells is precisely the point.

Later on, Pezim steps into his white Mercedes 420, punches a Sinatra tape into the deck, and cruises along streets with names like Gold Dust Avenue. He croons:

> Through the good or lean years
> And for all the in-between years,

17

Come what may.
Who knows where the road will lead us,
Only a fool would say.
But if you let me love you,
For sure I'm going to love you,
All the way.

Pezim has been more or less hiding out in Arizona for six months now. When the first of the stock-trading revelations broke in October, he took it hard. He says he couldn't work. He says he couldn't stand having his credibility questioned.

I ask him why he seems so down.

"Because the public perception of me is that I'm a crook."

He talks of how angry and betrayed he has felt. All those nasty banner headlines in the news. The press might as well be making allegations of rape, he says. The point is that once people have it in their heads that someone's guilty of stock manipulation, even exoneration won't make them change their minds, he says.

"I still think I'm the greatest thing that's happened to the Vancouver Stock Exchange. Who else has done for the mining industry what I've done?"

On Saturday morning, Pezim and Harvey go grocery shopping, looking like two lonely old men. Pezim loves grocery shopping. There's a second reason for the trip. Pezim, who worries incessantly about his health, was panicked by the persistence of his chest cold. So they stopped off at the hospital, where he had a chest X-ray.

When he returns, he has a look of invincibility. He proclaims that his lungs are free of cancer – which for Pezim is like getting medical approval to start smoking again. Pezim wears the orange hospital-admission bracelet for the rest of the day.

"My neurologist told me you can make up your mind. You can smoke or you can fuck. He meant it. He wasn't trying to be a wise guy."

Pezim mentions a recent piece in *Cosmopolitan* magazine about the delights of sex with older men – that is, one presumes, the virtues of younger women having sex with older men. He is minutes away from a Benson & Hedges.

He removes his sweatshirt and stands naked from the waist up in powder-blue leisure slacks. He grabs a carving knife and starts shelling a piece of beef, removing the bone the way he was taught to do fifty years ago in Toronto. He is happy puttering in the kitchen. He waves the knife in the air. If the press doesn't come around, he says, meaning if they don't start to play nice, he will . . .

And here he slashes the air once,

"Eh!"

Twice,

"Eh!"

"Ting. No balls."

Pezim comes up with a title for a book about his life. *Big Balls.*

June is beautiful. Reddish hair. Helluva figure, particularly for someone in her mid-forties with a teen-aged son. It is not uncommon for Pezim to import women for companionship. On this Saturday afternoon, his guest is June, who, as it happens, is a friend of Dotty's and who has flown in from Los Angeles. Dotty would like to see Pezim set himself up with someone nice. Perhaps Dotty disapproves of the calibre of some of Pezim's earlier associations.

It's hot-hot, probably ninety, and June arrives in a pair of tight-fitting black jeans, which she soon discards in favour of a fluorescent-lime bathing suit. As she glides toward the pool, a little sun visor on her head, one can't help but notice that she

19

overcorrects her posture, the way runway models do, so that her hips thrust forward and her shoulders thrust back. Professional models who earn their keep by staying thin monitor their thinness by whether they retain the little hollow right in the buttock. June has that. June has a languid walk. She likes it when people watch her.

June sells goo for your face. Good goo, she says, for an outfit in Los Angeles called Georgette Klinger, with offices on Rodeo Drive. She is smart-talking and Grace Kelly cool and I wonder if she has had her nose done. June says that Pezim's place reminds her of Rancho Mirage, a top-end California spa.

Later, she slips into a black cocktail dress for dinner. Pezim appears in pastel slacks and a pastel sweater. He had been wondering aloud the night before – sipping on an orange soda, which he drinks a lot of, eating jelly doughnuts and macaroons – whether he would sleep with June. He hadn't yet met the woman. Seeing the two of them together, the idea seems preposterous. June looks like pasta primavera; Pezim like corned-beef brisket.

June doesn't know Pezim or understand what he does for a living. At one point, she pontificates on the subject of gold-mining, on how she always thought the business involved sending a guy out into the bush with a pick and an axe. Which is true. It is just not Pezim's part of the business. It is second nature for people, especially unsuccessful people, to ask successful people what they do and how they do it.

After dinner, Pezim and June and Dotty and Harvey curl up in front of the television and watch a taped documentary on the discovery of Hemlo. There's Pezim talking about $12.5 billion worth of gold in the ground. There's Peter Brown talking about how Pezim would rather write a bad deal than no deal. Pezim points to one man on the screen and comments that the fellow was subsequently brought up on charges of child molestation. Pezim has seen this film a million times before. He is bored. It is yesterday's story. For Murray Pezim, whatever happened yesterday is of no interest.

Lying in his chaise beside the pool on Sunday afternoon, Pezim is trying to dredge up some family history from his foggy memory. The doorbell rings. Enter Elliott Middleton, who has arrived at the Pezim house to sell magazine subscriptions. Elliott has even more of a central-casting aura about him than did Ernie Gastineau.

Pezim is often a nice guy. He's nice to Elliott. He says he'll take subscriptions to *Esquire*, *Fortune*, and *U.S. News & World Report*. Elliott asks Murray if it would be all right if he sits down.

"You don't mind if I have a squat, do you?"

He is tall, thin, black, and overwhelmingly friendly. He will be president one day, if self-motivation is the key.

"When you first started out, you might have had rough times," says Elliott to Pezim. "What kept you motivated?"

"Never quit," says Pezim, which is what he always says.

"Never quit, huh? Is that right? 'Cause like, huh, Whitney, he told me, next door, he said, Stretch – that's my nickname, 'cause I got long arms – he said the elevator to success is broken, so you more or less gotta climb those stairs one step at a time. What kind of advice could you give me as far as pulling myself up?"

"Just don't quit," says Pezim. He lights up a Benson & Hedges.

Elliott, who's in junior college and was signed with Texas A&M University until he broke his kneecap and ruined his basketball career, thereby breaking his particular elevator to success, is probably looking for more helpful advice. Selling magazines is a job with a short ladder. "But when you're from out of state wanting to go somewhere, oatmeal is better than no meal."

After he gets Pezim's cheque, he makes a verbal salute. "Whenever I get a chance to work here again I won't knock on your door to sell you no magazines. I'll come over for some dinner and pick your brain. You motivate me. If you ever get a chance to come to Charleston, South Carolina, come by and see the Middleton family. But you gotta bring an empty stomach because Mom will fill you up for sure."

Pezim has seemed an empty soul since the Friday market close. Even with June, and Elliott, and Ernie, and the wealth to do what he wants, go where he wants, Pezim without trading activity seems dead all over. He seems depressed, lethargic.

I ask him where he keeps his medication. We walk along the marble hallway to his bedroom, big and lonely, through to the bathroom. He picks up his bottle of lithium carbonate. Pezim is supposed to take one capsule twice a day. He is manic depressive. Has been diagnosed as such for years.

There's no telling where indifference ends and sadness begins and where sadness ends and depression begins. But it is clear to me that something is wrong with Murray.

Pezim stayed in Phoenix for another two weeks, then one day drove to Tombstone with Pearl Whalley and her husband-to-be, a tattooed ex-biker named Mickey, and Pearl's teen-aged daughter, Jodi. They went to the Chiricahua Mountains, where Geronimo made his last stand, then checked into the Gadson Hotel in Douglas, Arizona. Murray once ran a lime plant there, which led to all sorts of trouble.

During dinner Pezim phoned the home of John Ivany, the come-from-Noranda lawyer who is president of Prime Resources. Tina Ivany, John's wife, answered the phone. She expressed surprise that Pezim hadn't heard the news: the securities regulators had spoken. Pezim, Ivany, and their associate Larry Page had been charged with insider trading.

CHAPTER 2

Gethsemane

A t 4:15 a.m., Murray Pezim slides naked out of bed, wraps himself in a full-length robe, and pads barefoot around the circular upstairs hallway in his $8-million Vancouver house. He stops at the bedroom door of Pearl Whalley, who is asleep beside her boyfriend Mickey. Pearl's job at this hour is not to remain beside the beautifully built man who will soon be her second husband, but to minister to Pezim, whose habit it has always been to rise early. She throws on whatever oversized T-shirt lies handy and sets about making Pezim's instant coffee, choosing his clothing for the day, and, most important, being a sounding board for whatever agony Murray Pezim is going through at that moment. She moves quietly about the house so as not to disturb Mickey, her daughter Jodi, and her two Shih Tzus, whom she affectionately calls her "zimbaloids."

Pearl looks less than stunning at this hour. Her blonde-enhanced hair is dishevelled, her face is creased, her eyes puffy. She seems older than her thirty years. She has the tough look of someone who hasn't had it easy, which in Pearl's case means a first husband who piddled away the couple's financial security on hard drugs and fast times. Few of the legion of women who have trooped into and out of Pezim's world have had it easy. Pezim picks these broken women especially. He says he likes to try to fix them, make them better.

Though Pezim hasn't slept, he looks sharp. He has been on his bedside phone to stockbrokers since 2:30, calling Europe, calling Toronto, touting a drill hole in the Eskay Creek gold field. Pezim always figures that when he can't sleep, which is often, no-one else should either. Now that Pearl's up he can prattle on about how he would have liked to have been a professional singer. People have told him he's pretty good on the mike, "You know, like Frank Sinatra."

It is April 19, 1990, nearly three weeks since Pezim returned from Phoenix. At ten a.m., he is scheduled to meet with the directors of Prime Resources, of which he is chairman. His preoccupation since his return has been the insider-trading allegations. The superintendent of brokers has charged Pezim, Larry Page, and John Ivany, all Prime directors, with fiddling the price of some stock options when they knew, or ought to have known, about positive drill results at Eskay.

The charges refer back to midsummer 1989, when Pezim et al. received spectacular geological information on "Hole 109." In the mining business, exploration projects are made up of drilling, and drilling, and drilling again. The drill core is tested for gold content, or copper, or zinc, or whatever. It is these test results, called assays, that force the cancellation or encourage the continuation of an exploration effort. Sometimes hanging in until Hole 40 or Hole 50 pays off.

Pezim drilled Hemlo like Swiss cheese in the early Eighties. He had to. It had what geologists call a die-base dyke running though it, a fracture that cut the run of the gold. Proving the run

(the continuity of the ore body) beyond the fracture was imperative in establishing the viability of the Hemlo ore body. Pezim hung
in at Hemlo until Hole 76, which gave the first clear sign of the
gold bonanza. Hundreds of subsequent holes had to be drilled to
delineate the size − and wealth − of the find. Hemlo made Canadian
mining history and Pezim neatly knitted his tenacious pursuit into
Hemlo lore. Hemlo has become a pat element in the Pezim story.

On August 2, 1989, one of the Prime group of companies,
Calpine Resources, released information that Hole 109 at Eskay
had intersected a fifty-foot interval containing sections of visible
gold. In the mining world, visible gold technically means doo-dah.
It's the geological equivalent of spotting bubblegum on the side-
walk. But for stock-market aficionados, specifically A-type Vancouver Stock Exchange players, even a rumour of visible gold is
enough to advance the stock price of a penny gold company. The
stock-player's objective is to buy in fast and bail out fast. The
good news very rarely hangs around.

Toward the end of August, however, Hole 109 looked as if
it might be one of the few exceptions to the rule. Subsequent
assay results proved there was a handsome grade of gold ore in the
rock. One section was unbelievably rich, showing nearly three
ounces of gold for every ton of rock. That's a motherlode. In the
right conditions, with the right economics, mining companies have
been known to pull a gold grade of one tenth of an ounce of gold
for every ton of ore and still make a profit.

Pezim and his pals issued a second press release on August
21 announcing their good fortune. Up until 109 they had been
stuck in mud similar to Hemlo until Hole 76. They knew there
was good gold, but, again, as at Hemlo, they ran into a geophysical
fault and couldn't determine whether the gold continued beyond.
Hole 109 proved that it did. With a vengeance.

It was still early days. There were many Eskay skeptics.

The territory, south of Stewart, east of the Alaskan Panhandle, is topographically tough, with wildly varying elevations. The lack of a road made the area, dubbed the Golden Triangle by the Vancouver brokerage community, difficult to get at. But the Prime people were indefatigable. They drilled throughout the six-month-long winter. They used Bombardier ski-slope groomers to attack the snow, shoving up to sixty feet of the stuff each time they moved a drill. The Prime people thought they could smell the next Hemlo.

Wade Nesmith, the superintendent of brokers, smelled something, too. He charged that Murray Pezim, John Ivany, and Larry Page knew the potential of Hole 109 before making timely and adequate disclosure to the public. In the interim, said Nesmith, Prime and Calpine carried on a merry subterfuge.

Included in the SOB's allegations were charges that the directors had lowered the strike price of Prime options – a right that entitles the holder to purchase a share at a particular price – while in possession of information that would certainly boost Prime's share price. In addition, he charged, the directors had issued Calpine options at seemingly cut-rate prices, again allegedly while in possession of information that would be favourable to Calpine's share price.

In July, Calpine had announced the arrangement of a private placement of two million share units, each unit consisting of one share and one warrant. A warrant is a sweetener entitling the holder to purchase a further share in the company at a specified price and time. In this case, the warrant was exercisable over a two-year period at a price of $2 in the first year and $2.30 in year two. On August 10, after the initial Hole 109 press release but before the more specific information was made public on August 21, Prime announced that it was the purchaser of the Calpine units. The purchase increased Prime's interest in Calpine (and thereby its hold on Eskay) from twenty-two percent to 31.2 percent. If Prime exercised the warrants that went along with the shares, it would end up with thirty-six percent of Calpine. On August 15, Prime arranged the further purchase of 1,370,000 shares of Calpine, boosting its stake in the company to forty percent. In short, Wade Nesmith wanted to prove that Prime had secured control of Calpine at bargain-basement prices. Calpine's share price had risen to more than $9 in late August from a low of $1.25 in July.

The SOB's office announced the details of the supposed infractions on Friday, March 30. The following Monday, shareholders were scheduled to vote on the proposed merger of Prime and Calpine. Lang Evans, the SOB's chief investigator, stationed himself outside the meeting room to await the results of the vote. It was Evans who had connected the timing of the drill-core samples to the corporate press releases. Pezim walked up to him.

"How the fuck do you sleep at night, you little prick?" Pezim asked Evans. "How the fuck do you sleep?"

One week later Nesmith laid another charge. Prime, he said, failed to report that for a twenty-three-day period in the fall of 1989 Peter Brown's Canarim Investment, the forerunner to L.O.M. Western Securities and Vancouver's most influential brokerage house, had reneged on its agreement to take up a million Prime units at $4.25 a unit.

Canarim had originally earmarked the units for the British brokerage Alexanders, Laing & Cruickshank, which in turn would work as agents for the units in Europe. In September, ALC withdrew from the deal. Brown, in turn, refused to take up the units. Prime's share price went on a market tumble, falling to under $2. Brown's firm did, eventually, make good on the deal, but, said the SOB, there was a three-week period when the purchase was in jeopardy. Prime, he charged, had breached disclosure rules.

All of which was enough to make Pezim long for the good old days on the VSE, when the rules were looser than loose, when he'd run into the SOB in a washroom somewhere and they'd have it out then and there.

On this Thursday morning in April, the SOB is giving Pezim a pain in the head, which isn't helped by the chest cold that lingers even after all that time in the Phoenix sun. He looks good, though. He puts on a monogrammed pink-and-white-striped shirt, a navy blazer, and grey slacks, then heads for one of the twin curved marble staircases in the still-dark mansion. As soon as his smooth black Italian leather loafer settles on the top step, wee iridescent lights recessed under the lip of each and every step turn on, sweeping down to the Italian marble foyer. Murray Pezim gets to start each and every day as if he's living in a Busby Berkeley musical set.

In the kitchen, Pezim decides against the pouf that Pearl has chosen for him. He finds it an unsuitable match for his tie, which is pink and blue on a taupe background. He stuffs his cigarettes into his jacket pocket, picks up his car keys, and makes his way through the sparsely furnished cavern that is his home. On narrow hallway tables lie fabric swatches – German cottons and Hong Kong silks. Entire bolts sit propped in corners of the living room, empty save for four chairs, a coffee table, and three brass candlesticks. Pezim's friends joke that he's the only guy they know with a 13,000-square-foot mansion with just one fully furnished room. This was meant to be Pezim's dream home, to be shared with his third wife, Susan.

Susan, tall, blonde, and thirtyish, had taken on the task of decorating, choosing the soft greens and pinks that she favoured, pale woods of bird's-eye maple and white oak, California shutters that would let in streams of light. But she never moved in. The marriage broke up, just as everyone said it would, a few months after it began.

Pezim has been trying to unload this monster house. He'd

take $6.5 million. No-one wants it. If you're going to spend that kind of money, why buy someone else's idea of paradise, even if it does have two swimming pools, a party-size twenty-eight-jet hot tub, a tennis court, a steam room that accommodates eight, temperature-controlled fur storage, and a master suite with his and hers bedrooms, each with a marble-faced, gas-fired fireplace, and a shared bathroom with sunken Jacuzzi, semicircular, two-sink, marble vanity, separate water closet, double-size shower/steam stall, marble walls, and a marble floor?

Pezim needs the money. He's being pressed on margin accounts, he has that $2-million tax bill, and he hasn't paid off Susan, whose prenuptial agreement stipulated that, should she and Pezim divorce, she would get a ski condo at Whistler, a house in West Vancouver, and $1 million cash – a $3-million package. That he has to sell the house doesn't bother Pezim. Everyone says he'd be much happier living in the Four Seasons Hotel, which is where he stays when he's womanless. Pezim wonders whether a one-week fire sale would move the property.

Later, Pearl reflects on the sadness of this situation. "What's the difference between loneliness in this place and loneliness in that place? It's just the same, only the colour of the walls is different."

After he closes the front door, Pezim stands under the portico, appearing a very small figure set against a Tara backdrop of a house. A gentle rain is falling on the newly landscaped property, a meagre collection of infant shrubbery that has none of the glory that the plum trees bring to the rest of Vancouver at this time of year.

He steps into his navy Mercedes, steers it along the circular drive, through salmon-coloured wrought-iron gates, and heads downtown. As the Benz rounds onto Point Grey Road, Pezim lights a Benson & Hedges. The windshield wipers make silent, parallel moves. In this luxury, he is cocooned from the dark and the rain and the wind. He talks about Prime Resources, and Jimmy Pattison, and how he, Pezim, is trying to stir up interest in Prime from Placer Dome, a Vancouver gold-mining giant. He thinks the board meeting is going to be a fight over strategy. He's still angry that Ned Goodman wasn't in there buying the stock when Pattison was.

When the dust had settled, the Jim Pattison Group had emerged with 11.7 percent of Prime, making Pattison the number two shareholder after Ned Goodman's Corona. Pezim and Clemiss, if they combined their position, held third spot. The Pezim people have been telling Placer Dome that getting Prime would ultimately get them 800,000 ounces of gold a year. Placer's engineers have been holed up periodically in Prime's offices, studying geological reports, eyeing drill cores.

At this point, Pezim thinks he'll be facing a cash offer for his shares from Placer Dome. Or else a share swap from Goodman. He says he doesn't like Goodman's paper. What he doesn't say is that he needs to sell out.

He pulls the Benz into the underground lot of the Prime Capital Building on West Hastings Street in downtown Vancouver. As he walks to the elevator, his hands rammed in his pockets, he moves, slightly stooped, with the early signs of an old man's shuffle. He looks contemplative and worried. He wonders aloud whether he should have worn power yellow instead of the pink-and-white stripe.

"I want to go into the meeting angry," he says. "I don't want to fall for that soft touch from Tim Hoare [a member of the board] and Ned. The pats on the back. The how are you, Murray."

Pezim figures he is in for a shitty day, his third shitty day in a row.

On Tuesday, he appeared before the securities panel for the initial meeting on the insider-trading charges. Pezim (along with six lawyers) was the only principal to show. Everyone knew the hearing would be postponed until July to give the parties involved more preparation time. But Pezim wanted to put on a brave face for the media, who would be obliged to attend regardless of the non-event nature of the meeting.

He psyched himself up for his session with the television cameras – "I fear nothing. What could they do to me? Retire me? I could go to Toronto, Los Angeles, New York. There's nothing wrong with living in Beverly Hills, sweetheart."

But Pezim knew this wasn't true, wasn't possible. The Canadian penny-mining game flourishes only in Vancouver, not in Toronto. And Pezim is too old to start fresh in the U.S. The day's trading was all the proof anyone needed to believe this was so: when the numbers were tallied after the market closed, Prime and a little Pezim penny called Adrian Resources traded nearly $5-million worth of shares, one third of the day's total for the more than two thousand companies listed on the VSE.

Wednesday morning of the second lousy day, Pezim had looked as grey as grey. At six a.m., sitting in his office, Pezim was listless. All the agony of the sleeplessness the night before came pouring out.

"The business used to be fun," he said. "It's not fun any more. I find a huge mine and I'm miserable. I'm at the point, this summer, I'm out of the business. I have to sell out before the result of the trial. I could be wiped out."

The day grew worse. An internal report from a gold analyst at Yorkton Securities on Adrian Resources was faxed to the Prime offices. It sent Pezim into a fury. The report said that disputes over mining claims and the questionable economics of mining the ore were of sufficient concern that clients should be advised to cash out their positions. As soon as the market had opened, Adrian stock started to tumble.

The Adrian collapse was the last straw. Pezim figured that

31

just about everyone was dumping on him. He turned to the ever present Harvey Gould. "Get me Peter," meaning Peter Brown.

Both men were at Pezim's control station, a bending piece of Corefam, maybe faux granite or maybe faux marble. Definitely faux. It is perhaps eight feet long, with twists here and curves there. Pezim's war-room table accommodates not only Pezim himself, but Harvey, and a changing cast of young guys from inside Prime and from outside brokerages who drop in, sit down, and take over a terminal and a phone or two. Murray himself faces five machines: one for commodities prices and stock averages; a second that follows a Pezim-selected group of TSE- and VSE-listed companies; a third that runs through the trades and the broker-ages behind the trades for the same group of companies; a fourth that shows the floor markets on these stocks – the runup on the offerings and the rundown on the bids; and, finally, one screen that simply shows every single trade on every single company on all Canadian exchanges.

"Peter," said Murray, when the connection was made, "I'm getting down. The stock's getting killed." He pounded the table. Within minutes he was hysterical, on the verge of tears.

"The exchange," his side of the conversation went, "shit 'em, fuck 'em. Will you come over after?" He meant after Brown's meeting that morning with the VSE officials. The man was pleading.

It was 7:45. The market had been open for little more than an hour. As the morning progressed Pezim became increasingly agi-tated. "I'm leaving town," he said. "I swear to God," he said. "Incompetent people," he said. "From fuck they don't know."

Vancouver was socked in that Wednesday. It looked as if the skies would dump rain any minute. The entire scene was about as cheerful as an Ingmar Bergman flick. Pezim walked out to the balcony that juts off his office. The view, even on a grey day, is lovely, a panorama sweeping Burrard Inlet and the exclusive

British Properties on the north shore. "What do you think? What's going to happen to me? What are they saying?" Pezim was distracted, off in space.

Nell Dragovan, pleasant and plump, walked into the office. "Come here," she said to Murray. "I want to tell you a rumour I heard."

The story on the street was that Pezim, Page, and Brown bought size positions in Adrian after British Columbia's gold commissioner dismissed a complaint over one of the company's property claims. The threesome, so the story goes, then blew off all their paper. That would make Pezim and his associates responsible for the drubbing the stock was taking. Dragovan was smiling because she found this absurd.

Pezim asked his nephew Larry (the son of his brother Norman and a local broker) to buy some Adrian for his own account, then caught himself and cancelled the purchase. VSE rules prohibit a trader from trading for his own account when he's already trading on behalf of his company, which Pezim is. Stock-exchange rules also dictate that an insider may pick up only two percent of the stock of a company at one time. Pezim picked up 125,000 shares for Prime that day near the low. Then he worked the phones, exhorting everyone to buy, buy, buy. Adrian traded 800,000 shares in two hours.

The share price rose to $2.44 from $1.85. Pezim raised his fists and attempted to conjure the allegory of the phoenix rising from the ashes. By the time he got on the phone to VSE President Don Hudson, to tell him he was a "nervous, bloody wreck," he was, in fact, in a much restored frame of mind. Adrian was on its way to trading close to three million shares for the day. Pezim sold before the market close at $2.30, for a profit, before commissions, of $56,000.

Peanuts. Lunch money. Pezim and his friends and his business pals and the cadre of hangers-on who leech off the Pezim success still had hours to go before lunch. The Pezim people are used to watching him swing from hope to despair and back again regularly. Daily. Hourly.

Shortly after 10 a.m., geological information on the Prime Resources property in Eskay Creek was transmitted to head office. Pezim phoned the exchange, halted the stock, and issued a very polished press release announcing a twenty-foot intersection of gold. A visible intersection, mind. No assay results, but a geological estimate of a gold grade of one to two percent. The intersect was not as phenomenal as Hole 109, but impressive nonetheless.

Halting the stock and issuing the gold guess to the public was Pezim's way of mooning the securities commission. He was bending himself out of shape to do what the SOB's office alleges he failed to do in the insider-trading case. It was Pezim's way of telling them they couldn't have it both ways. If they wanted disclosure, he'd give them disclosure. In spades.

Before Pezim took off for dinner with the broker-groupies who hang on his every word in the hope of being favoured with his business, Pezim made a feisty display of optimism.

"What's the whole case about?" he asked of no-one in particular. "Take my licence away from me? They wouldn't dare."

Back home toward the close of the day, Pezim pulled himself from the hot tub and wrapped a peach towel around his waist. He gabbed with his son Michael, the Vancouver surgeon, who rarely hangs out at the Pezim mansion. Michael is thirty-six, balding, pale, and reserved. Pezim, in this mood, at this moment, with the tan he has brought with him from Arizona, seemed younger than his years, vibrant, healthy. He has lovely hands, gentle hands, and with these he starts motioning in the air as if he were a conductor moving a symphony.

"If you were to fill this room," he said to Michael, "if the grade were to hold, how much would it be worth?" He was talking about the "visible gold" results at Eskay. The puzzle was

34

to estimate the value of the gold if this room in his multimillion-dollar mansion were to be dumped full of Eskay rock.

"Twenty million dollars," guessed Michael.

"Fifty million," said his father. And with Pezim, it's more than likely that if someone were to do just that, dump a bunch of Eskay rock in that pretty, bare house, he'd be right on the money.

Pezim goes to bed. He doesn't sleep.

At 5:45 a.m. on Thursday, the elevator doors deposit Pezim at his penthouse office. The receptionist hasn't yet arrived, but John Ivany is already doing a coffee-in-hand cruise through the office. This is uncharacteristic. Ivany is an operations man. It is not his habit to arrive at this ungodly hour.

It takes fewer than ten minutes for Pezim to lose it, the way he lost it the previous day – patience, rational thought, good humour. This time, though, it is worse. During a phone conversation with a Calgary broker, Pezim learns that Ned Goodman has struck a deal on behalf of Prime to take control of a gold-mining company called Stikine Resources. Stikine has fifty percent of the key Eskay Creek property, Prime the other, thanks to the Calpine merger. Goodman's plan is to merge Stikine with Prime. Prime will thereby seal control of the gold play. Goodman's Corona controls Prime.

What riles Pezim is not that Goodman has done the deal, because everyone agrees that, if it works, it's a fabulous deal, but rather that he was left out of it. The previous week, Goodman went to the California ranch of John Toffan, the president of Stikine, and reached a tentative agreement. He reeled in Ron Brimacombe, a broker at Yorkton Securities, for support. "The Brim" had a whack of Stikine snugly in the hands of friendly accounts. Tendering to Goodman meant a $2.1-million commission for Yorkton, big money for a small firm.

Goodman broke the news to John Ivany the night before at

Goodman's hotel room. Goodman didn't call Pezim. He tells Pezim later that he didn't want to wake him. He didn't want to wake the man who doesn't sleep. What is more likely is that he didn't want Pezim blabbing to the media, which is Pezim's habit. Pezim likes pre-empting corporate releases by bestowing the latest news on whichever of the local reporters is currently in favour. He loves to gab and reporters love him for it. He has burned the Corona group in the past by leaking confidential information.

The other reason for excluding Pezim is that he and Goodman have had their problems in the past, and Goodman knows that Pezim, when he feels like it, can be the loosest of loose cannons. Goodman is a brilliant and calculating numbers man. He knows the importance of bringing a deal in tight. He knows how easily a deal can get jinxed.

Pezim is furious. He's pissed that Ivany was told first. He's probably pissed that Goodman was able to do what he couldn't. He, Page, and Ivany had made two runs at Stikine, in January and in March, but Toffan wouldn't bite. Goodman is a tenacious deal-maker who could get along with the devil to get a deal done.

At about six a.m., Pezim phones Peter Brown, who is sound asleep in his Belmont Avenue house in Vancouver's Point Grey neighbourhood. For Brown to be awakened by Pezim at unconventional hours is not unusual. Brown is one of Pezim's touchstones. The conversation is brief.

"He's your friend," says Pezim, referring to Goodman. "Stick him up your ass."

At ten a.m. the Prime board assembles around a black oval table: Pezim, Goodman, Ivany, Page, Tim Hoare, chairman of the international mining division of Alexanders, Laing & Cruickshank, John Ing, president of the Toronto brokerage Maison Placements Canada Inc., Paul Carroll, who for twenty years has been Goodman's lawyer, and Jacob Brouwer, a newish board member

unknown to some of the men in attendance. The Toronto financier
Myron Gottlieb, a long-time ally of Goodman's, is on the speaker
phone from Toronto, as is Alan Lenczner, executive vice-president
of Central Capital. Lenczner became a Corona associate in the
Hemlo days when he and Ron Slaght, both litigation lawyers with
McCarthy & McCarthy in Toronto, successfully wrested Hemlo's
Williams mine from its adversary, Lac Minerals.

The directors first listen to legal briefings on the state of
the securities investigation from the three lawyers defending
Pezim, Page, and Ivany. Then Goodman unveils his plan: for
Prime to merge with Stikine; for Prime to seal control of Eskay
Creek once and for all; for Prime to sideline Pezim. Pezim stays
quiet. There is no yelling or screaming.

Fourteen hours later, a group gathers at Chartwell's, a posh
restaurant in the Four Seasons Hotel, the kind of mahogany and
tapestry dining room that favours Vivaldi and candelabra. Pezim
feels at home, not for the atmosphere, and not for the food (which
is quite good, and therefore not to Pezim's taste), but rather
because he's known here and gets pampered.

The first to arrive is John Ing, who quietly comments that
Pezim has lost again. Pearl Whalley arrives, looking gorgeous and
rested, with her daughter Jodi, and Pearl's sister Shirley, who has
phenomenal, gravity-free breasts. Jodi dips heavily into the champagne. Mickey, Pearl explains to Pezim, has decided to sit this one
out. It's not really his kind of thing, and anyway, he doesn't own a
suitable jacket. Pezim is disappointed. He's extremely fond of the
former Hell's Angel who lives in his house, runs his errands, and
tends his yard.

John McPhail is in attendance. He is one of the Pezim
groupies, a broker at Yorkton Securities and the son of Gus McPhail,
who up until his recent death was a friend of Pezim's and one of
Vancouver's securities kingpins. Art Clemiss, one-time broker, now

multimillionaire Pezim acolyte, makes an appearance. There are three empty places. The party is awaiting the arrival of the four horsemen.

The women have their shrimp and champagne; Pezim has his Coke, overdone steak, and, later, his chocolate ice cream. When the four horsemen arrive they seem in roistering good humour. There is Tim Hoare, a tall, pigeon-toed Londoner with a mess of black curly hair and the look of a ruddy-faced, over-fed pub owner. There is Peter Brown, impeccably dressed, still handsome at forty-eight, his looks marred only by a slightly pugified nose that makes him appear as though he took a bad tumble into cement as a youngster. And Paul Carroll, the Dudley Moore of lawyers, impish and of pygmy proportions next to Hoare. Soon to follow is Ned Goodman himself. There is no place for him at the table. There is some juggling of chairs.

The men recount the events of the day. They joke about how Art Clemiss was initially angry about the Prime-Stikine deal until he counted all the money he'd make. Each of the men is happy for his own reasons. Peter Brown got to play broker to the event. He was Pezim's broker, Goodman's broker, Pattison's broker, and he was on the board. It is because of deals like this one that Brown is a multimillionaire. Goodman is happy because he did the deal his way: for every Stikine share, shareholders will get a share and a half in the new company, 5.33 Class A Corona shares, and the greater of either $15 or 0.0273 ounces of Eskay gold – dubbed the gold nugget. Pezim and Clemiss and Page will swap their Prime shares for Corona shares, which is exactly what Pezim said he didn't want to do. But he had no choice. Goodman had the right of first refusal on those shares. There were no competing bids. Pezim is the least happy of them all.

There is some table talk of the securities investigation, of how Pezim has it on good authority that Wade Nesmith, the SOB, is an anti-Semite. Pezim has come to believe this because someone somewhere in the rumour mill told him of Nesmith's affiliation with the Jim Keegstra case in Edmonton. This was in the days when Nesmith was a Crown counsel and Keegstra was a teacher who told his students the Holocaust didn't happen. Nesmith, in fact, did work in the special prosecutions branch of the Crown's office in Edmonton, but he had nothing to do with the Keegstra case and is no anti-Semite. Nevertheless, Nesmith has become Pezim's bête noire.

"No one person should have the power to destroy people," Pezim will say, again and again. At this point, Pezim and Nesmith have not met.

Through a couple of vodkas, Brown entertains the table with tales of Pezim, antics of a man he has known for twenty years, through a ride of fortune and misfortune, depression and elation. He tells of the time Edwin Land walked into the New York offices of Pezim and his then mentor in promotions, Earl Glick. It was a highly tacky operation, with stationery imprinted with a caricature of a Chinese man and the words, "Buy low, sell high," and business cards that said, "Click with Glick." Anyway, says Brown, in walks Land with a prototype for the Polaroid camera, trailing oil and grease across the office's hideous orange shag.

"Get the fuck outta here," Glick yelled at Land, or so Brown's rendering of the story goes. Land, of course, went on to make billions with his camera. Glick and Pezim instead backed Colonial Aircraft, an amphibious plane that managed to draw a full-brass lineup for its inaugural flight. It sank.

When Brown tells the story, he paints a picture of a Securities Exchange Commission official presenting himself at the door of Glick and Co. to ask hard questions about the Colonial venture, suggesting that New York was too big and too tough for people like Glick. "I've got the plane tickets right here," says Brown, playing Glick in an anxious sweat, waving the imaginary tickets in the air.

The diners love such stories because Pezim has been known

for putting himself and too much of his money behind wacko losers, because he has a reputation for being a man of good humour who will laugh at himself, and because some of those at the table, including probably Brown, really love the guy in their fashion.

At the head of the table, Pezim laughs along, appreciating the fact that Brown, an eloquent speaker, a private-school kid with polish, tells Pezim stories better than Pezim himself. There are no obvious indications of animosity among any of the people present, though it's clear that not all are the warmest of friends. Pezim, sitting next to the tall, fleshy, bespectacled Goodman, has the demeanour of a prematurely aging child.

Now that Goodman has effectively rolled three companies into one, Prime becomes a real gold-producer. He no longer needs Pezim. So Goodman punts Murray into a new corporate entity called Prime Equities. It will be a repository, as was its predecessor, for junior concerns that are unproved prospects.

Pezim swears up and down that he's happy with the arrangement. That, really, he prefers to run with the small stuff. That he was never meant to be an operator, a manager. He suggests a corporate moniker for the new company: "Son of Prime. Blazing in the sky. Just like the second coming of Jesus Christ."

But if Pezim is so happy, so optimistic, so full of himself, how come he looks so miserable? As the party departs there is much nudging and ribbing and chumminess among Hoare and Carroll and Brown. Goodman seems in an upbeat mood. The four men head for an Italian restaurant. None of them ate at Chartwell's.

Pezim hits the escalator first. The other men pause. As Pezim descends to the foyer he turns around and stares up at these younger men who have come to control him. He seems small and enfeebled. He heads for home with John Ing, where the two have a hot tub together. Pezim has a hot tub most nights – though sometimes he has a quick swim or, more accurately, a quick float.

Pezim goes to bed, but he doesn't sleep. So he gets up and wakes Jodi, and tells the reformed drug addict that she really ought to get an education and perhaps she might like to go to school in Arizona, where Tammy is studying video arts. This is a sincere offer on Pezim's part.

It is Friday morning and Pezim is working the phones, pummelling the speed lines, barking at Harvey Gould to get him his connections. He's selling Goodman's deal to the street.

"I try to explain what the deal is all about," he says. "They go like this." He opens his eyes wide, raises his arm and scratches his head, pointing his elbow high into the air. Like a monkey. Like a stupid, brainless monkey. Usually, the Vancouver street prefers a Pezim deal to a Goodman deal.

John Ivany, tall and heavyset, his face overrun with crooked teeth, and cheeks that flush easily, scrums with The Pez. Everyone talks about how honest John is, John the family man who quietly does his job. Quietly, but with ambition. He hopes one day to run the big gold-mining company that Ned Goodman is trying to create by combining Corona's gold assets with Prime's. The insider-trading charges are as tough on Ivany as they are on Pezim. Probably tougher.

There's a sad story going around about just how badly Honest John is hurting. His son Neil came home from public school one day carrying a book that had been inscribed to him by his father. Under Neil's name someone had written "Son of a Crook."

Ivany walks up to Pezim in the great lumbering quarterback style that he has and says, quietly, "We're going to have to halt this visible stuff." He's talking about the gold showings. He knows that it looks bad for the company to be making such announcements even in the good days when the securities people aren't breathing down their necks. It looks almost as if Ivany wants

41

to put some distance between himself and Pezim. Would-be friends and one-time allies like Ivany are positioning themselves for the outcome of the hearing. It was as if the stock community had made a decision in concert: if anyone falls, it will be Pezim alone.

Even Pezim, who in his more ebullient moments thinks the whole damned world is his buddy, believes this to be true. "Blood has to be spilled," he says. "Who's the easiest person to sacrifice? Probably me, eh? It stinks."

When Pezim retires to that big, empty house at the end of the week, the bigness of it and the emptiness of it are unbearable. It is at times like these that the woman thing becomes an issue. It is at times like these that a man in the Pezim entourage with the unlikely name of Basil Pantages comes in handy. What Pantages does is unclear. Records show that at one time he was a restaurateur who may have popped into Pezim's life through a Pezim penny venture called Adera Mining. These days Pantages hangs around Prime headquarters. He looks like an overly oiled, overly tanned George Hamilton. He has recently, according to Pearl Whalley, who monitors such doings, lined Pezim up with someone named Larisa, who wears her blonde hair in cornbraids à la Bo Derek some ten years after the fashion.

On Friday night, Larisa and a female pal come to entertain Pezim. The previous weekend, when Larisa and pal had first come to play with Murray, Pearl had closeted herself in her bedroom upstairs. When she thought she heard the party break up, she had peered over the upstairs balcony and seen the two fauns — starkers — streaking across the hallway. This weekend is pretty much a repeat performance.

Pezim doesn't sleep in. He gets his cargo out of the house early Saturday and heads downtown for a haircut and a steam, leaving Pearl to cluck over the pancake make-up Larisa and friend have left smeared on a couple of Prime Resources T-shirts. To Pearl's way of thinking, Pezim's personal life is not at all satisfactory. There isn't much to Pezim's life right now that looks appealing.

Pezim then waited three agonizing months for the Securities Commission hearing. In the meantime, he tried to mess up the Stikine deal. Even though he agreed to sell his Prime position to Goodman, he spent the subsequent weeks working furiously to heighten the interest of the mining giant Placer Dome, which eventually got a forty-five percent stake in Stikine and went on to fight Corona for control.

Pezim worked flat out trying to beat Goodman. The Corona camp felt his behaviour was actionable. But all Pezim wanted was a better buck. He hoped the hoopla would result in increased share prices all around. He demanded an exchange of his Prime shares for Corona Gold shares, the proposed new Goodman company designed to house gold assets exclusively — not the oil-and-gas or diamond-mining-in-Botswana interests or whatever else is in there.

Pezim and Clemiss and Page ended up accepting one Corona share plus a buck a share; Pattison got a little better than that. Pezim cashed out at $25 million. Pezim's interference cost Goodman an extra $10 million or so.

On July 9, Murray Pezim presented himself, as he would every day in the five-week-long hearing, at a claustrophobic hearing room in the B.C. Hydro building in downtown Vancouver. The media seized the moment. The Pez and his co-accused were splashed across the business pages and television screens. The entire spectacle was wonderfully Vancouverish. Early in the proceedings, one of the commissioners referred to Howe Street as "shady." "The twilight world of Howe Street" was another of his descriptions. Then he and his biases stepped off the Commission panel.

Ivany distanced himself further from Pezim by testifying that he wasn't privy to assay results before their release to the public.

Prime's geologist, Chet Idziszek, gave convincing testimony that the company had an effective Chinese Wall – that is, a communications barrier that prevented the transfer of undisclosed assay information from the geologist's side of the wall to the directors' side.

Everyone waited for the point man in the story. Observers really only wanted to see Pezim in action.

In the second week of August, Murray Pezim began his testimony. He pointed out that even though he had the opportunity to benefit from certain share options, he didn't. He explained that he lost $4-million when brokers made margin calls on his Prime position in the fall of 1989. The share price had fallen to $1.61 from $5.25 when investors bailed out of the market to take advantage of a new Prime offering. Pezim said the brokers sold him out at $1.83. Pezim argued that if he had done anything wrong – and he wasn't saying he had – he didn't make a penny out of it.

He attempted to look upbeat. He sported a variety of blazing neckties. He made various appearances at B.C. Lions games. One day, he wore a black-satin Lions' jacket to the hearing room.

In private he railed against his accusers. He said Gregory Walsh, who led the Commission's case, was a "thirty-seven-year-old prosecutor who doesn't know how to wipe his ass." Wade Nesmith was nicknamed "The Phantom," for he never came to the hearings. Pezim flared when he was informed that two days before the conclusion of the hearing, Nesmith was seen at a yacht club in Vancouver dining with Doug Hyndman, the chairman of the British Columbia Securities Commission, though the two had actually attended a dinner for twenty, sponsored by the VSE and the Securities Commission. Pezim accused his accusers of threatening witnesses. The spectacle – he said, he hoped – was the biggest farce in history. It was they who should be charged.

But he was worried. He was blue. What scared him the most was that he was being "tried" not in a formal court of law but by a securities group that had never dealt with a case as tough as this one. He stopped trading. By mid-September he was estimating that dollar losses – in postponed share underwritings and jobs lost in the mining camps – exceeded $100 million. He said he couldn't raise two cents. His newly named Prime Equities (Son of Prime) had struck a deal with Kennecott, a giant U.S. mining concern, in which Kennecott would undertake a $6.8-million private placement with Prime Equities. The contract stated that the funds would be placed in an interest-bearing trust account pending the outcome of the hearing. The deal stipulated that "In the event that the Commission prohibits Pezim from trading in securities and/or acting as a director of a reporting issuer for a period exceeding six months, Kennecott shall have the right to rescind the private placement." The condition was a blow. Pezim refused to sign. It was, he said, a matter of pride.

He was obsessed with the Commission inquiry. Obsessed with Chairman Doug Hyndman. Obsessed with SOB Wade Nesmith and chief investigator Lang Evans too. What bothered him most was the thought that these know-nothings, these pups, these well-educated men in tasselled loafers and overcut Italian suits could end his capricious fifty-year career.

"If the Commission says I'm not fit to serve as a director, then regardless of the appeal, honey, I'm finished."

By the fall, Pezim had retreated again to Arizona. The VSE Index, a monitor of the performance of a substantial portion of the more than two thousand listed companies, fell to under 600 points in the first week in October, half its high during the initial Eskay ride. Share prices averaged eighty-five cents, when not all that long ago three dollars was the norm. The Pezim hearing, everyone

45

agreed, was responsible for much of the malaise. When Pezim doesn't work the phones, not much happens. The excitement over the Eskay gold play petered out. There was, too, the general economic slump that was making for tough times for all exchanges. It was a bear market.

Pezim told reporters that Art Clemiss had retired. He later told reporters that he too had retired. He didn't mean it. He simply wanted to deliver an object lesson in how hauntingly quiet the stock business can get. Pezim, as always, was dealing in hyberbole. The press played along. If The Pez were shut out, they said, the Vancouver Stock Exchange would wither. Perhaps die.

The announcement that ABC's *PrimeTime Live* was going to broadcast an exposé of the exchange certainly hadn't helped. The program sent a producer and his wife under cover, posing as New York investors searching for junior companies with the potential of big returns. In the wife's hairdo was a camera lens; winding down the back of her neck was a fibre-optic cable. The investigation yielded three instances of what certainly appeared to be securities violations. Adrian du Plessis, a one-time VSE floor trader turned anti-corruption crusader, told the journalists that the exchange was a network of institutionalized fraud. More than fifty percent of the listed companies, he said, were sheer scams.

Chris Wallace, son of the *60 Minutes* host Mike Wallace, spent eight hours with Pezim for the *PrimeTime* show. Pezim came off looking like the buffoonish king of the exchange. The following day, Don Hudson, the president of the VSE, decried the lack of balance of the report. Wade Nesmith said it was "*National Enquirer* goes video."

In Paradise Valley, the VSE spectacle was pre-empted by Arizona's gubernatorial race. Pezim had a friend in Vancouver place a telephone receiver beside the television so he could listen in. He couldn't see himself moaning through "Pennies from

Heaven" at Chardonnay's, a Vancouver broker hangout. He couldn't see himself cavorting with a belly dancer. He couldn't see what a fool he seemed.

For Pezim it was a rehash. "We know who the bums are," he said. "We want to throw the bums out." Why single out the VSE? "I can go to New York and find a bunch of bums and phony stock promoters."

The show did not connect Pezim with any junk deals. But it did point out that he was being investigated for insider-trading violations. There was a television clip of a very sombre Pezim during his Securities Commission testimony.

The show didn't help Pezim or the VSE. The exchange draws a third of its trading dollars from foreign investors. Don Hudson told me once that on any American statutory holiday, VSE trading drops by twenty-five percent. Anyone interested in dropping a dollar into the VSE who happened to catch the ABC program would very likely think twice about investing with Pezim.

On Friday, November 16, 1990, the British Columbia Securities Commission released its report on the Pezim investigation. It found that Prime and Calpine had failed to make disclosure of Eskay drilling results before the repricing of stock options; had failed to disclose the purchaser of a private placement of stock; and had failed to make timely disclosure of the default by Canarim to purchase the Prime units. Significantly, the Commission found "no fraudulent intent on the part of the respondents, and did not find that Messrs. Pezim, Page, and Ivany had knowledge of any undisclosed material changes when they engaged in the securities transactions."

Pezim was cleared of insider trading. The Commission did find, however, that the three "failed to carry out their duties to ensure that Prime and Calpine complied with securities regulatory requirements." Prime and Calpine had contravened Section 67 of the B.C. Securities Act by granting stock options without making material changes known to the public. Pezim himself had misled the exchange. The Commission reserved its findings pending final legal arguments.

A month later, the Securities Commission ordered a one-year trading ban against Pezim, Page, and Ivany. The three appealed. Peter Brown's firm was subsequently fined $50,000 for its failure to disclose the default on the taking up of Prime units.

Four days after Christmas, Pezim turned sixty-nine. There were bright spots. He planned his first financing in months, for a company called Consolidated Rhodes, one of the many junior mines under Prime Equities. Chet Idziszek, the geologist, stuck with Pezim on the new venture. John Ivany moved over to the Corona offices, which had made the move from Toronto to Vancouver, to work alongside the chief executive, Peter Steen.

Best of all, the *Northern Miner*, the industry Bible, held a New Year's lunch honouring Pezim and Idziszek as 1990's Mining Men of the Year. The award, said the paper, was being given in recognition of the importance of Eskay Creek as one of the most significant Canadian ore discoveries since Hemlo. Pezim, of course, had been there for both plays. The securities investigation, said the paper, was immaterial.

In its editorial the *Miner* described Pezim as someone who "arouses strong reactions in people, but whether one considers him a hero or a rogue, we believe that when he goes to that great stock market in the sky – and we trust that is many years away – he'll join the Pantheon of mining greats and be remembered for his contributions, not his shortcomings."

It was pure schmaltz, perfectly Pezim, a premature obituary of an unconventional man.

CHAPTER 3

Who's Responsible for This?

*"To find out why Sammy really runs so much
faster than anyone else, you'd probably have to
know what kind of infancy he had, and whether
his kindergarten teacher used to slap him, and
under what conditions he learned the facts of life,
whether he ever suffered from malnutrition – the
whole works."*
        BUDD SCHULBERG, *WHAT MAKES SAMMY RUN?*

The white stretch Lincoln could barely navigate the corners of the
streets that define Toronto's Kensington Market – Nassau,
Baldwin, Augusta, Kensington itself. They are narrow streets,
made more so by the hordes of shoppers who park illegally to get
to this greengrocer or that poultry store. Kensington is a hodge-
podge of earthy entrepreneurship, a shoppers' paradise for those
who don't like their chicken slapped on polystyrene or their herbs
prepackaged.

    Murray Pezim was nestled in the Lincoln's rear upholstery,

looking not at all like the kind of guy who gets squired in a stretch. Pezim is not an ostentatious man. He doesn't have the appearance or the bearing of someone whom others defer to. Even when he examines his fingernails, as pampered men sometimes do, with their hands half curled toward them, Pezim bears a closer resemblance to Charlie Chaplin imitating a rich man than a rich man in reality.

As the stretch rounded the corner of St. Andrew Street, Pezim leaned forward, then strained his neck down and to the side, in order to see out of the window and up. It would have been easier for him to get out of the car to take in the passing scene. But there was some showmanship involved. Pezim was performing for a documentary film crew that was shooting a segment on the financier behind the Hemlo gold discovery. They wanted to know the beginnings of this outrageous stock promoter, who was in truth a very rich man.

So Pezim stayed put as he showed the crew his first home in what was once Toronto's Jewish ghetto, just west of Spadina Avenue, which was itself dominated by the Jewish rag trade. By the eighties, when Pezim had become a celebrity and therefore movie material, the neighbourhood had acquired a distinct Portuguese-Asian flavour. Retro clothing stores had taken over locations once fronted by the fruit stalls and meat markets of Pezim's youth. Asian merchants and restaurateurs had remade Spadina Avenue. But Kensington stubbornly retained much of the personality of fifty years ago.

Finally, in a "there it is, boys" sort of way, Pezim pointed to a quaint-looking dormer with a little peaked roof – just the kind of spot Hollywood would pick for a poor Jewish kid with big dreams to grow up in. Yup, it was tough being a Jew in those days, Pezim told the camera. "If I wanted to stay out of fights I'd have to walk about eight miles to get to school."

50

Cut.

Wrong window. Wrong house. Pezim, in fact, started life two doors over, in the small end house in a row of poor, red-brick lookalikes. Nor did he grow up in this so-called Jewish ghetto; his family moved from poverty to a handsome seventeen-room house on a ritzy street when he was three years old. It is not that Pezim means to deceive. He has often told the tale of his family's move from rank working class to middle class, even upper middle class. But Pezim has perfected fast, pat answers to predictable questions. He isn't particularly interested in the early years, when he wasn't pushing stock or making money.

Murray's father, Isadore, who was always called Izzy, arrived in Canada in 1904 as an adolescent, one of seven children born to Morris and Sarah Pezim. Morris made barrels for the wine industry in the town of Focsani, 160 kilometres north of Bucharest. Though he was relatively well-to-do, he wanted more for his family than a life in the Romanian vineyards. So the couple packed up Izzy, who was twelve, and his six siblings, Jacob, Jenny, Fanny, Samuel, Harry, and Harriet. They took a train to Germany, travelled to Holland, then took a ship to Canada, each of them arriving with a money belt containing the family's life savings in gold coins. They were not refugees, but they didn't understand, or perhaps didn't trust, the notion of funds transfer.

Toronto was a seventeen-square-mile city of 280,000 when the Pezim family arrived. It hoped even then to be a centre of commerce, the country's financial heart. But the city – or the "Logical Location," as it billed itself – was just beginning to grow.

Morris started his new life as a labourer, earning five dollars a week. It wasn't what Sarah had in mind. So they moved into a house at 70 Elizabeth Street, a Jewish enclave in downtown Toronto, with a grocery-store front. There they sold dry goods

and potatoes and onions and pickles, as well as candies for the
neighbourhood children. Morris was not without financial sophisti-
cation: he issued and redeemed his own currency. The family lived
in the back.

The streets then were unpaved. Horse-drawn buggies tra-
versed roads of wooden planks. When Jacob, Morris and Sarah's
eldest child, died of tuberculosis, they travelled to the funeral by
horse and buggy.

Later, Morris moved his family to a second store, Pezim's
Grocery Store, at the intersection of Phoebe and Huron streets.
Morris and Sarah's brood had pretty well grown by this time, but
a new generation of children came to the shop, sometimes to steal
the penny-candy grab bags. Morris didn't mind the thievery, being
a benevolent and good-humoured man. What he didn't like were
the impromptu craps games that would start up on the pavement
directly outside the store. Then Morris would call the police. "Get
out of here, you bums," he'd yell.

Gambling he didn't like.

But Izzy did. He was very much a risk-taker and a gambling man, though this wasn't immediately evident. His first job,
as a button sewer at Eaton's, which at that time had a tailoring
operation, was traditional enough for the immigrant labour force.
His brother, Samuel, also started out at Eaton's. But Izzy had
bigger dreams.

In his early twenties, he married Rebecca Faibish and they
moved to the house on St. Andrew Street, right beside the Berlin
Butcher, across from a lumber yard, down the street from the
Minsk Synagogue, and very near a chicken-plucker. Few houses in
the neighbourhood were simply residences; embroiderers and
leather workers and all manner of one-person enterprises were
dotted throughout. The neighbourhood had the feel of a small
world, closed unto itself, which indeed it was.

Who's Responsible for This?

As much as the Jewish Market smelled of the Crown Bread Bakery and open-to-the-air pickle barrels and the fruit stand of the immense Mr. Five by Five — "Hey, lady, don't squeeza the peaches" — there was a toughness to it. Young cops on the beat steered clear. There were stories of pickpockets and street ruffians. The local boxers — Baby Yak and Sammy Luftspring — only added to its reputation. Billy Grife, whose parents had a bakery, went on to become a famous weightlifter. Joe Goodman became a wrestler. The neighbourhood bred scrappers.

Rebecca bore Murray, just plain Murray Pezim with no middle name, on December 29, 1921. He was the baby, the fourth child after his sisters Rose and Frances and his brother Norman.

By the time Murray was born, Izzy was a store clerk at Benjamin Rapp, a drugstore on Dundas Street. Riches — he imagined, he hoped — lay in the pharmacy business. So he returned to school to get his senior matriculation, which was all he needed to own and operate a drugstore. He even took a couple of chemistry courses at the University of Toronto. By 1923, he was running Don Pharmacy, with two downtown locations. The stores became profitable not through prescription drugs but through a brisk traffic in the alcohol business. These were Prohibition days. According to family lore, the local police were Izzy Pezim's best customers.

He was always on the lookout for a way to make some extra cash. One summer he set off with a friend for Atlantic City to set up a weight-guessing operation on the boardwalk, which was no hardship on Rebecca, given that she was the one who always held the family together anyway. Becky, as she was called, was protective of her children, scrupulous in the care of her home, and kept a beady eye on the family finances. The Atlantic City escapade was perfectly in character for Izzy, by all reports a rakish man with a twinkle in his eye and a penchant for flirting, a good dresser who smoked White Owl cigars. He was handsome and fussy about his appearance. He was a hustler.

When Murray was a toddler, Izzy did a very smart thing. He sold the pharmacies while the going was good, sold the St. Andrew Street house, and moved Rebecca and the four children to a seventeen-room house on Palmerston Avenue, just down the way from the Westons, the millionaire bread men. Palmerston was a prestige address, a street with a stone entrance at one end, and fancy Edwardian carriage lamps lining the sides of the road. Comfortable, middle-class Jewish families had started to filter into this once-WASP enclave. On one side of the Pezims lived the McLennans, on the other the Rothsteins.

From a neighbourhood that smelled of fish heads and chicken feathers, the Pezims had gone establishment. This is not to suggest that Murray's father was rich. His down payment was probably minimal, and it is more than likely that he was overreaching himself by making the move. Nevertheless, Izzy had done so well in selling his stores that to celebrate he hired a nanny, pulled the family's big-box Buick out of the garage, and took Rebecca on a six-month trip through the U.S. The kids stayed home with the nanny.

The large sunroom at the back of the house on the second floor was Murray's favourite room. He craved the sun. The warmth. Even then, he loathed Toronto winters, which is probably why he fondly remembers spring runoff, throwing a stick or gum wrapper into the flowing gutters, then racing along with the other children to see whose stick or wrapper made it to the finish line first.

Murray and his brother Norman, older by two and a half years, went to Clinton Public School. It was a short walk, down Palmerston, then west over to Manning Avenue and into the twenty-three-room school. It had two playgrounds, the south-end yard for the girls, the north-end yard for the boys. The Jewish boys kept to the Manning side of the school yard, and scrapped often with the Irish and with the Italians. Sometimes they'd agree to meet at Christie Pits to really have it out. It was tough being a Jew.

The playgrounds were covered with wooden planks, so the children would play marbles in the cracks between the boards. The cadets would train with wooden rifles in the schoolyard. After lunch and after recess, school rules required that the children line up outside the building, then march in rows inside as a teacher named Major Wilkie played "Men of Harlech" or whatever struck his fancy on the piano. And no talking. Every so often, cows would march up Clinton Street to the nearby slaughterhouse.

At the end of the school day, Murray would run home up Palmerston, with its wide road and lush trees, and maybe get in a fight along the way – maybe even stage a fight and charge admission. He did that once, but then his mother arrived and put a stop to it. Norman was different. He would often take detours to avoid trouble. Tom Hardy was a particular bully. Used to beat Norman up every time he saw him. Fifteen years later Tom Hardy was sentenced to twenty years for armed robbery.

Murray and Norman weren't really chums. Norman hung out with his contemporaries Louie Weingarten – later to reinvent himself as the comedian Johnny Wayne – and Frank Shuster, Wayne's lifelong show-business partner. Murray's buddies, Henry Sussman and Ralphie Ashburn, were younger.

Murray's sisters were much closer. Though Rose was the older of the girls by eighteen months, Frances was the leader, and it was with her girlfriends that they would hang out. Neither was beautiful. Rose had a lazy eye and wore glasses with thick lenses. Frances weighed more than 160 pounds as a teen-ager; she may have ballooned as high as 200. But she seemed happy. "When *meine Fegele* used to laugh," Rebecca would say of her daughter, "the whole world would laugh." The girls were smart as whips, with an aptitude for mathematics. They adored their parents. They were raised to adore their brothers, too, which they did forever.

These were the twenties. Girls sported side parts, their hair swept low over one eye. The boys wore argyle V-necks and hair styles that could have marked any generation of schoolboys, except the long-haired sixties. When Commander Byrd left New York for the South Pole, when a fire took the lives of seventy-five men at the Hollinger mine near Timmins, when Gordon Sinclair's travels through India were printed in the *Daily Star*, the children would study these events and sometimes write stories for the *Clinton Clarion*.

Not Murray. It was math that pushed him onto the honour roll again and again. He was like his dad. He could do numbers in his head better than just about anybody. "Take these numbers down," Izzy would say, then reel off a list of fifteen or so. "Now multiply them. What's taking you so long?"

"Maa-rry," John MacFarlane the math teacher would call from the front of the class, with a soft A, and a roll in the R. "Do some multiplication tables for us, Maa-rry."

And Murray would. "He truly loved me," says Pezim of MacFarlane. "He thought I was the brightest son of a bitch in the world."

These early years were happy ones. College Street lay directly to the south, and served as a kind of promenade for the kids, who would stroll past the delis, the occasional Chinese restaurant, moving in packs, the girls travelling separately from the boys. Murray and Norman would sometimes run across the railway ties that supported the streetcar tracks to get a smoked meat on rye at Becker's or maybe at Peter Wellts's deli, with a Verner's ginger ale or a cream soda to wash it down. When the Pezims first arrived in the neighbourhood, you could get a smoked-meat sandwich for a nickel, which wasn't a hardship for the boys.

The Alhambra Theatre was on the north side of Bloor Street at Bathurst and the Madison just across the road. A nickel would buy a whole day's worth of Tom Mix. And there was Shea's, where you got a spot of vaudeville with your movie. On Queen Street, south of College, there was a burlesque house called the Casino Theatre. Murray loved that kind of show. Still does. Men in baggy pants, or playing women with absurdly oversized breasts. Slapstick routine.

The Pezims were orthodox Jews. Morris, Murray's grandfather, was one of the founders of what was then known as the Romanian Hebrew Synagogue on Centre Avenue, just south of Dundas Street. Much later, it moved to the north end of Toronto, to Bathurst Street and Wilson Avenue, and changed its name to Adath Israel. There is a founding-members plaque there today bearing Morris Pezim's name.

He was known as Big Zaida to generations of Pezims and neighbourhood children. In later years, he trimmed his beard to a small goatee. (Later still, the family called him The Colonel, because of his resemblance to Colonel Sanders, the Kentucky Fried Chicken king.) It was The Colonel who smoked four packs of Lucky Strike daily, and who would live to ninety-six.

On the Day of Atonement, the Pezims all went to synagogue. Once, while the adults prayed, Murray, Rose, Frances and Norman took off for Shea's. It wasn't often you got to see Cab Calloway in person for only a nickel. And the show was grand, for Calloway did his famous rendering of *Minnie the Moocher*.

But as they approached the synagogue on their return, there was their father, waiting on the synagogue steps. Izzy was not one for punishment, but he was looking very stern nevertheless.

"You'd better go stand by your grandfather," he said.

When they approached, Morris continued to sway back and

forth, murmuring his prayer. He didn't miss a beat. "And how," he said, swaying forward, "was Cab," he said, swaying back, "Calloway?" for he wasn't mad at all.

Murray was always a wilful child. Even his mother, who was tough as nails, couldn't force him to attend Hebrew school, as Norman did. Nor could she get him to sit still for the piano lessons she paid for. Rebecca thought Murray had beautiful hands, a pianist's hands. But it was Norman she would plunk down on the piano stool because she didn't want to waste her fifty cents. She would chase Murray around the block with a broom. Murray adored his mother.

The extended Pezim family – Izzy's siblings and their spouses and their offspring – was as stereotypically close and Jewish as any in a Woody Allen movie. When the group sat Passover, folding tables were added to the dining-room table. Sometimes, it snaked its way to the front door. Izzy and Rebecca would often get together with one or another of Izzy's siblings and their offspring and take the entire brood over to High Park, or Sunnyside Park, or maybe Centre Island.

Decades later, when Murray's sister Frances lay dying of Parkinson's disease, she pieced together some of her childhood memories in a scribbler for her only grandchild, Jaimie. She wanted him to know how happy her upbringing had been.

"Mother said her floors must be made of honey because there were always lots of kids and people running in and out of our house."

The good times didn't last. In 1926 Izzy went into the real-estate business, which went nowhere. The following year, he established a wholesale dry-goods outfit with his brother, Sam, who knew the business. Sam had started his career as a travelling salesman for a dry-goods wholesaler, working for Chamandy Brothers when he left the service after World War I. So it followed that Sam would be president of the new enterprise – Pezim Bros. – and Izzy would be secretary. Sam was the salesman; Izzy was the inside man.

In those days, the entire strip of Wellington Street between Yonge and York streets was filled with wholesalers, most of them light manufacturers. They fed into the still-newish buildings that had sprung up after a fire in 1904 swept through much of what is now Toronto's financial core. Sam and Izzy first set up shop in a basement in Wellington Street, then moved around the corner to Bay Street near King Street, just around the corner from the Cunard Shipping Line and the Toronto *Telegram*. For three years, they tried to make a go of it, selling on credit, which was the practice of the day.

Then came the stock-market crash of 1929, followed by the Depression. Izzy and Sam crashed along with everyone else. Murray believes Izzy had invested in the stock market before the crash, but to what degree, and whether it had a direct effect on the failure of Pezim Bros., is uncertain. Whatever the case, Pezim Bros. went bankrupt. The family was now poor once again. Becker's raised the price of their smoked-meat sandwiches to two for fifteen cents. They remained the Sunday treat for the Pezim boys. Lunch was often bread and jam.

Frances said in her memoirs that she left school at thirteen because the family was having financial problems. She told her only child, Vicki, that after the bankruptcy she walked to school one day with Rose, Murray, and Norman with her head hidden under her coat. Frances was shamed by what had happened. The other three were unperturbed. "Big deal, Pa will make it back," they said.

As adults, after Murray became addicted to the stock market, Rose and Norman and various other family members became speculators and investors. Never Frances.

Murray and Norman were students at Harbord Collegiate

Institute by this time, not five minutes from their home on Palmerston. Murray was still a skinny kid with a huge honker and wild hair. Unlike Norman, who bore a resemblance to their father, Murray looked Jewish. Harbord's population was ninety percent Jewish in those days, with students such as Louie Weingarten, Frank Shuster, Sam "Blondy" Shopsowitz, Eddie Goodman. More than a handful were on their way to becoming famous – Weingarten and Shuster in show business, Shopsowitz through smoked-meat riches, Goodman via the back rooms of the Conservative party. Weingarten and Shuster belonged to the Oola Boola Club, which called itself the "Society for the Propagation of Irrationality." A skit troupe, the Oola Boola members would sing ditties like this one:

> "Hush little Monday, do not cry,
> You'll be Friday by and by."

In his second year at Harbord, Murray got a hundred percent in math two terms in a row – and even started to tutor kids older than himself – while flunking English composition and literature.

The house on Palmerston Avenue was now, of necessity, filled with boarders, as Izzy tried to stave off personal bankruptcy. He took out a second mortgage to try to make a couple of other investments work, such as an apartment building on Dundas Street. That went sour, too. But as had always been his custom, he continued to host poker games every Sunday night – with the men playing high stakes of a couple of dollars a bet in one room while the women played for smaller stakes in another. Norman and Murray liked to scrounge the quarters that the men sometimes dropped on the carpet. These games weren't in the league of Murray's Uncle George, who went to Montreal for real adventures. He could afford to lose $5,000.

How poor was poor? When the time came for Murray's bar mitzvah, it was a stretch for Rebecca and Izzy to provide the traditional celebration, even though in this case it was just sandwiches and ice cream. The worst of it was that there wasn't enough ice cream to go around and Murray was told he'd have to go without. So he crawled under the dining-room table, which had a tablecloth grazing the floor, and refused to come out. Finally, Norman promised him his ice cream. The fountain pens and handkerchiefs and other gifts that Murray received were sold to pay for the festivities.

The bar mitzvah was Murray's second coming-of-age event. He says he lost his virginity a year earlier to a woman of 25. The story may be apocryphal. It is difficult to reconcile with the image of an immature thirteen-year-old, hiding under a table, crying for a bowl of ice cream.

Izzy Pezim hadn't known the pharmacy business. He hadn't known the wholesale dry-goods business. He didn't know the meat business either, but being as broke as he was, and facing few options, he took a loan from his nephew, Nathan "Nick" Schwartz, who had become a successful meat retailer and was willing to show Murray's father the ropes. Izzy started with a butcher shop on north Yonge Street in 1932, then moved to the Rogers Road Cut Rate Meat Store. To Rogers Road he added the Pape Avenue Cut Rate Meat Market, then replaced that with the Quality Cut Rate Meat Market. Frances worked as a cashier at the Pure Food Meat Market, which was also part of the growing empire. Rose did the same at the Victoria Cut Rate Meat Market, which wasn't.

By 1936 Izzy had built himself a substantial business. But he never cut a slab of meat. He was more the managerial type. And he wasn't calling himself Izzy now. He was Peter, a name more in keeping with the non-Jewish neighbourhoods in which he did business.

In January 1937, Murray dropped out of Harbord. For the first time, he was having a completely dismal academic year – even in geometry, he scored just sixty-nine percent. Besides, the meat business was meant to be a family-run enterprise. Murray started as a trainee at the Quality Meat Market. The butchering business wasn't what he had in mind for his life's work.

There is a huge family photo of the golden wedding anniversary of Murray's grandparents, Morris and Sarah, taken when Murray is thirteen, two years before he quit school. Gathered at the Old Spain banquet hall on Dundas Street, they appear a somewhat sombre group. But Murray looks skinny and eager, like someone just dying to find out what life has in store. Even then Murray had chutzpah. He could have been a model for the young Sammy Glick, the central character of Budd Schulberg's novel, *What Makes Sammy Run?*, who came to epitomize any brash, ruthlessly ambitious, come-from-nowhere Jewish kid, a hustler with confidence to burn and a monumental ego to match.

Everyone – Murray and Izzy and the girls – worked hard to make a go of the new venture. Frances made forty-five cents a week. Of that she gave fifteen cents to Murray, fifteen to Norman, and five to Rose, and kept ten for herself. Even so, the business went nowhere at first, and the bank foreclosed on the Palmerston Street mortgage. The Pezims moved to a rented, though not immodest, home on Turner Avenue in north Toronto, where they continued to take in boarders.

Murray probably had it the toughest of all of them. He was the one who arrived at the store at four a.m. and actually cut the carcasses. God, it was cold, those winter days, riding his bike through the Toronto slush, hacking at slabs of meat in refrigerated rooms, thrusting his hands into pails of warm water so that he could still hold a knife. But in those pre-supermarket days, meat at least had the promise of being a good business. Whatever meat Izzy brought into the store on Monday was pretty well gone by Saturday night. No inventory. All cash. No credit.

Every Friday night the family would gather for lively Sabbath dinners of chicken and chicken soup. In addition to being an immaculate housekeeper, Rebecca Pezim was a good cook. She eventually had a gas stove installed in the basement of the Turner Road house so that she could make an eggplant specialty, a dish that required the searing of the eggplant skin over an open flame, giving the flesh of the vegetable a delicious burnt taste. Another favourite was mamaliga, a cornmeal with either a thick borscht or cheese poured on top.

On Saturdays, the family held their weekly business meeting. Norman, the only one to have stayed out of the butcher business, had set up a little company called the Mercury Distributing Service, which delivered advertising fliers door to door. Norman would have liked to continue at university – he had stood second in his class at the University of Toronto at his December exams in first year. But the registrar demanded his $60 in overdue tuition fees.

"I went to my father and he cried," says Norman. "He said, 'I can't give you the money.' He actually broke into tears."

Norman was not a stellar businessman, family members recall. Certainly, much of the dinner-table talk focused on his entrepreneurial problems. It was the type of family that shared all its affairs. Besides, Norman used the cashier's box at his father's Bloor Street store. There could be no business secrets.

In 1940, when Izzy had made his comeback, he said he wanted Norman to return to university. It was too late. It was too late for Murray, too, who by this time was chasing women with his friend Mickey Wolfe. The two of them kept a split of Scotch in the glove compartment of Mickey's car and promised it to any young flesh that would come across. Sex in those days was hard to come by. "I want you to know that for maybe two years that bottle was never opened," Pezim says today.

But he made himself a reputation as a ladies' man nevertheless, charming the local housewives at the Rogers Road shop, which he eventually managed. "And how are you, Mrs. So-and-So? My, you're looking beautiful today. How young you look."

He was just flirting. It was the other employees who would occasionally jump a housewife on the sawdust bags in the back of the store in exchange for a couple of sausages. Or so Pezim says.

Rebecca, in her own way, kept a watch on the family enterprise. Saturday evenings she would sit in the family car, right outside the Rogers Road butcher shop, and wait for the week to come to an end. As she stared into the shop window she'd see the meat displays that Murray on occasion would win a prize for. Before Murray could shake loose for Saturday night, he had to head back to Turner Road and watch while Rebecca scrutinized the books. Then he would slick on the Brilliantine and Aqua Velva and head down to the Palais Royale dance hall, where the doors opened wide over Lake Ontario and where he would find some young thing to dance with to the strains of Bert Niosi and his band.

In the years just preceding World War II, Izzy's stores were in the money. In those days, if a man had $100,000 he was considered wealthy. Norman believes that Izzy achieved that. He remembers that one week one of the shops did a volume of $7,000 – a windfall. In her memoir, Frances referred to her father as a "shtickel," or little, millionaire.

The Turner Road house, meanwhile, had become a marriage bureau for the Pezim children. Rose married Moe Langer, who had been a tenant first on Palmerston and then on Turner. In 1940, they had their first son, Paul. After Moe enlisted in the RCAF and with Rose working for Jacomo DelZotto, a budding real-estate developer, Paul was virtually raised in those early years by Rebecca. The Langers stayed with the Pezims for fifteen years. Another tenant, Izzy Wagman, who changed his name to Irwin Arthur Wallace (everyone called him Wally), married Frances, and they moved to an apartment. Frances, who also went to work for DelZotto, often said that Wally fell in love with the Pezim family before he fell in love with her. Helen Kriger, who married Norman, was a young woman from Fenelon Falls who became a boarder when she arrived in Toronto to study pharmacy at the University of Toronto.

As the family grew, Rebecca happily slaved over Friday-night dinners for the brood. The household gained a reputation as a meeting place. There was always an argument going. It was good argument, without spite or malice. There was always a card game going, like Clubbyish, which Izzy and Wally would often play. Other family members would hover and place side bets.

By the early forties, all the children but Murray had settled down. Murray was single. Murray was carousing. Murray was sowing his wild oats. Or trying to.

Feeling the fullness of life and the lust for adventure, Murray, Norman, Louie Weingarten and Frank Shuster drove to Newmarket and joined the army on St. Patrick's Day, 1942. It was spring break-up, when the snow melts and runs through the streets, the time of year Murray loves. Norman immediately volunteered for active service. Murray didn't.

Weingarten and Shuster went into the Army Show, where they became famous. The Pezim brothers joined the Brockville Rifles and were shipped to Nanaimo on Vancouver Island. While there, Norman and Murray and anyone they could round up would head to Vancouver, rent a hotel room, and run a craps game.

Eventually, Norman was sent overseas. He was assigned to

an infantry battalion as a signals officer, and crossed the English Channel on D-Day with Le Régiment de la Chaudière, a front-line French Canadian battalion.

Men like Norman had wartime experiences. Murray had wartime exploits. He was shipped with the Brockville Rifles to Jamaica. He says he was variously a truck driver and a prisoner-of-war guard, and he stood sentry over thirty thousand Germans – "big Germans" – who had served with the Afrika Korps.

Pezim liked to gamble with the other soldiers, win their leaves, and lie on the beach. There are pictures of him, then twenty-three or so, propped up on one elbow on the sand. There are girls about, and he has the look of a happy guy. In Jamaica, he spent a good deal of time at the Casablanca Hotel at Montego Bay. He sent Norman pictures of naked Jamaican women.

Pezim fell in love with the island. It smelled of bougain-villea and free-form sex. Life was good. Now all he had to do was figure out how he could live the same good life in post-war Toronto.

CHAPTER 4

The Game

J erry Singer pulled his car to a stop in front of 39 Turner Road. It was a snowy December night in 1946, one of those rare evenings when Toronto, usually mired in slush at that time of year, seems a pretty winter place.

Beside Jerry sat a beautiful seventeen-year-old named Bernice Carol Frankel, his date for the evening. They had stopped at the Pezim house to pick up Fanny Kriger, the sister of Norman Pezim's wife, Helen. This was turkey-buying month in the butcher business, of course, and Fanny told Jerry she couldn't be sprung until the Pezims – Murray, his parents Izzy and Rebecca, his sister Rose, and Rose's husband, Moe – had returned from buying the season's load of turkeys. Fanny was baby-sitting Paul, the son of Moe and Rose.

Jerry returned to his car, shut off the motor, and ushered Bernice Frankel into the Pezim home, a nice house, large and wel-coming. Bernice, Jerry, and Fanny had been talking for about half an hour when the turkey buyers returned, the coldest-looking, most unappealing group of tired, over-bundled travellers imaginable.

Murray Pezim didn't register at first with Bernice Frankel. There were no fireworks. But looking back on that evening many decades later, she says she believes Jerry Singer was put on this earth to introduce her to Murray. Looking back on that evening many decades later, Murray – and this may be apocryphal – says he told his mother, Rebecca, that very night that Bernice Frankel was the woman he was going to marry.

Rebecca was not impressed. She and her friends had tried to line up her younger son with all manner of plump, dark-haired Jewish girls who they felt would make good, plump wives. Besides, Rebecca had hoped to see Murray take up with someone from money. Bernice was blonde and slight, and though of Jewish Romanian descent, didn't look Jewish enough. And her family was poor. Which is why Rebecca is said to have screamed something like, "You will not marry that shiksa!"

Murray Pezim had left Jamaica a year before. He was flat. He says he had to borrow $100 from someone at the British Consulate to finance his way home. All of his gambling winnings had been put back into the Jamaican funfest. His life since his return had gone nowhere, romantic or otherwise. The fact is that until he met Bernice Frankel, Murray, then almost twenty-five, had shown no interest in serious relationships, Jewish, shiksa, or otherwise.

The two started to date. The daughter of a furniture salesman, Bernice was working as a dental assistant and still lived at home. Her father had lost his dress business during the Depression. In the forties, the Frankels lived on Manning Avenue, a working-class street just two streets west of Palmerston Avenue. When Murray first asked her how old she was she lied and said nineteen.

"He had been running around with many women even at the time," recalls Bernice, who wanted to appear sophisticated. "He was quite worldly. I was just a very sheltered little kid who was making $10 a week in a dentist's office and giving $5 to my mother."

To a teenager like Bernice, Pezim was cosmopolitan, funny, and compassionate, and could charm the birds out of the trees. Or at least this is the way he seemed early on. He was boastful, certainly, but Bernice was not put off by that. And though Murray was no millionaire, he was ambitious and in any case made a good living at the Rogers Road shop. Perhaps most important, he was protective of Bernice, who hadn't had a particularly happy childhood. Murray offered security. Certainly, it wasn't his looks that appealed. Her mother called Murray a toothpick; Bernice agrees he was not an attractive man back then. His best feature was his warm brown eyes.

Bernice has fond memories of their courtship. Once, Murray took her to Sunnyside Park, a popular waterfront spot for swimming or just strolling to the background strains of classical music. And there was the amusement park. Bernice recalls a ring-toss game at which Murray landed three rings and picked out the prize that Bernice had asked for: a black serving tray hand-painted with shocking-pink roses. But even as the proud Murray, his chest puffed out like a pouter pigeon, basked in her admiration, the gamesman handed Bernice a small toy dog. Murray rounded up a security guard or two, and made a fuss until Bernice had her tray. He couldn't stand being taken for a sucker.

In those days, Murray drove a Ford Monarch. Even today, he loves cars. He has a slow down-the-road kind of driving style. He likes the edge, always parking right at the mouth of a driveway, so that no-one can park in front of him. It was in the Monarch that he taught Bernice to drive.

Bernice tells this story as an illustration of how thoughtful and attentive Murray could be. She had signed up for professional driving lessons, but the first night the instructor pulled up to a bar and suggested they go for a drink. "Forget the lessons," said Murray, when he heard this. He taught her himself. On the day she went for her driving test, Murray went too, going so far as to motion a Simpson's truck out of the way so Bernice would have less trouble.

"Is that man," asked the examiner, "going to follow us through the entire test?"

Murray Pezim and Bernice Frankel were married on January 6, 1948, at an art gallery in downtown Toronto. There were about two hundred guests in attendance. Murray wore tails and a tophat. Rented. Bernice wore a white floor-length gown. Borrowed. A film of the affair shows how very thin Murray was, and how very happy he seemed. The band played, the women clutched their cigarette cases as they danced. The sisters, Frances and particularly Rose, had grown pretty. In one clip a jovial Izzy grabs his wife and kisses her in a big, warm way. It was a wonderful party. The Pezims and the Frankels split the bill.

Bernice says today she believes she is the only woman who didn't marry Murray Pezim for his money.

The post-war forties were a hustle. As the veterans returned home they poured into university, where they were given dibs on the available places. The diaspora of Kensington Market tried to make a buck any which way. Some hustled chickens. Others hustled securities. Pezim hustled beef. But he had bigger dreams.

"Picture this," he would say to Bernice, cutting a swath through the air with his hands to make an imaginary corporate banner, replacing his Jewish surname for a fashionable Manhattan district. "Murray Hill Butter. Murray Hill Dairy." And Murray Hill this and Murray Hill that. You wanna believe, he would tell his wife, that Murray Pezim, butcher, would in very short order be transformed into Murray Pezim, titan.

Meanwhile, bigger gamblers, entrepreneurs, and cheats hit the Toronto Stock Exchange. There were two games to play, and each was ruled by a very specific type of player. The straight game offered investors the relatively low-risk investment opportunities of stocks in banks, insurance companies, senior industrials, a couple of railways, established resource operations, and a handful of debentures. A century after a dozen men came up with the idea of instituting a thirty-minute trading session, the Toronto Stock Exchange liked to think it had come of age. The securities firms that ruled this side of the board were run by good, grey men with names like Doherty and Trebilcock and Tudhope, who had carried on the mission of good, grey men before them with names like Ames and Cox. They hoped to make investors of solid, middle-class citizens who liked the notion of getting dividends on time while contributing to the economic growth of a nation.

These smoothly tailored securities men became part of the country's still-young establishment. They mingled at the Royal Canadian Yacht Club and the Canadian Club and the Albany Club. They took up residence in the city's tony Rosedale district or to the northwest in Forest Hill. They supported their chosen charities and they gave generously to the arts. In truth, the game they played wasn't very much fun at all. While it was profitable to paper out successive issues of companies such as Massey-Harris and Canada Packers and Bell Telephone, the market wasn't getting jazzed from these firms.

It was the penny game that held the promise of spectacular returns. It was the small stuff that caught the eye of the little guy and fired up the Toronto Stock Exchange. This made sense. It might cost $60 to buy a single share of Abitibi Power and Paper. Bell Telephone offered handsome dividends for those who could cope with the $200 share price. But everyone could play the penny-stock game. A nickel buys a share, a hundred nickels buys

71

a block – just five bucks a gamble to double, triple, quintuple your money. On the TSE, this lottery, the penny game, was usually synonymous with the exploration game: oil and gas, base metals, gold.

You could not grow up in Toronto in those days and not know something of the mining business. Since the turn of the century, Ontario prospectors had been turning up gold at places such as Madoc, Larder Lake, Red Lake, and, most spectacularly, the Dome Mine near Timmins. These finds revived memories of the California Sutter's Mill find in 1848, of the gold boom in Rossland, British Columbia, that started ten years later, and the frenzied Klondike gold rush of 1898. It was the Rossland boom – magnificent finds in the Kootenay and Slocan districts – that led to the establishment of two mining exchanges in Toronto. The Toronto Mining and Industrial Exchange opened in 1896, and the Standard Stock & Mining Exchange in 1897. In 1899, the two merged, kept the name of the latter, and set about giving the Toronto Stock Exchange, which had been around since 1852, a run for its money.

The silver finds at Cobalt, Ontario, in 1903 gave the newly merged mining exchange its first mining boom. After World War I, frontiersmen pushed into the copper-gold field at Rouyn Noranda in Quebec and the lead-copper-zinc discovery in the Sudbury basin. In 1929, mining stocks crashed along with everything else. Gilbert LaBine's radium discovery the following year at Great Bear Lake in the Northwest Territories started another prosperous cycle.

By the mid-1890s, a gold standard had been adopted by most European countries, as well as the United States and Canada. Bullion was used to balance international payments and provided a full convertibility of currency into gold. Inflation after World War I threw the system out of whack, leaving some currencies exchangeable for less than half the gold convertibility before 1914. The replacement Gold Exchange Standard permitted central banks to use foreign currencies as well as gold and government bonds as monetary backing.

In the succeeding years, countries went on and off the gold standard. Conflicting national policies, particularly among the so-called three pillars of international finance – France, Britain and the United States – started to force balance-of-payments discrepancies in the late twenties. By 1931, this system of currency management had fallen apart. The failure of the largest commercial bank in Austria had repercussions for other currencies, most seriously for Britain's sterling. That country's foreign liabilities were four times its gold reserves. In the fall of 1931, Britain suspended the convertibility of currency to gold. The *Financial Post* in Toronto reported that even when the London Stock Exchange closed in the chaos following the abandonment of the gold standard there, the mining exchange in Toronto maintained daily trading sessions and suffered no significant loss of membership.

In 1934, the Gold Reserve Act, brought in under President Franklin Delano Roosevelt, pegged the price of gold at $35 (U.S.) an ounce. The act stipulated that gold could not be used as a medium of domestic exchange and made it illegal for individuals or private companies to own bullion. Nevertheless, the act was good news for gold-miners. In the twenties, an ounce of gold was worth just $20 (U.S.). The Gold Reserve Act encouraged established gold-producers to look again at seemingly tapped-out sources – that is, to study the feasibility of mining ore that was harder to get at and therefore more expensive to mine. Eventually, however, as mining costs rose, the pegged price put a squeeze on gold-mining profits, forcing the mining industry to look elsewhere for its windfall.

Prospectors turned their talents toward the base metals – zinc, copper, nickel, iron ore. They would tromp into the Ontario bush – and the Quebec bush and the Manitoba bush – blazing posts to mark their mining claims. Any mineral find, it seemed, would fuel a staking rush of prospectors and marauding claims-jumpers. The base-metals discoveries made the mining giants of the day – Hudson Bay Mining & Smelting, Sherritt Gordon, Noranda, and Falconbridge. There were plenty of base-camp stories of ribald, unpoliced, oversexed, booze-sodden communities. The goal for the prospectors, of course, was to sell their claims, if not to an established mining house, then perhaps a Bay Street promoter who would funnel these claims into a dormant corporate shell with a live stock-exchange listing. Then flog the hell out of the stock.

In 1933, the mining exchange outperformed the Toronto Stock Exchange by fifty percent in dollars traded. But the various mining booms that had marked the exchange's four-decade existence had attracted countless scoundrels and bad actors, as well as endless shell companies flogged by pitchmen who would push a nickel stock to fifty cents, then bail out. The mining exchange was for speculators and risk-takers. From its headquarters on Temperance Street, the operation appeared respectable enough – or, at least, everyone wore a suit. But it did a terrible job of self-regulation.

In the thirties, the most talked-about mining promoter in the country was Joe Hirshhorn, a Latvian-born American who set up shop on Bay Street in 1933. Much envied and often reviled, Hirshhorn started out as a stock trader, then moved into the underwriting and promoting of resource issues. By the end of his first year in Toronto, he had the heads of the established mining concerns calling for a securities investigation into his manipulation of the stock of Gunnar Gold, a company run by Gilbert LaBine.

In its report, the Ontario Securities Commission concluded that Hirshhorn, who had been an earlier financier for Gunnar and had more than half a million shares in the company, had indeed played fast and loose. Said the Commission:

> As a result of this manipulation, he created an arti-
> ficial market into which was lured the unsuspecting
> public, and that the purpose of the manipulation
> was the disposal of his own shares at the highest
> possible price. The process of manipulation is by
> buying and selling to create in the public mind the
> impression of great activity in the stock. It soon
> gets abroad that there is something doing. The
> public is attracted and joins in the activities of the
> manipulation thereby making it possible for him
> gradually to force the shares to a point far beyond
> their real value. This Mr. Hirshhorn succeeded in
> doing with very great skill, even losing substantial
> blocks of his own shares on the way up. On July
> 19th, the shares reached a high of $2.50 Mr. Hirsh-
> horn's last sale was at $2.48, which might be consid-
> ered a profitable transaction in view of the fact that
> the shares had cost him originally about eight cents.

Such pointed sarcasm is rare among securities regulators.
This judgement came from John Godfrey, the securities commissioner. What was particularly disturbing to him was that Hirshhorn had not violated the rules. "Manipulation is per se not a
crime," he wrote.

> It is the conspiring with one or more persons to
> manipulate which is punishable . . . . With the com-
> plicated mechanism of the modern stock exchange,
> however, manipulation can be accomplished in a
> perfectly legal way. The manipulator can sit in the

centre of his operations surrounded by telephones and by using a three- or four-way jitney (clearing trades through a number of brokerages) can buy and sell stocks without brokers who are doing the buying and selling knowing that the manipulation is in process. One broker may know only that a certain party is buying; another broker may know only that a certain party is selling. A skillful manipulator can cover his tracks so that the broker he uses in the transaction may never have a guilty knowledge of his operations and without that guilty knowledge there can be no unlawful conspiracy.

Months before the report was released in early 1935, the Toronto Stock Exchange governors decided to merge the two exchanges, in the hope of keeping the mining promoters in better check. The *Financial Post* published a cartoon of George Drew, who preceded Godfrey as the province's securities commissioner, pointing a shotgun at the two exchanges. Years later, Frank Kaplan, a reporter with the *Post*, wrote that the forced wedding was meant to "clean up the then high, wide and handsome tactics and financial troubles of the mining brokers." On a more mercenary — and cynical — level, the stock-exchange governors surely had another reason for wanting a merger: there were fistfuls of money to be made from mining stocks.

The trading headquarters of the TSE were located on the second floor of the National Trust Building at 24 King Street East. National Trust itself shared the main floor with A.E. Ames and Co., one of the most respected securities firms of the day. Right next door was Dominion Securities, owned by George Cox, who also owned the National Trust building and, in fact, National Trust itself. This was the heart of the securities establishment. In 1934,

341 million shares went from buyers to sellers and sellers to buyers, for a share value total of $415 million.

In 1937, the exchange moved with great fanfare to its spanking new Art Deco headquarters on Bay Street, where it remained for more than forty years, a panoramic frieze marching across its stone face of a fisherman, farmer, factory worker, clerk, banker and miner.

When World War II began, the exchange moved quickly to ban short selling, fearing the practice of borrowing stock in anticipation of falling share prices was too easy a mark in such bad times. The TSE sewered between 1940 and 1942, then crept up through 1943 and 1944. As one might expect, 1945, with the war over, was an excellent year, with 442 million shares bought or sold, for a value of $618 million.

While base-metals prospects flourished before the war, the hopes for oil and gas had been less promising. A powerful monopoly in the United States had cornered the industry there. In Canada, Imperial Oil, with the oil fields in southwestern Ontario fast approaching depletion, was frantically looking for new sources of crude. In February, 1947, Imperial hit a bonanza at Leduc, twenty kilometres south of Edmonton.

Everybody and his cousin were playing the market. In 1948, the *Financial Post* reported that "more and more Canadians are trading on the stock market without anything to show for it — either profits or stocks. The ding-dong action of post-war markets has produced a lot of stock but few millionaires."

The average Joe wouldn't make a million. The average Joe would get suckered. Murray Pezim, being an average Joe with long-shot dreams, poured his savings of $1,300 (in some accounts of this story the figure is $13,000, but $1,300 is more likely) into a penny-mining outfit called Duvay Gold Mines. One of the regular

Rogers Road patrons was a broker named Max Guthrie, who worked for E.T. Lynch and Co. He would tout this or that stock to anyone who would listen – and Duvay was one such property. Pezim knew nothing about the stock market, but to him the operation smelled of the main chance.

Duvay was like many penny-mining businesses. Incorporated in November 1944, it had an asset base that consisted of a bunch of unpatented mining claims on about 750 acres of property in good mining country near a Quebec town called Amos, just north of Val-d'Or. In its TSE listing statement, Duvay reported that "spectacular showings of gold have been disclosed in the areas blasted." The accompanying engineer's report is full of references to visible gold, a concept that even the novice Pezim would understand. In its financial statements for 1945 it lists office petty cash of $5. Its cash balance: $26,000.

The company was run by a well-known promoter and lawyer named Sam Ciglen who, years later, was found guilty of a little tax evasion here, a little stock fraud there. Ciglen was sentenced to two years in Kingston Penitentiary and disbarred. But in 1945, Ciglen was a prominent man about town, a partner in a law firm in the Concourse building on Adelaide Street. Duvay had no taint about it. Pezim made staggered purchases that started out at 25 cents a share, watched the stock fall to 12 cents, then sink into oblivion. He lost every nickel.

"Murray lost $1,300 as though it was being sucked into a vacuum cleaner," says Bernice. "He didn't know what he was doing."

For Murray Pezim, the experience was an epiphany. Pezim then as now didn't like to be burned, pushed or cheated. After he blew his brains out on Duvay, he started studying the stock business. He didn't get any quarrel from Bernice, either, who didn't really care for the idea of being married to a butcher

forever. It was such a dirty business. Butchers didn't get dressed
up to go to work.

It's not difficult to guess which of the two stock-market
games appealed more to Murray Pezim in 1949. Not that he had
much choice. An uneducated, over-eager Jewish kid could never
enter the world of the Upper Canada College-educated future
masters of the universe. It was the penny hopefuls for him. He
would get spruced up and head down to watch the trading action
on the stock-exchange floor, the butcher-floor sawdust puffing out
of his pant cuffs, the aroma of his aftershave billowing in his wake.
Murray Pezim's ambition was to get on the inside of penny deals.
He knew the potential rewards far outstripped anything he would
ever see in the butcher business.

He was ready to play. He was ready to blow his brains out
again and again and again.

Like the soberminded men who ran the reputable securities firms,
the exchange itself had a smart, businesslike veneer. This was no
longer a frontier operation, officials would tell the news reporters
of the day. Why, the average brokerage was a shirt-and-tie, leather-
furniture-and-mahogany type of place. It was open for trading
from 10 a.m. to 4 p.m. daily, 10 a.m. to 1 p.m. on Saturday. There
was a one-and-a-half-hour weekday close for lunch. A raucous,
boozy bunch, the traders often had a tough time keeping their
orders straight in the afternoon.

In the forties, stockbrokers were called "customers' men."
They were licensed and regulated by the TSE, and made their
living from commissions, drawing one-third of the amount that the
brokerage charged the investor. The term "salesmen," on the other
hand, applied to licensed sellers of bonds and mutual funds. The
mechanics of the job of customers' men were simple enough. They
would take a trading order either over the telephone or in person,

write it out, and give it to the order clerk. The order clerk would then phone one of the firm's trading clerks scattered through the 140 trading desks on the exchange floor. The clerk in turn would summon his firm's floor trader by hitting a numbered light above a trading desk. Each brokerage, then as today, was identified by a number.

The process worked well during slow markets, but when there was real action on the floor, the clerk would either shoot the order to the trader through a pneumatic tube or use an exchange runner to get the order quickly to the floor trader. The floor trader would take the order and head to whichever of the nine trading posts listed that particular stock. The posts themselves were hexagonal, listing perhaps ten stocks (identified by the companies' trading symbols) on each of the six sides, along with the bid (the offering price) and the ask (the desired selling price) of the stocks.

There were rules and regulations, the governors of the exchange told anyone prepared to listen. There were listing requirements, trading regulations, audit requirements. The public, the exchange commissioners proclaimed, was being given a fair run for its money. Unscrupulous practices, they promised, were being sought out and eradicated. This was a house of integrity and fiscal responsibility.

The truth was that even after the mining exchange was swept under the TSE's regulatory umbrella, the penny-mining game was home to legions of liars and hoodwinkers. Bay Street was filled with boiler rooms from which high-pressure stock salesmen worked. Greenwood Securities, for example, had orange crates nailed to the walls with a phone in each crate. Salesmen would flog stock to Europe, to the United States, wherever. Americans loved the penny mines. Promoters would place advertisements in foreign papers, sell securities by mail, always making extravagant promises of quick profits.

The boiler-room business was straightforward. The "lead getter" would telephone a potential client, usually an offshore client, offering "research" on a stock from the firm's "analysts." He would quote a mention of the company from a reputable publication such as the *Northern Miner*, or send the potential client a crassly self-serving tout sheet. The "line opener" would follow up on the lead getter's leads. It was the line opener's responsibility to get the sucker on the hook. The companies being sold would usually have exotic names such as Keyboycon or Harricana. Names that the American poet, Stephen Vincent Benét, once affectionately called the "snakeskin titles of mining claims."

A man who was a player then (and is still a player today) tells the story of one lead getter during the oil boom. He was nowhere near an oil field. He was, in fact, in a Bay Street boiler room. There was road construction nearby — complete with the persistent racket of a jackhammer (which, to be fair, is a rock driller of sorts).

"Hear that?" said the lead getter to the sucker, holding the phone out the window. "They're drilling right now."

The man telling the story is Isadore (Izzy) Rotterman, a figure who looms large in the Pezim saga. And he doesn't mince words when explaining just how lucrative the boiler-room business was in those days. "You wouldn't buy a $5 bill from the guy for fifty cents." It wouldn't end once the sucker had been reeled in, either. A "loader," then a "reloader," each time a different salesman, would get the client to swallow more stock — and to keep swallowing until he and the stock went under. The promoters on the inside track, who got in at a nickel, would always get out at the top.

The boiler-room salesmen would work until the small hours of the morning, clocking the time zones across the U.S. At

81

two or three in the morning, they would crawl to the Cork Room on the west side of Bay Street, or the TRAC (the Toronto Radio Artists' Club) on Yonge Street just south of Wellington, and have a few drinks. A lot of these men were carnival types, veterans from the Royal American Shows. In the thirties, the Ontario Securities Commission had hired a 350-pound tough guy named Frank Crowe as inspector to bust the boiler rooms. But the Securities Commission was just a handful of people, and the boiler rooms flourished.

Between the scoundrels in the boiler rooms and the blue suits in the brokerages were scores of other firms that were also big trouble. There were the bookies and druggies who became brokers. There were brokers fronting for promoters, advising clients to buy while simultaneously filling the promoters' sell orders. This particularly popular practice, called backdooring, was rampant. Every promoter backdoored. It was just another part of the game. (In fact, Murray Pezim backdoors all the time and he'll defend it to this day. In Vancouver, he explains, there are no market-makers. By market-maker he means a trader who is ready to buy when another trader wants to sell; who moves to sell when another trader is ready to buy. So promoters like Pezim serve the purpose of maintaining an orderly market. A promoter, once he really gets a stock moving – with an upticking in the stock price – must start selling, otherwise he'll go broke. "That doesn't mean I'm blowing off all my paper," he says, in his own defence.)

Back in the forties, there were no filing requirements for insider trading. There was no way for the investor to know that the promoter himself was saying good-bye to the shares at the same time as the chump was saying hello. The fact is, says Izzy Rotterman, there wasn't a promoter on Bay Street who wouldn't backdoor a client in the old days.

"There's no such animal," he says. "I'd have to dream up

someone from the depths. If they didn't backdoor stock there was something wrong with them. We're talking pre-sixties. We're talking moose-pasture days. We're talking about crooks. We're talking about skulduggery. You might as well go back and talk about the Morgans and the Kennedys and the Rockefellers. They're all crooks."

Another technique was for promoters to keep nominee accounts at a number of brokerages, creating the appearance of trading activity while concealing the fact that the shares were being repeatedly bought and sold through the accounts of one person.

Regulations governing mining companies also raised problems. The TSE was the only exchange in the world that permitted a listed company to raise money through the sale of shares on the trading floor. The system didn't require a share prospectus, so purchasers couldn't judge the merits of the stock or the financial status of the company, or determine why the money was being raised. It was an excellent opportunity for promoters to get their stocks to shareholders without shareholders being aware they were buying from promoters. This form of financing, permitted only for mining companies, was a huge supervisory headache. The system raised millions of dollars every year for purported mining outfits, but as often as not a huge percentage of the draw, if not all, went into individual pockets, not into exploration. You could do a financing in fifteen minutes. For the men on the inside track, it was an incredible bonanza.

Best of all, promoters didn't have to break the law or even bend the rules to get rich. The primary financing of mining shares allowed for options tied to treasury shares. The options, a right to purchase further shares, would be tied to escalating "strike," or exercise, prices. The potential windfall was all the incentive any stock-pusher needed to get the shares pumping higher and higher. A promoter could busy himself backdooring his stock through the early run-up, then exercise options as the price gained speed. This was no casino. The odds were far more favourable. The players with the highest windfall potential were those men – and they were almost exclusively men – who served as financiers or underwriters and promoter at the same time. They could broker the deal, backdoor the stock, switch hats to promoter, tout the stock while selling it, then exercise the options. And the windfall was tax-free.

The floor traders in the forties were unregistered. They could trade for themselves at the same time they were trading for a brokerage. The potential for personal profits was immeasurable. Unlicensed brokers fronting for unscrupulous promoters vending rumours of mining riches, mythical deals, imaginary returns, made for a fabulous match.

Izzy Rotterman synthesizes it nicely: "A promoter could take a piece of peed-on property and sell it as ocean frontage." And yet, the little guy could make a buck at this game. He could hang around the boardroom of, say, Frank Leslie's brokerage, in the basement of the Ogilvie Building on Bay Street (which actually had steam pipes running overhead, giving it a real boiler-room ambience). The customers' men would be sitting around the periphery, and the client could say, "Hey, Joe, buy me 500" such and such, all the while watching the board markers and the ticker tape.

In 1949, the stock market received a boost from the federal government. The country needed capital, craved growth. In his budget speech the finance minister of the day rose in the House of Commons and said, "We depend and must depend for full employment and the creation of new wealth on the willingness of our people to risk their money in constructive enterprises." The TSE took this to mean stock purchases. The exchange was going crazy with the oil boom. It was a fabulous time to get in on the action.

Murray Pezim was sharpening his elbows, dreaming of winning his very own million. He needed access to the inside rail of the business, that is to say, the money-making rail. Max Guthrie, who sold Pezim into his first learning experience in the form of Duvay Gold, wasn't the only securities type to frequent the Rogers Road store. Another regular was Archie Hart, an account executive at Thomson Kernaghan, the Bay Street brokerage. He advised Pezim to talk to Ed Kernaghan. Though Kernaghan had no job to offer, he did agree to let Pezim hang out at the brokerage to learn the business. For four months – though he continued to work at the butcher shop – Pezim immersed himself whenever possible in the stock market, hanging at the brokerage, hanging around the trading floor, hanging around the hangouts.

Kernaghan also put Pezim in touch with a New York trader named Milo Green, a partner at the brokerage house Hentz and Co. A one-time Zurich commodities trader, Green was, says Pezim, simply brilliant, "a beautiful man . . . a concert pianist." Pezim has said this hundreds of times in hundreds of interviews. It was Green, says Pezim, who gave him the oft-quoted saying that hangs on his office wall.

I saw a man chasing the horizon. I shouted to him, "You'll never reach it." He replied, "You lie," and rushed on.

This has become a Pezim motto. He says Green taught him about life! about people! about emotions! Pezim says that Bernice disliked Green, as she came to dislike many of his associates. Bernice, for her part, says she never heard of Milo Green, nor did she know what her husband was doing in New York, which is odd for a still-fledgling relationship. That Pezim moved on to Chicago as a commodities trader for two months isn't mentioned by her at all.

But soon Murray was back in Toronto, back at the butcher business. His father, Izzy, was prospering, so there wasn't much pressure put on Murray to get his act together. He was, after all, one of the Pezim golden boys.

His first real job in the securities business was in the early fifties as a broker with E.T. Lynch, the firm at which Max Guthrie worked. One of his buddies was a promoter named Morry Kessler, who brokered stock out of Standard Securities. Kessler introduced Murray to Al Rosen, who had a little mining play called Ascot Metals. Pezim started pushing the stock. He believed it was a winner. It wasn't.

Pezim had failed. Pezim was bugged. He scurried once again back to the butcher business, back to the family, back to the security of a pay cheque. He felt deflated. Even then, he didn't handle defeat well. Even then, his moods swung from elation to depression. Later, he came to believe that it wasn't the failure – the failures – that drained him, but the fear that next time he wouldn't make a rebound. Fear gave Pezim the night sweats.

The year before, in 1950, Frances, Murray's sister, had a nervous breakdown. The fat, seemingly happy child had grown up, married a notary public, and had a child of her own. But *meine Fegele* was not content. After the breakdown, she had a series of electric-shock treatments. Frances never completely recovered. She was nervous, insecure, quick to weep, terrified she would become ill again, embarrassed she had fallen ill in the first place. She suffered migraines. She would take to her bed. She would retch. In the Pezim family, there were no secrets. Everyone felt sorry for Frances. Her parents, Izzy and Rebecca, were surprised that their daughter was not as well adjusted as she appeared. They probably didn't realize that Murray, their golden boy, wasn't all that stable, either.

On the home front, he had already turned any dreams of conventional domesticity that Bernice may have harboured to dust.

He would complain that she was too fastidious, that he would get out of bed to urinate and come back to find the sheets stripped. In late March 1951, Bernice went into her first labour. Pezim went to get the car. When he returned, he found Bernice in the bathroom combing her eyebrows.

"Get into the car!" he screamed.

Within a year, still shelling bones out of slabs of meat, Pezim was headed nowhere. He was going nuts, climbing the walls. He was hanging out with a crowd of Jewish rounders, promoters, bookies, and boiler-room artists. Every one of Pezim's friends was a sharpie in one way or another. He was going daily to Jackie Beale's card club in north Toronto. Beale was a bookmaker, and he handled Pezim's business. Beale ran a steambath, too. Pezim loved to steam. To eat. To gamble, especially on the fights.

What he needed was an angle. It was clear to him that the big money – and the easiest money – was in the penny mines. Maybe Duvay was an unfortunate fluke. Perhaps Aseni was, too. Perhaps if he tried again in the penny-stock business he would be third-time lucky.

CHAPTER 5

Grift Sense

"My boy . . . always try to rub up against money,
for if you rub up against money long enough,
some of it may rub off on you."
DAMON RUNYON, "A VERY HONORABLE GUY"

Every morning, Murray Pezim hustled himself down to the offices
of Jenkin Evans in the Northern Ontario Building at 330 Bay
Street, picked up a pack of cigarettes at Alex Savein's smoke shop
on the ground floor, and headed to suite 904, an unassuming little
operation situated between Chateau Gai Wines and Gulf Lead
Mines. Pezim was a pipsqueak. Just another broker. Just another
salesman pushing any old stock any which way.

The Northern Ontario Building was a veritable brokerage
palace. Through its sixteen floors were scattered the likes of
J. Bradley Streit, Draper Dobie, Wesley Davidson, Wardrop Gardiner,
Seguin Barrett, Ross Milner, and G. H. Rennie. Brokers all. On the
fifteenth floor was Royal Securities, bond dealers. On the sixteenth
were the Boy Scouts of Canada and the Kiwanis Safety Council.

Some of the brokerages were not what you would call blue chip. They churned their commissions on the penny mines, shamelessly sporting the monikers of hopeful mining juniors on their name plates. J. B. Streit, for example, was not merely a brokerage but the backer behind Wesley Gold Mines, Dillam Gold Mines, Boycon Pershing Gold Mines, and Orenda Gold Mines. The company names and the corporate backing would change as their fortunes ebbed and flowed. A penny mine would fall dormant, only to have its name picked up by a new band of promoters in search of an existing stock-exchange listing into which they could pour the latest handful of mining claims.

Jenkin Evans himself was an affable Welshman, who had started as a mining contractor in the Kirkland Lake area of northeastern Ontario – sinking shafts, building headframes, that sort of thing. Because of his working-man beginnings, he lacked the establishment patina of the Bay Street men we know today. He marched around the office with a cigar stub sticking out of his mouth, often unlit, the uncut end growing moist and bitter through the day. He weighed in at maybe 240 pounds. If the stock business had made old man Jenks wealthy, it didn't show.

Pezim was fond of Jenks, at least in part because he could teach him about gold. Even though base metals were the more interesting mining finds in the fifties, Pezim liked to study Jenks's gold hoard, a collection of nuggets and a few large rock samples showing gold quartz veins. The two men played crib together for a nickel. Pezim today says that when he looked away, his boss would move the peg up a notch or two. Jenks sounds, from all descriptions, like the addled and lovable Uncle Billy in *It's a Wonderful Life*.

Several promoters ruled the penny operators in 1952. Down at Draper Dobie, Louis Arthur Chesler, whom everyone called Lou, was indisputably a kingpin on the street, along with Bud Knight, another Draper associate and a big man around town. The

Peterborough-born Chesler had started out as a customers' man at Draper before moving into the financing and promoting of mining ventures. He was a big talker and a big man, a Sidney Greenstreet type who weighed about three hundred pounds, with short, wavy hair crowning his pudgy, boyish face. Chesler was then in his late thirties, but already a millionaire with a ritzy home on Old Forest Hill Road. When Chesler bet the ball games, he'd wager fifty grand. Maybe a hundred grand. Draper Dobie in the fifties was a big house, a real action house. This was long before Montegu Black III, Conrad's brother, came to run the place.

After work, guys like Pezim would head to the Savarin, a cafeteria-style eatery and bar run by a couple of Greeks, two doors north of Jenkin Evans on Bay Street, just past the Grand & Toy store. Or maybe the Towne Tavern on Queen Street, run by Sam Berger, a salesman at Davidson's. Guys like Chesler would hang out at the Club Norman on Adelaide Street, one of the first licensed establishments in the city, a classy joint with live enter- tainment, dancing, and little lamps on the tables. Very New York, the kind of place one dressed for. Later, when Nat Sandler bought the Club Norman he changed the name to the Club One Two. Sandler himself had a small brokerage, specializing in junior industrials. Not only was Chesler a One Two regular but he may have owned a piece of the club.

Jewish wealth was burgeoning in Toronto then, and Chesler was part of it. There was the Levy family, millionaire owners of an auto-parts outfit that made a big score by salvaging military vehi- cles after World War II. There were the Dunkelmans, the people behind Tip Top Tailors, and the Shopsowitzes, who built their empire on hot dogs and corned-beef sandwiches. The WASP establishment kept its distance from this new wealth. The Toronto Club, the most venerable men's cloister, barred Jews. Similarly, Jews were not welcome at the WASPier summer retreats. So they built their own. The Dunkelmans bought acreage at Balfour Beach, near Jacksons Point, on the south shore of Lake Simcoe, and put up a string of cottages; the Dunkelmans, the Cheslers, the Levys all holidayed there. The Shopsowitzes built the Monteith Inn on Lake Rosseau; it too became a popular Jewish get-away.

Meanwhile, Murray Pezim, little man, was still living with Bernice in their apartment on Bathurst Street. They were not wealthy, but they had a close group of friends. Socially, they would have dinner parties amongst themselves, the Pezims one week, then another couple the next and on from there. Hallowe'en, 1955, the party was at the Pezims', and Murray wore a nightshirt of sorts, pinned all over with stock certificates. Bernice was a geisha girl, with black braids made out of exercise tights.

The couple would get out of town from time to time, maybe down to Miami, where Pezim once in the early years of his marriage made a killing of a couple thousand dollars shooting craps at the Colonial Club, which bought an extra week's holiday. He came to favour the Fontainebleau Hotel in Miami, the mobster Meyer Lansky's place, with a gambling casino and a chicken-curry entrée for $1.65. Pezim and his male pals – some of them small-time mobsters – would occasionally take the train to Chicago, then go over to Las Vegas, gambling all the way. This was all penny-ante stuff. To reach Chesleresque heights, Murray needed connections and fat-cat clients. He had to get in on deals. He had to find a partner.

In a building at the corner of Bay and Front streets were the offices of Maris Investment, run by an entrepreneur named Earl Glick. The Earl, as he was known, was almost a year older than Murray. The son of Russian immigrants, he had arrived in Canada as a three-year-old, and his name then had been Isadore. In the twenties, when the Pezims were living on Palmerston, his father, David Glick, was selling rings and repairing watches from a small store on nearby Dundas Street. The Glicks took rooms for a while on Palmerston, a few blocks south of the Pezims, though Earl and Murray were not boyhood friends.

In the fifties, Pezim started hustling Glick's business. The Earl, a nondescript, actuarial-looking man, was a big stock-market player, the kind who generated handsome commissions for brokers. It is this business that Murray wanted at first. But the two came to forge a much stronger alliance as partners in penny promotions. The Earl called the shots, deciding which corporate shells to hunt down and which new ventures to promote. Pezim, the hustler, Mr. Personality, was charged with selling the stock, finding the investors.

The partnership quickly found itself in one of those penny-mining booms that had made the Toronto Stock Exchange famous. So famous that *Life* magazine trumpeted the TSE mining hustle in a 1953 feature. "These days Toronto, Canada, an ordinarily staid community known as the 'City of Churches,' is atwitter," the article said. The TSE had surpassed the New York Stock Exchange as the busiest exchange on the continent. Penny stocks, or "drill-hole securities," as they were called, were offering "people of humble income a chance to become minor-league Hetty Greens and Jay Goulds overnight." Jay Gould? The same bandit who craved a little stock manipulation now and then, who tried to corner the gold market, who became the definitive robber baron by monopolizing more railroad miles than even the Vanderbilts did? Hetty Green? The miserly Wall Street operator, the most famous woman financier of her day, who was adept at engineering bull markets in railroad stocks? These were role models?

In truth, there were many examples of small man made big in Toronto. They weren't on a Gould-Green scale — even Chesler wasn't that big — but they were money-makers come from small beginnings. "A Toronto commercial artist who had bought a thousand shares of one penny stock and departed for a January vacation in Barbados, returned to discover he had made $10,000 while sunning himself," said the magazine, making winning sound so deliciously easy. "A group of ladies working together in Haileybury, Ontario, once the home of famed mine developer Gilbert LaBine . . . pooled their slender resources last fall and bought 30,000 shares of one of his stocks. All are now independently wealthy."

The article didn't mention the Morris Blacks or Irving Goulds of the day. The dirty-deal promoters. Or the infamous Frank Kaftel, a one-time ballet dancer who turned into a swindler of spectacular proportions. Next to him, all other promoters were choirboys. The Kaftel legend can't be verified. It is said he was a man who had promoters salaaming before him in hopes of drawing his business, a man who made a billion dollars, who owed the Ontario government $16 million in taxes, who would spend $2,000 daily, who favoured the lemon steak at Domenic's and a young girl who bore a resemblance to Audrey Hepburn. Kaftel eventually relocated to Paris where, according to the legend, he had an apartment on avenue Foch and a mail drop at Hotel Georges V – George Sank.

The article went on to explain that the rapid growth of the TSE was a reflection of a new self-esteem, an emboldened national psyche:

> Canada is growing in self-confidence, after decades of feeling inferior to its mother country and bustling neighbour to the south . . . . The result . . . is a national need for risk capital, money which is frankly gambled on the long chance and which pays the long price when it hits. Canada is encouraging this with lenient tax laws in investment profits – no capital gains taxes, for example, and a very generous "depletion" exemption on mining stock profits.

The year before, in 1952, Gilbert LaBine's Gunnar Gold, the same stock that Joe Hirshhorn had manipulated twenty years earlier, had driven the exchange wild. Now LaBine, the *Life* article said, was searching for uranium along the north shore of Lake Athabasca in northern Saskatchewan. In the thirties, LaBine had discovered the Eldorado mine, a radium project at Great Bear Lake that expelled what was then unmarketable uranium as a waste product. Eldorado didn't flourish as a radium producer, but the mine's prospects had revived after 1939 following the discovery of nuclear fission. In fact, Eldorado provided some of the uranium that was used in the Manhattan Project and ultimately fed Robert Oppenheimer's nuclear bombs at Los Alamos.

The strategic importance of Eldorado moved a wartime Canadian government to take over the mine in 1942, eventually turning it into a Crown corporation. LaBine and his brother were removed from its operations. That didn't stop LaBine from sending Albert Zeemel, his chief geologist, into the same vicinity in 1952 to search for more. According to *Life*, Zeemel's Geiger counter "started ticking like a 98 cent alarm clock, and he presently concluded that he had made the find of a lifetime." Gunnar Gold moved to $14 from $2.

There was precious little skepticism in the magazine piece. The TSE offered a stock-market Eldorado to even the smallest, most ill-equipped beginners. The *Life* writer found a clerk, a "girl clerk," no less, who earned a paltry $30 a week, saved what she could, and invested all she had in a 17-cent stock. "Today, no longer a clerk, she is living in comfortable retirement in western Canada."

If some girl clerk could do it, Pezim could do it a thousand times over. A million times over. A little divine intervention wouldn't hurt, however. And as fate would have it this is just what Pezim found in a lucky uranium strike called Denison Mines.

There was another promoter about town in 1953. His name was Stephen Boleslav Roman, a stolid, square-faced, 32-year-old Slovakian immigrant who was as desperate as Pezim to get rich quick. In business, he was aggressive, rude, probably anti-Semitic. Pezim says none of this bothered him, since Roman seemed to be anti-Protestant, anti-anyone who wasn't a God-fearing, guilt-ridden, ultra-devout Roman Catholic. By 1953, a couple of penny ventures had already taken Roman into the money – not the big chips, but bigger chips than Pezim had ever seen.

In June, 1953, the same month the *Life* piece slavered over the TSE and Gilbert LaBine's revived search for uranium, Joe Hirshhorn was financing the now fabled Big Z uranium-staking rush in the Algoma bush of northern Ontario. Hirshhorn was banking on the smarts of a prospector named Franc Joubin, who had an office on Adelaide Street in the heart of Toronto's mining district. Joubin and Hirshhorn masterminded a staking spree that resulted in the simultaneous recording of 1,400 separate properties covering 56,000 acres of bush – an outrageous, audacious accomplishment. From this grew the Rio Algom uranium mine.

But Franc Joubin's blanket prospecting had overlooked the richest uranium deposit of all, at Quirke Lake, about forty-five kilometres northeast of the town of Blind River. A mining engineer named Arthur Stollery staked these leftovers and went knocking on promoters' doors, looking for someone to back him the way Hirshhorn had backed Joubin. Steve Roman took the bait. Consolidated Denison Mines was the corporate shell that absorbed the Stollery claims.

While the Denison team started drilling, the TSE was hitting new trading records, primarily because of a multimillion-tonne lead-zinc-copper discovery near Bathurst, New Brunswick. The mining plays of Hirshhorn-Joubin and Roman-Stollery helped the mine listings swamp the performance of the blue-chip industrials. The *Financial Post* reported that the two discoveries meant that "staffs of the larger brokerage houses have been working to midnight to keep records up-to-date with the mad daily market pace."

By the spring of 1955, Consolidated Denison and Can-Met, another Roman vehicle, had started to set huge trading volumes. After the Algoma euphoria in northern Ontario, and comforted by handsome government contracts that guaranteed sales at profitable prices to uranium producers, even the most cautious traders started making big bets on Roman's properties. Roman needed other promoters to help flog Denison. Jenkin Evans underwrote 100,000 Denison shares at forty cents. Murray Pezim was in.

Denison was Pezim's first high ride. The TSE was at that time trading twelve million shares a day, sixty percent of it coming from uranium issues. In one day, Can-Met traded very nearly half its entire capitalization. To promote these stocks didn't require intelligence, foresight, or a knowledge of geology. It would be foolish to suggest that Pezim played Denison for any reason other than that it was another penny opportunity. Only this time, the opportunity wasn't getting in at ten cents and out at a buck. Denison was a winner. Its properties were real. The uranium was there by the truckload. Pezim started pushing Denison at forty cents, and he was into Can-Met as well. He bailed out of Denison at $17 a share. It eventually went to $85. Even though he got out early, Pezim may have made as much as $4 million.

The story gets a little murky here. The Earl says he and Pezim raised funds for a number of hopeful mining companies, including Denison Mines. It was Denison, he says, that launched the twosome into the strata of big-shot promoters. Pezim says that's bullshit. He says that Steve Roman was his contact, Denison was his play, and The Earl was nowhere near the deal. What can be confirmed is that Roman pinched Bernice's bum at a Christmas party, that she found him a vulgar man, that she told Murray that he'd better give up any ideas of friendship. The partnership of Pezim and Glick, however, continued, which in Bernice's eyes wasn't a better pairing.

Bernice found Glick unfriendly, uncompromising, and an unwelcome infliction on her marriage.

Today, Glick is retired, seventy years of age, and partially paralysed after suffering a stroke. He lives on the Bridle Path, millionaires' row in north Toronto. He would not agree to an interview, but he did send a letter responding to some questions. It was a nice letter, the kind that one assumes was written by a nice man. But those who knew Glick when he was Pezim's partner say that while he was a brilliant financier, he had a nasty personality.

The Denison success allowed Murray and Bernice to leave their rented quarters on Bathurst Street and move into a swank home on Stormont Avenue, in upscale north Toronto. More acquisitions followed. One Saturday, Pezim and Morry Kessler, a promoter friend of Pezim's who, with his wife Daisy, socialized with Pezim and Bernice, bought four Ford Thunderbirds: two sedans and two ragtops. Murray's were blue and green. He also started buying a better cut of suit. In their circle of friends, Murray and Bernice became trend-setters: the Pezims had the first television, the first dishwasher, the first air-conditioner.

Murray and Bernice saw less of Izzy and Rebecca. They had had a second child, Michael, and together the family worshipped at Bernice's parents' synagogue, not Adath Israel. Holiday celebrations, as in most families, were a balancing act between the two sets of in-laws.

But gatherings of the Pezims were still a good time. Murray and his brother Norman threw themselves prostrate onto a couch as soon as they arrived. When Murray rose, the fastidious Bernice would plump the cushions. If Murray had a crude joke to tell, he'd tell it out of earshot of the women. When he went to play his recording of a farting contest, a British import, he played it privately for the men. He was a popular uncle to the offspring of his siblings. He picked five-year-old Vicki up from hospital once, and didn't seem to mind a bit when she whoopsed on the lovely blue interior of his new blue T-bird.

In Pezim home movies, usually taken by Murray, Cheryl and Michael and cousin Vicki mug for the cameras in the back yard on Stormont. They were happy children, playing on swings and in blowup plastic swimming pools. Seeing them then, carefree on hot summer days, one wishes for them what one would wish for all families — that they would remain warm and close and loving, and capture that forever something that few families do.

Pezim would often hit the town without Bernice, chumming with his gang of rounders, sipping Cutty Sark and soda at the Top Hat Club on the lakeshore. One crony was Izzy Rotterman, who had graduated from selling linings and buttons and bobs to furriers to moving paper for people like Earl Glick. Rotterman, like many others in the business, would be rewarded when he came to exercise all those nice options on junior companies. He became a very wealthy man.

Away from his wife and family, Rotterman was crass and foul-mouthed. His friends called him Pansy, which wasn't a problem since it referred to the flower he sometimes sported in a lapel. Rotterman wasn't, isn't, without a certain charm, today an aging representative of a bygone era. He and Pezim would spend an occasional weekend carousing at the Monteith Inn on Lake Rosseau. A favourite pastime was the "Oh May Gag." Here's how Rotterman tells it:

"Let's say your name is Phil. You're from Pittsburgh. Phil's sitting by the water. I say 'Phil, I've got a girl. She's so beautiful. She's got a figure. You've never seen a figure like that. She drives me crazy. She's sex crazy. I can't keep up with her. I can't keep going. Her husband is a brakeman on the trains. He works at nights. He's a big sonofabitch. Big rough bastard. But he's always away at night.'

"So Phil would say 'You don't know me. Why pick on me?'

"'I'll tell you why. I don't want to lose her. If I introduce her to my friends they're going to stick it to me.' I says, 'Ya gotta go up.' I always pick a house, always dark at night, up the road. I tell him I whistle first, then I call 'Oh May.' I whistle three times as I come near the window. And on the third 'Oh May' she gives me the signal that the coast is clear. We would steal all the light bulbs in the Monteith Inn. We'd have the bulbs in our pockets ready for the gag. We'd dance with the girls. They'd go crazy. Think we were excited. So Phil comes up with all these parcels. Says he can't wait. I whistle. As we get near this place I got guys hiding behind the trees. Murray could put on a deep voice. As I said 'Oh May' the third time he'd yell, 'You're coming to screw my wife.'

"All hell would break loose. The bulbs would go off as they were thrown against trees. This one guy ran straight into a ditch, broke his leg. We didn't mean to harm anyone most times."

Most times, says Rotterman, they'd have their victim hide in a Monteith privy – for hours – until he was told that the coast was clear.

Rotterman believes that Damon Runyon heard of the gag and subsequently wrote it up as a short story. Trouble is, Runyon died in 1946 and the Oh May Gag was being played out in the fifties. Runyon did, however, write a short story called "The Brakeman's Daughter" in the twenties. That's the difficulty with so much of the Pezim story. Huge chunks of reality have drifted away, replayed into fantasy.

Pezim enjoyed hanging out with Rotterman, but his partnership with Glick was more important. Murray was still employed at Jenkin Evans, which did well by the mining boom and moved to more spacious quarters at 360 Bay. Glick moved his Maris Investment to the same building, which was convenient, given that he and Pezim were all but inseparable. Glick continued to play back-room financier. Pezim was the up-front promoter, the one with the personality, the indefatigable Sammy Glick who could charm and shmooze an investor into a stock until sundown and long past.

Often, Glick and his wife, Essie, and Murray and Bernice would socialize. Glick was rough on Essie, often swearing at her. Pezim may have picked up some tips on how to handle women from him.

"Wear your black dress and wear your pearls," Pezim would say to Bernice, "and don't open your mouth."

If The Earl and Essie were travelling to Nassau on holiday, Pezim and Bernice would follow. This was a hardship for Bernice, since Earl would slap her down verbally when she disagreed with him.

"What do you know, you from Manning Avenue?" Earl would say, reminding Bernice of her humble beginnings, ignoring the fact that his were equally impoverished.

Then he'd leave the table, Pezim would follow, and later blast Bernice for being uncivil to his pal. His own language was growing vulgar, though not in front of Bernice, and it's likely he was running around on her at this point — which is no big deal to Pezim's way of thinking.

Pezim today will say that a woman's brain capacity is twenty-five percent that of a man. That is what he told me. A man has four times the brain power of a woman.

When the market was going Pezim's way, he'd wear the same tie day after day in the superstitious belief that he would keep winning as long as he didn't change. When the market wasn't moving in his favour, he would head home, crawl into bed, pull the sheets over his head, and stop talking.

When things were going his way, nobody could beat Pezim in the Big Thinking department. Except maybe Earl Glick. The Earl realized in 1954 or so that their uranium successes in Canada provided an obvious entrée into the New York market. He needed connections. He went to see a man named Bill Coldoff, a Toronto broker who had retired two years earlier after a market crash and a heart attack had wiped out his millions and his health. Coldoff had had a big book, as they say in the stock business when speaking of a long list of fat-cat clients. He had connections in Toronto and New York, the very connections Glick needed.

So The Earl, with Coldoff's help, opened an office on Park Avenue and bought a seat on the American Stock Exchange. Pezim followed. He wasn't a principal, this time, but a hanger-on.

It was into this office that Edwin Land took what would one day be called the Polaroid camera, leaking grease all over the shitty orange shag.

"It is true," says Glick in his letter, "that Edwin Land once had come into the New York office with a prototype of the Polaroid Camera, as the office was always keen to underwrite new products and enterprises. However, the Polaroid Camera did not appeal to the group running the office at the time."

Colonial Aircraft, the amphibious aircraft that they did decide to back, never quite got the approval of the Federal Aviation Authority.

There is no information at the Securities and Exchange Commission to suggest that Colonial was investigated by the Commission, or that Glick was pushed out of town. Bill Coldoff recalls that another Glick outfit, Spartan Air Services, was enjoined from trading by the SEC. The Commission slapped a cease-and-desist order on Spartan, he says, on evidence that the company was a boiler-room operation. Coldoff says he and Glick together flew to see the securities officials in Washington, faced their adversaries off over, as he describes it, a "sixty-foot table," and convinced the Commission there had been no wrongdoing on the part of the principals. The trading ban was lifted.

Nevertheless, the New York operation of Glick and Co. was a failure, and the office, lacking capital, soon closed. Besides, Glick preferred to concentrate on Toronto, where he figured he was smarter than just about anybody else.

Pezim figured he was the smart one. Much as he needed Glick, he always had the grand notion that he could be bigger and definitely better on his own. But The Earl had his strengths: under his tutelage, for example, Pezim could have mastered the art of never losing your shirt when those about you are losing theirs.

The land where the bougainvillea bloom, where firm-breasted women wander the beach topless, where it never snows, was Pezim's idea of the land of opportunity. Jamaica.

In 1957, a twenty-two acre oceanfront property came up for sale. It tied right onto Ocho Rios. The beachfront ran for three-quarters of a mile. A hedonist's paradise.

Here's how The Pez tells it: "So I bought the thing and started to invite people down there. We had a party going for about two years. It was wild, okay? Everyone running around in the nude. It was like a nudist colony. They said what a great place for a hotel. They talked me into it. That destroyed everything. The hotel's still there. Called the Carib Ocho Rios. Nuts. What can you do? Hugh O'Brien and Lorne Greene worked for me on that project. Lorne was nothing then. Hugh O'Brien had a secretary named Goody. Very romantic island. The minute you step off that plane you feel charged up, the adrenaline starts to go up. I was a horny guy in those days. Always had a hard on. No matter where I looked. Bang."

The hotel in Ocho Rios was supposed to cost a million and a quarter. Jackie Beale, the bookie, a guy named Jimmy Ponzo, a sprinkling of questionable types, were involved in that deal. Rotterman too, in a very minor way.

During the summer of 1958, with the Jamaica beach party still in full swing, the Pezims rented a cottage at Balfour Beach near Jacksons Point. Nanci Ellen Pezim, their third and last child, had been born the previous October. Murray and Bernice and their children and Murray's brother Norman, his wife Helen and their children, all headed to Balfour for the season. A number of Murray's friends like Beale and Ponzo who had become part of the Jamaican scene, dropped in on the Pezims at this Ontario retreat. Bernice hated being treated as if she were running a hotel; she resented the way Ponzo dropped his towels on the floor, expecting her to pick up after him. The guys were full of themselves and their southern adventures. It didn't take much for Bernice to catch on to the fact that her husband had been screwing around.

It also wasn't long before the Jamaica beach party went bust. The highly sexed adventure failed on two fronts. For one, Pezim dived into a near-empty swimming pool and ruined his back, which got him started on pain-killers. Sometimes he couldn't get out of bed. Even today, he walks a bit bent. As for the hotel, Pezim poured $4 million into the place. Then the Bank of Montreal called its loans, stepped in, and squeezed Pezim out of his ownership. Pezim could have made a bundle if he had held onto the land and sold it vacant when Jamaica became a tourist hotspot a few years later.

In the caper that is Murray Pezim's life, this is the first time he blew his brains out in a big way.

After the Jamaica debacle, Pezim went scurrying back to The Earl. Shuffling, actually, because his back was giving him a lot of pain. The partnership he discovered when he returned included Bill Coldoff and a doctor named Nate Hurwitz.

Pezim, meanwhile, had kept his job at Jenkin Evans, his hotel ambitions being more or less a crazed if expensive diversion. But the market had changed during the Jamaica episode. Although volumes were still high, it was mainly a result of large institutional trades of large establishment companies, not the high-risk, high-reward penny mines. The metals markets had slumped, leaving small brokerages to battle a lack of investor interest in their small mining issues.

Investors had been burned too. In the summer of 1957, shares in Aconic Mining Corp. had collapsed to $2 from $11.14 in a day's trading on the Toronto Stock Exchange, the worst stock plunge for a single company in memory. Aconic had been touting an iron-ore project, and had plans to develop a magnetic-sand deposit near Natashquan, in southeastern Quebec. The collapse forced brokers to make margin calls on their clients. Stop-loss orders – orders given by clients to their brokers to sell out if a certain stock falls to a certain price – were touched off. A subsequent securities investigation led to charges against a former corporate official for wash trading – creating the appearance of active trading and boosting the market price by using the accounts of a single individual to volley trades back and forth. The official declared bankruptcy two weeks after the stock collapse. Shareholders lost $23 million.

Glick and Pezim, while not giving up on mining altogether, started looking for new opportunities in junior industrial concerns – companies involved in hosiery, publishing, electronic equipment, that kind of thing. There were all sorts of promotional possibilities beyond mining.

Pezim's connection with Jenkin Evans was key, for he and Glick needed an underwriter, and who better than old man Jenks, with Pezim shouting the potential for this stock or that company right there under Jenks's nose?

The Glick-Pezim plan was to revive ailing small industrials and issue shares to the public using the successful junior-mine method. The first venture of note was Spartan Air Services, an aerial-survey company with an unfailing ability to lose $1 million a year. In November 1960, Maris Investment stepped in through a complicated manoeuvre that allowed Spartan's controlling shareholder, Bristol Aeroplane of Canada, to back out. The new Spartan hoped to follow the junior-mine style of taking a primary distribution of shares directly to the trading floor to be sold at whatever prices the promoters could muster. There would be no prospectus. There would be no predetermined share pricing. In street lingo, the shares would be sold "at the market."

The TSE balked. While the Exchange was lax in its regulation of penny mines, it had a different attitude to the baby industrials. Exchange officials rather liked the idea of detailed prospectuses, shares that were issued at a predetermined price, and operations that could at least be seen to have a shot at achieving profitability.

The Glick group was unfazed. They packed up their paper and floated it instead on the Canadian Stock Exchange in Montreal, which then resided beside the Montreal Stock Exchange and had a much looser attitude toward securities regulation.

Spartan initially was a Glick promotion; Pezim was the salesman. Under new management the company did, somewhat surprisingly, start to turn around. Spartan later entered into an agreement with an American outfit called Fotochrome for Canadian rights to a one-step colour camera. It was the Fotochrome affiliation that took Coldoff and Glick before the SEC. Fotochrome's shares were suspended because of what the SEC deemed were misleading promotional statements regarding the availability of financing and the potential of the camera. Spartan eventually wound its way back into debt and out of business.

In May 1961, Glick took control of a company called National Hosiery, a Hamilton-based firm that a year before had fought a takeover battle launched by an eccentric financier named Michael Jay. The company had been a money-maker in the fifties, but had started to lose money at the time of its takeover troubles. In announcing his victory the previous autumn, Jay had said he had received congratulatory cables from the Shah of Iran, "a personal cable from Nasser, and another from de Gaulle." Jay's takeover ultimately failed and months later Glick and Pezim stepped in and took control of the company.

The new controllers renamed the enterprise Phantom Industries and listed it on the Toronto Stock Exchange. Jenkin Evans was the lead underwriter. E.H. Pooler – a frequent player in Glick-Pezim enterprises – was the number-two brokerage. Earl Glick was director and president; Murray Pezim director and secretary treasurer. Norman Glick, brother of Earl, was then a salesman at E.H. Pooler and his name was often interwoven on corporate filing statements with The Earl's.

Glick announced that the company would streamline and modernize manufacturing operations and acquire new lines of merchandise to tag onto the company's existing line of lingerie, gloves, and the like.

Through the Jenkin Evans underwriting, shares in the company went out at $5.75. In 1962, Glick stayed on the board but handed the presidency to a man named Harrison Verner. In the summer of 1963, Verner proclaimed that Phantom had come through the bad times and would be posting a profit for that year. Seven months later, Phantom's bankers called their loans. It was penniless. The company was placed in receivership. But Phantom didn't stop trading until the TSE pulled the plug seven months later, complaining that it ordered the suspension for failure to "publish a report for the year ended nine months ago despite a three-month extensive allowed by the exchange. The firm is in bankruptcy."

Phantom shared head offices with another Glick-Pezim enterprise called Leland Publishing. There is a picture of Pezim hanging on the wall of his brother Norman's den in Arizona. He is crouched, with a pair of dice in one hand, wearing a New Year's Eve Guy Lombardo-style foil hat. He looks as if he's playing craps. He's actually celebrating the launching of Leland Publishing with a bunch of other fellows, including Norman.

The Pezim pose is apt. Leland was a crapshoot. Until 1960, Leland had been a company specializing in the sale of educational books and records through food-chain outlets. Then it was folded into Norman Pezim's Mercury Lithographing, which had grown from the flier enterprise Norman started just after the war. Once again, Jenkin Evans led a share issue. Once again, Harrison Verner stepped in as president. By 1964, the company was bankrupt.

There are numerous examples of the failed corporate escapades of Murray Pezim and Earl Glick. When Pezim talks about the defeat of this deal or that deal, he usually says: "It could have been the greatest thing ever. It just didn't work out." These companies don't grace the corporate landscape; they grace alphabetized lists of predecessor and defunct companies. Either that, or they are rolled into other ventures by other promoters. Tangible contributions to the commercial effort of the nation are nil, although these companies very likely made hundreds of thousands of dollars individually for Glick and Pezim through the initial promotion of share offerings.

Glick kept his. Pezim often didn't.

When Murray was in the dough, he would buy Bernice fabulous diamonds. When they went out of the town he'd say to her "Let them see your jewellery."

While these Glick-Pezim junior industrials were piddling through investors' hands, the junior mining issues on the TSE were also headed for a day of recovery. Nineteen sixty-three was a bonanza year for the little mines, exciting enough to revive the interest of Lou Chesler. Chesler had moved to the United States years before. After making his millions on Bay Street, he decided to become a wheeler-dealer on Wall Street with a penchant for Bahamian real estate and corporate takeovers. Chesler's raiding style was to go after companies with fat treasuries, pay shareholders a premium to sell out, then use the cash to finance other projects.

In 1963, Chesler re-emerged in Toronto to make a pass at Gunnar Mining, or at least what was left of Gilbert LaBine's creation. Gunnar had $32 million in the kitty; Chesler, it was rumoured, needed the dough to bail out one of his stalled Bahamian land projects. Chesler's takeover raid failed, and, aside from a brief flutter in the late sixties, the one-time promotional king of Bay Street was yesterday's man.

The junior-mine revival had the regulators worried. The Aconic episode was still recent, painful history. The rules that governed the penny-mine industry remained lax. It was still possible to float a useless stock issue without a prospectus, leaving the investor with no way of analysing the merits of the offering. The supervisors were caught in a double bind: they didn't want unwitting investors to be abused; on the other hand, they feared that a prospectus requirement would seriously dent mine financings, and that, of course, would in turn damage the health of the exchange itself.

In April 1964, Texasgulf Inc., an American sulphur producer and burgeoning mining conglomerate, announced the kind of discovery that has made the Canadian mining industry legendary. On this occasion, it was an unprecedented copper-zinc find near Timmins in northern Ontario. To this day, the Kidd Creek mine is a prize. Bought from Texasgulf by the Canada Development Corp. in 1981, it was subsequently sold to Falconbridge in 1986, which in turn used it as high ransom during Noranda's takeover of Falconbridge in 1989. When news of the 1964 discovery got out, hundreds of prospectors flooded to Timmins to tie thousands of claims onto those of Texasgulf.

Pezim was in the wrong spot when the excitement began. He was in London with Bill Coldoff and Jenkin Evans, skimming along in a rented Rolls-Royce – the same one that the television talk-show host Jack Paar, then at the height of his fame, used when he went to London. Pezim and Coldoff had spent six hours suffering the stink of Jenks's cigars as they made their way to a godforsaken part of Wales. They were looking for lead prospects. Jenks's idea.

The news of Texasgulf brought the three men back to Toronto like a shot. Earl Glick was already in Timmins setting up a string of mining bets within a twelve-mile radius of the Texasgulf find. He set Coldoff up in a Timmins motel, where he stayed six months, fronting for Glick, purchasing as many properties in the area as possible. Glick had taken control of a handful of mining shells. The claims that Coldoff purchased from prospectors were poured into these dormant companies. Eight claims were dumped into Norgold Mines, four into Kirkland Minerals, eight into National Explorations, of which Pezim was president. Gulf Lead, another Glick company, bought four claims from a trio of prospectors who had set up a claims-sales shop in a suite of the Empire Hotel in Timmins. Two of these men – John Larche and Don McKinnon – would become well known to Murray Pezim years later.

The Glick claims-spread was a classic area play, dispersing the potential for profits through a handful of companies. The greater the number of stock issues, the greater the reward. In the first feature profile of Earl Glick, Frank Kaplan, a reporter with the *Financial Post*, wrote that when Glick was working on something like the Timmins play, he "can maintain a feverish pace that leaves visitors gasping for breath. He is in the best of physical condition, works out regularly on karate and judo. The ample expanse of soft off-white broadloom in his Bay St. office makes an excellent mat."

Viola Rita MacMillan greased in even faster than Glick. She made her fortune prospecting the Kirkland Lake gold-rush years earlier, and by the mid-fifties was already a legend. *Saturday Night* magazine published a profile of her in 1955, accompanied by photographs of the lady prospector in the bush and in her luxurious penthouse suite on top of the downtown Toronto office building where she had her corporate headquarters. She was five feet flat and less than 110 pounds.

One of MacMillan's companies was Windfall Oils & Mines. Another was Consolidated Golden Arrow Mines. Both had claims tied onto the Texasgulf property. While the Glick-Pezim companies moved up thirty cents here, forty cents there, Windfall went from fifty cents to $5.60 in July of 1964, moving on rumours of impressive drill-core findings. MacMillan, who at the time was the president of the Prospectors' & Developers' Association of Canada, would corner potential investors, touting what she said were spectacular assay results on her properties. The claims, in fact, were worthless, and the share prices collapsed. By October, Windfall Mines had fallen to 23 cents.

It was too much for the regulators to ignore. A royal commission was formed to investigate what came to be known as the Windfall scandal. MacMillan faced charges of manipulating both

111

Windfall and Consolidated Golden. Three years later, the courts found that MacMillan had manipulated a quarter of a million shares of Consolidated, which caused the share price to rise forty cents within an hour, for a profit of more than a thousand dollars for every minute of trading time. She was convicted of wash trading on Consolidated and sentenced to ten months in prison. The maximum sentence for wash trading was five years. MacMillan was paroled after serving six weeks of her sentence. She was subsequently cleared on charges of fraudulently manipulating Windfall shares.

MacMillan wasn't the only one to face charges. A geologist named Ken Darke, sent by Texasgulf to map the area initially and the first man to recognize the wealth of Kidd Creek assays, was found guilty of insider trading by the U.S. Securities and Exchange Commission. Darke had bought stock and options on his assay knowledge before any information had been released to the public. He had also passed the information on to various tipsters. None of this was unusual penny-mining practice. Getting caught, however, that was almost unheard of.

The royal commission, chaired by Mr. Justice Arthur Kelly, professed surprise over the practices of these companies. Here were these companies without assets, all of a sudden brought to life on the basis of two or three mining claims, which, without interference, could distribute, say, a million shares to the public without so much as examining the property purchased, let alone making any promises of actually undertaking any exploration.

Promoters like Glick, who took the claims into the shell companies, would start by taking a mark-up on the purchase price of the claims, a nice spread between what they paid for the claims and the price for which they subsequently sold the property to the company. Prospectors like Larche and McKinnon would receive free shares in the newly active companies in exchange for the claims and sometimes handsome cash payments. Larche and McKinnon, for example, received 250,000 shares of Windfall when they sold mining claims to Viola MacMillan. Underwriters like Jenkin Evans would receive options that could be exercised at accelerated prices that notched up at short-term intervals – say, at forty cents in three months, sixty cents in six months, and so on. The promoters themselves were usually granted options to buy shares at a certain price, which gave them all the more encouragement to push the stock to investors, thereby raising the price of the stock, and thereby making their options even more of a bargain when the time came for them to be exercised.

It was a rigged game that favoured the promoter, who got his money at the outset. If the company went under months or years later, it wasn't the promoter who would suffer, provided he extracted his equity at the front end, as Glick did.

Were there honest men in this business in the fifties? Irvy Rotterman told me that if I could show him an honest man in the market he'd eat this book. He meant any market. Anytime. Anywhere. The Toronto records show that Pezim wasn't called before any regulatory body, never had his broker's licence suspended or revoked. An index of securities cases that goes back to 1949 lists various grievances against other brokers – backdooring, boiler-room operations, cold calling. There was the broker who, in his application for a licence, neglected to mention his drug convictions in Afghanistan, his criminal record for accepting bribes, his various aliases, and his bookmaking convictions. "Bookmaking is not a major offence, but not suitable background for a securities salesman," said the decision-makers of the day.

There was also the problem of promoters placing fictitious buy orders, which would, of course, move the stock price up. This practice was rampant. There were advertisements placed in German newspapers claiming that investors would double or triple their money without risk of loss. The biggest supervisory headache was the primary distribution of shares, which were exempt from the prospectus provisions of the Act to Mining and Oil Securities. About the only regulation that was in place was the illegality of buying on margin shares that cost under $1.

The Kelly commission didn't have any answers to the mine-financing conundrum, it said. It suggested that the mining community might be better served by a separate exchange, forgetting, or perhaps not knowing, that decades earlier Toronto did have a mining exchange – two, in fact – and the system served to fatten the same people in the thirties as it fattened in the early sixties.

Long before the commission report was released to the public, however, another commission on banking and finance had voiced its complaints about TSE procedures. In response, the exchange had set up its own committee to study speculative issues.

The conclusions were blindingly obvious. It was clear that stricter rules and tighter enforcement would be needed if the TSE were to be accepted as a world-class exchange. To this end, it adopted mining-share regulations that squeezed out the small-cap, highly speculative issues. Shell companies could no longer be sheer shells, but would have to have liquid assets of $25,000 and would have to be able to prove previous exploration and development work. After being dormant for twelve months, companies would be delisted and would not qualify for reinstatement through a new underwriting. Financiers would be prohibited from short-selling against issues not yet disclosed. Staggered options were eliminated. And so on.

The change in Toronto suited the Vancouver Stock Exchange nicely. The VSE had been established more than fifty years earlier, but was only just beginning to challenge the power of its Toronto cousin. What the VSE had was the appearance and the substance of a frontier exchange. What suited this image was the very issues that Toronto wanted to exterminate. After the Windfall exposé the junior-mining game moved west. Pezim says this was a colossal error on Toronto's part. The TSE would have had Hemlo, he says, if it hadn't been so rash.

That may be true. But the new rules forced Pezim to a new playgound. Vancouver made Pezim. Vancouver transformed Murray Pezim into The Pez.

CHAPTER 6

Booze, Broads, and Baloney

I n the sixties, downtown Vancouver after dark had a gangster smell. Family groups ran the girls and the drugs and the clubs. The popular hangouts were the Penthouse Night Club on Seymour ("Rendezvous of the World's Greatest Celebrities"), the Ritz, the Palomar, the Kublai Khan Supper Club. Tony Lemur had a hot spot called Numbers, on Davie Street, which then, as now, was a business strip for hookers. The Filippones and the Philliponis ran the Penthouse, a cabaret night club. But for all its nighttime electricity, Vancouver in those days was not much more than a small town with a nice view.

The favoured hotel, more popular even than the dowager Hotel Vancouver, was the Hotel Georgia. Stately, brown, and boring, the Georgia abuts Howe Street, which was home to the VSE in those days. The Georgia was a hang-out for the VSE crowd – the boiler-room artists and broker-dealers and brokers and promoters. There was a lot of money being made, a lot of money being spent, and much of what was spent was spent at the Cavalier Lounge, the street-level bar in the Georgia.

The room had a Knights of Olde theme: dividers fashioned from chain mesh that hung from the ceiling separated the tables in the bar, a deuce on either side; heraldic banners hung from spears that jutted from the walls. It sounds awful, but Mary the bar waitress and John the bellhop who worked at the Georgia then and work there now swear it was a cool spot. From the Cavalier the regulars could place bets with their bookies, place bets with their brokers, then go over to Davie Street and lay some dough on a girl or two.

As soon as Pezim hit Vancouver, in March, 1964, he started hanging out at the Cavalier, drinking CC and ginger. Pezim was known as a modest drinker but a respectable tipper – three bucks, sometimes five, which thirty years ago was a handsome sum.

The Cavalier Grill had the best prime rib in town; it was known, too, for its scampi. The hotel had its own bakery in the basement. Everything was Number One, top class. Nothing was brought in the back door. Pezim would order a burnt steak and tomato-and-onion salad. If the steak wasn't done right through, until the meat was drained, dry and colourless, he would send it back to have it done some more. Celebrities would drift by, have a drink, have a meal, maybe stay the night in one of the rooms upstairs. The American celebrities were the big spenders, guys like Milton Berle.

The Cave Supper Club on nearby Hornby Street was another favourite stop for Pezim. Jack Benny, Liberace, the Righteous Brothers, Joey Bishop, Wayne Newton – just about every Ed Sullivan regular played the Cave in the Sixties. Pezim has always had a celebrity fixation; being in the same room as Joey Bishop, well, that would be Nirvana for him. When there wasn't a celebrity act, the Cave would put on a show like "Vive Les Girls!" keeping the "sensational French Revue," "an all-star cast of 24," running for weeks on end.

Pezim took a room at the Georgia right away – "Room 707 at $7 a night," he says, though the Georgia staff recall that Danny Franks, another local promoter, had that room, not Pezim. Sounds snappy though. Safe to say that Pezim's rooms at the outset were very likely modest. Nevertheless, Pezim maintains that the local brokerage community started talking about him the moment he arrived. "I was the action," he says, adding his name to such already established Vancouver promoters as Lou Wolfin.

Pezim wasn't the only Toronto stock-pusher to move west. George Caldough was there; he achieved a kind of immortality when Errol Flynn died in the arms of a sixteen-year-old on his yacht in 1959. The son of Wally Caldough, who had run one of the most audacious Toronto boiler rooms out of the old CPR building at King and Yonge, Georgie Porgie ended up in jail years later for his involvement in a stock scam. Pezim and Caldough were typical of the kind of guys who arrived in Vancouver in those days. The Toronto Stock Exchange was shutting down the penny-mining crowd; the boiler-shop artists and the bad-deal promoters were heading to the States and overseas. And to Vancouver.

The city was made for Pezim's kind of action. Technically, he was still a sales rep for Jenkin Evans, but was fronting for Earl Glick and the minority partners, Bill Coldoff and Nate Hurwitz, just as much. The Earl came to town and took up residence at the Georgia from time to time. He, like Pezim, wanted to rub up against the new local heavyweights, people like the Capozzi brothers – Joe, Tom, and Herb – who were often seen in the Georgia. There were other fresh young entrepreneurs about town. Men like Jimmy Pattison, who was already making it big with his first solo car dealership, Jim Pattison on Main. People such as Pattison – risk-takers, self-made money men – had the look of potential stock-market players, size players.

Pezim looked good, swank even. He was always manicured,

119

cologned, barber-shaved, and smartly dressed in a smooth sales-manish kind of way. He was always cruising in and out of the Georgia. Everyone at the hotel knew him. And he touted stocks to them all. John the bellhop told me that when Pezim once tried to sell him on a penny deal, he phoned his stockbroker, and his stockbroker told him to steer clear of Pezim.

Vancouver in those days offered easy pickings. Not only easy, but low profile. There was precious little coverage of the Vancouver Stock Exchange by the media in the sixties, either locally or nationally. The *Financial Post* probably did the best of the lot, but even it didn't consider coverage of the exchange a high priority.

The VSE had been around for nearly sixty years when Pezim arrived. It had been slow off the mark. Some of the mining booms that had forced the creation of the Toronto exchanges and contributed to their prosperity were actually made in British Columbia. The profits from the Rossland gold discovery, which made for a twenty-year mining boom running through World War I, for example, were funnelled through Toronto's two mining exchanges, draining potential stock commerce from the West.

In 1907 a group of westerners, including a man named Charles Loewen, got smart and decided to set up their own marketplace for stocks. The plan, naturally enough, was to fuel western Canada's economic expansion – and to most people economic expansion meant resource-based growth. British Columbia had lots of rocks and trees and was close to Alberta, the home of oil and gas. At its inception, the VSE had twelve members. Each paid $125 for a seat on the exchange – situated in one room on Pender Street where the rent was $35 a month. In its first day of business, on August 1, 1907, a thousand shares of Alberta Coal and Coke traded at forty-three cents. Two one-share transactions of Burton Saw Works traded in excess of a hundred dollars. That was it. The guys scraping the trades with chalk on blackboard probably knocked off early.

The early years were unimpressive financially, though marked by an unbridled capitalist spirit. After World War I, Vancouver brokers found themselves clearing more government war bonds through the exchange than stock trades. Leading up to World War II, there was considerable interest in gold, but like the Toronto exchanges, the VSE turned its focus to uranium and base metals after the war. Consolidated Mining and Smelting, for example, was hailed for its world-beating lead-zinc operation in British Columbia. Uranium Cobalt Co. was the most active VSE stock in 1951, mirroring the excitement in the East. By then, the VSE was generating $56 million in dollar volume of sales on something on the order of fifty-two million shares, for an average share price of just over $1. In reality, of course, the larger, established companies might trade for, say, $20 or $30. Numerous companies at the other end of the spectrum traded for pennies.

The exchange didn't want to be seen as an exclusively small-stock market. After all, the likes of Atlas Steel, Southam, George Weston, and Abitibi, the fast-growing paper giant, were all listed on the VSE, as was the lion's share of the country's chartered banks. Again, the reality was that these companies were interlisted on the Toronto Stock Exchange, and sometimes a U.S. exchange, as well as the VSE. A 1952 article about the exchange in *Saturday Night* magazine said that such listings had "given a new sense of service and power to the exchange, which has long sought to shake off the assumption that it deals only in the more speculative issues associated in the public mind with mines and oils."

It was the speculative issues that the investing public craved. And it was the speculative issues that the promoters wanted to push, for the very same reasons they pushed them on the TSE: fast profits and to hell with actually trying to find a gold

121

mine, a copper discovery, or an oil strike. When *Saturday Night* interviewed Johnny Jukes, a VSE member, he said this: "We've had our ups and downs, but we have a solid background now. The stocks on the VSE represent many mining companies that have consistently paid dividends for years, oil companies that are on the threshold of a period of enormous expansion, and industries allied with really basic production with large payrolls – industries that will be in business generations from now." Nowhere in the piece, not in the smallest corner, was there the slightest suggestion that the VSE was a high-rolling haven for gamblers.

While the Toronto market was getting caught up in the Texasgulf euphoria, the West Coast exchange was also flourishing. In 1964, the VSE broke all trading records: share volume reached more than 263 million, and share-price value totalled $220 million, almost double the previous year's tally. The real excitement came at the end of the year, when the province experienced an impressive mining boom, particularly in copper. Much was made of the heightened interest of the Japanese in buying Canadian minerals and investing in mines in British Columbia. The Japanese had become the province's biggest ore customer, pushing the value of production to $300 million annually.

On November 11, a *Financial Times of Canada* writer sent this wire to his editor at the paper's Montreal headquarters. A broker at James Richardson Securities was his source: "HE THINKS LAST WEEKS ACTIVITY SPARKED MAINLY BY SPECIALLY ENCOURAGING COPPER ASSAY REPORT NOVEMBER FIVE FROM NEW AREA OF NEW IMPERIALS YUKON OPERATION STOP IN PRESENT FAVORABLE SITUATION SUCH A REPORT FROM SINGLE COMPANY CAN SET WHOLE MARKET SKY ROCKETING WITHIN HOURS QUOTE IN MANY CASES THE PUBLIC BUYS BLIND THEREFORE SOME MINING COMPANIES FOR WHICH NO ADVANCE IS JUSTIFIED ARE CARRIED UPWARD ON THE COAT TAILS OF THE LEADERS UNQUOTE STOP AS BROKER THOMPSON SAYS QUOTE I

WOULD LIKE TO SEE PUBLIC USE A LITTLE MORE CAUTION UNQUOTE STOP."

During its six decades, the VSE had changed its quarters six times. In 1964, it moved once again, packing up its possessions at 540 Howe Street and moving next door to spanking new headquarters that presaged the electronic age. It boasted eight television cameras, which scanned the quotation board, then relayed the information to television screens in the various downtown brokerages. The camera system was supposed to get trading information to stock-watchers faster than the ticker could. But on busy days, the board markers, who scurried around the quotation board on a raised platform, using the pre-space-age tools of chalk and brushes, couldn't keep up with the action. It was amateurish, at best. It was, however, exciting. By 1964, there were 254 companies listed, 107 industrials, 106 mines, and forty-one oils. More than half the mining issues were trading at under twenty cents.

Pezim initially went west to gain control of a company called National Explorations. Texasgulf was just starting to fly in northern Ontario, and Earl Glick needed publicly listed companies into which he could pile the claims he had acquired in the area of the Kidd Creek discovery. National Explorations was such a company. It didn't have much to show for itself, save for a bunch of investments here and there in penny mines like Redstone Mines and New Privateer. National was authorized to issue 7.5-million shares, but had papered out only 4.75 million. If The Earl could get National, he'd get the opportunity to send new shares to market, and fast. Moreover, National was an easy target: Pezim and Nate Hurwitz already had a piece of the company sitting in a holding company of theirs called Beubern Enterprises.

Corporate control of National was then in the hands of a Vancouver broker named Tom Laidlaw who ran one of the small brokerage houses that dotted the West Coast market landscape. So when Pezim arrived in Vancouver, one of his first missions was to talk to Laidlaw. Here's how Pezim tells it:

"I told him I was looking to get control of a few listed companies. One of them was called National Explorations. The stock was 9 1/2 to ten cents. I asked him how much stock was issued and he said three million shares, or whatever. I said, 'Do you think you could get me 100 of that?' He came back and said, 'I bought you a hundred at 10 1/2.' I said, 'Well, buy me another hundred.' Came back, bought me another hundred at 10 1/2. Meantime, the market is still 9 1/2, 10. I said, 'How much have you bought for me?' He says three hundred. I says three hundred thousand? He said, oh no, three hundred shares. I could see him looking at me, and I know what he was thinking. Where's this three hundred thousand going to come from? I said phone the Toronto Dominion Bank. That was their mentality at the time. They were doing no business."

Well, come on. Why would any broker buy three hundred thousand shares, no questions asked, from some antsy, unknown promoter? Pezim, though a broker with Jenkin Evans, was acting on behalf of the Glick gang in this instance. Tom Laidlaw would have to eat the house loss if the promoter-broker didn't pay up. Pezim, of course, had that "Hey, look at me, I'm the New Big Guy About Town" attitude and figured that people like Laidlaw would just have to catch on.

In April 1964, Tom Laidlaw, president and director of National, reported to shareholders that under his officership company officials had "looked at a number of prospects, but were unable to find anything that we thought was suitable for the company." Laidlaw reported the Beubern approach. "After considerable thought and discussion, your directors have decided to turn over the management to this new group at the annual meeting and trust it will be most advantageous to shareholders."

On April 24, National shareholders approved a change in ownership from the Laidlaw group to Beubern. National became part of the Texasgulf play. Glick paid $30,000 in cash and 40,000 free shares for the four township claims that went into the company. Shattuck Denn Mining, a U.S. concern, must have been mightily impressed by the Glick pitch; it put up more than $100,000 for shares in the five Gulf-area plays and struck a deal to finance all future exploration in exchange for fifty percent of the properties. Jenkin Evans, of course, did the National underwriting, and so was nicely positioned for investor enthusiasm for the Timmins race. There was also a pile of options for the insiders, the first 200,000 exercisable within sixty days at fifteen cents a share.

Pezim was president and director; Glick, vice-president and director; Nate Hurwitz and Bill Coldoff, both directors. The fallout from the Windfall scandal would eventually cream National Explorations, as it did the other companies that rode the Texasgulf boom. In the end, the whole affair was remarkably similar to the one described by the Richardson's broker to the *Financial Times* writer at the end of 1964 – just a bunch of worthless paper carried on the coattails of someone else's mining success.

After the Windfall fiasco, National – like many other Glick-Pezim endeavours – sought to metamorphose into whatever form would best attract investor dollars. After it had abandoned the Texasgulf area, it became First National Uranium Mines, under which banner it searched for uranium in the Beaverlodge area of northern Saskatchewan. Pezim stepped away from its corporate operations and Glick became its president, to be joined by his brothers, Norman and David. In the late sixties, the company was suspended from trading on the TSE for failing to file the required financial reports. The shares had, at the time, risen a dollar in heavy trading on the news that the company was looking to buy a

Bahamian construction company for a pile of treasury shares. And on and on and on in a seemingly endless corporate maze.

The Windfall affair afforded the VSE an opportunity to be tremendously self-righteous – such venality as insider trading, stock manipulation, and wash trading were not part of the Vancouver scene. Sure. And bears don't pee in the woods, either.

Increased VSE activity rarely caught national media attention. One exception was an article by Barry Broadfoot in *Maclean's* magazine headed, "Everybody's Gambling on the Poor Man's Bay Street – and Some of Them are Winning." Broadfoot wrote of a nineteen-year-old newspaper copy boy who had made "about twenty thousand dollars so far on a copper stock called Western Mines. . . . Less spectacularly, there's an elevator girl in a Georgia Street office building who made $350 last month on a silver mine." It seemed a replay of the *Life* article on the Toronto Stock Exchange a decade earlier, though citing much smaller winnings.

The exchange, said Broadfoot, was "in the middle of a penny stock boomlet that has obscure new issues trading hands like trading stamps." Some days saw more than a million shares swapped. More than half the mines were trading at under twenty cents, and Broadfoot had one example of a twenty-cent stock called Craigmont Mines that had soared to $18. Broadfoot, unlike the *Life* writer, introduced some refreshing skepticism into his piece. No-one seemed concerned, he said, that many of the stocks in question were little more than "fairly expensive wallpaper." He quoted a broker who likened the VSE to a bingo game: "Everybody's into the market this year," the broker sang gleefully. Another said that the VSE community was grateful for the Windfall debacle because it had shaken confidence in the Toronto market.

The supercharged VSE was certainly to Pezim's liking and, initially, to Glick's as well. Before long, the two men opened up what was to become the Glick-Pezim Suite, if you please, at the Hotel Georgia. It became a revolving door for babes and booze, a platform for doing deals, unveiling new promotions, putting on dog-and-pony shows, shoving stock every which way.

Actually, the suite was officially the Lord Stanley suite, two units made into one. The Lord Stanley was considered the poshest digs in the hotel, still is, though today the $450 per night cost seems dear given the drab state of the rooms.

The door to these quarters had – and still has – the Lord Stanley arms, stallions rearing up on their hind legs. The motif, one supposes, was meant to blend with all the Cavalier heraldic stuff twelve floors below. The living room of the suite measures thirty-six by twenty feet, has an enormous wet bar made of pecan, a fireplace that casts an electric glow, and cushy, ugly furniture. The bathroom has a vaguely Egyptian motif and includes among its features gold sprayed, fish-shaped faucets.

Under the lip of the bar in the living room was a button that flushed – and to this day flushes – the toilet in the washroom. The remote-controlled flusher is legendary at the Georgia. Pezim is a born gagster, low-brow variety, and when beautiful broads went to the beautiful bathroom, Pezim loved to press that button. They'd reappear and he would say something like, "Have a nice time, dear?" Something clever like that.

Pezim unstintingly worked the Pezim charisma on the Vancouver investment community. The set-up required someone who didn't need much sleep, given that the parties at the suite would last long into the night. He was an impromptu crooner: "Fly me to the moon, and let me play among the stars . . . Don't wanna be like Madame Curie, Discovering things means nothing to me. It's all been discovered what I'm thinking of, I love to live." Jive, jive, jive.

Pezim would psych himself up for the following trading day, which starts at 6:30 a.m. (to coincide with the TSE, which

127

opens at 9:30). He was inexhaustible. Rising at six or even earlier – whether he'd slept or not – he'd quickly hustle out to breakfast, drawing his stock customers and customers-to-be around. He'd tour all the brokerages, pushing, pushing, pushing.

He'd present himself on the VSE floor, exhorting, touting, loud-mouthing. Ba-ba-ba-ba-ba-ba-ba. That's how Pezim's friends imitate his loud-mouthing. Ba-ba-ba-ba-ba-ba-ba, with those graceful hands in motion all the time.

On weekends, he'd fly home to Stormont Avenue in Toronto, where he would do the kid bit – perhaps take them to Edwards Gardens to feed the chipmunks. Pezim says he has a way with animals, says they'll come right up to him. The point, one presumes, is to emphasize how warm and endearing Pezim figures the real Pezim is.

Bernice and the children never went west. Pezim says she didn't want to live there, didn't want to raise their three children there.

During his sojourns in Toronto, he was often seen in the company of Marilyn Murray, the plump daughter of a minister and secretary to Earl Glick and Bill Coldoff. Sometimes Pezim and Marilyn would rendezvous at the home of Les MacConnell, who became a fast friend of Pezim's. His wife also worked for Glick. Pezim started getting a reputation for shtupping women in the Glick offices. Perhaps Marilyn became more important than the others because of her importance to Glick.

Despite her husband's infidelities, Bernice seemed to have a good life. She had money. She had jewellery. Pezim would buy her beautiful gifts. She liked to travel to spas when he wasn't around. And he still took her to Florida.

One time, she recalls, they met a friendly couple there, a fellow married to a fat, short little girl, as Bernice describes her. The husband asked Pezim whether he would be interested in wife-swapping, switching the fat little girl for the beautiful Bernice? Bernice later asked Murray whether he had given the proposal any serious thought.

"Did you see the wife?" he cried. "She's such a fat dog."

It wasn't, says Bernice, that her husband was repelled by the idea, but rather by the individual. Murray the mover.

"I love women," he always says. "I love women."

At one point in late 1964, maybe early 1965, the group controlled as many as twenty-five companies listed on the VSE. Bill Coldoff recalls one day when he, The Earl, and Nate Hurwitz were gathered in The Suite at the Georgia. When Pezim arrived, he was even itchier than usual. He had just come from a meeting with a Texan, he said. This particular Texan, had, like most Texans, oodles of money. The Texan wanted to buy stocks. Did the group think, asked Pezim, that he should deal him some shares? Are you kidding, the other three said. Sell to the guy. Stuff him full of all the stock you can get your hands on. Which Pezim said he would do.

The following day the volume trades on the group's shares doubled, or maybe tripled. (Who can remember such details?) The investing syndicate quite naturally had a question to put to Pezim: who the heck was this Texas big shot and could they meet him? Sure, said Pezim, who promptly scurried out of the suite. Twenty minutes later, he returned.

He was solo. And he was wearing a very nice stetson.

The story was funny; the partners applauded, even though they never would have sanctioned Pezim's buying spree had they known what he was up to. The skit serves to illustrate why Pezim is a fallible market player. He has always believed that he can support a stock by buying it. What's more, he has a reputation for believing his own stock pitches long after his closest partners have taken their profits and headed home. There have been times when

Pezim, watching his pals dump his stocks, has started to cry. Then he starts buying the stock himself in the mistaken belief that he will prove them wrong.

Pezim ate Glick's paper, Rotterman's paper, Clemiss's paper. Years later, after he became famous, the Vancouver stock community honoured Pezim with their Promoter of the Year Award. Peter Brown, head of Canarim Investment Corp., the largest firm on the West Coast, rose to skewer his friend.

"Murray is reported to have made and lost $1 million or more, twenty-seven times in his career. He is believed to have lost more than $25 million on each of two go-rounds on Hemlo. If we assume that on the other times he lost an average of $1.4 million, then over the thirty-year period he has lost $90 million, or an average of $3 million per year over his working life. Stated another way, $250,000 per month for thirty years. This is an astounding and consistent achievement."

In the sixties, this flaw was less amusing. Glick was the one who was the most adept at keeping Pezim in line. He knew that when Pezim was up he had an unbeatable ability to promote stock, which, of course, meant profits for Glick. But Pezim was increasingly volatile, increasingly out of control. One friend says that when Pezim's stocks were down, you could tell because he would be grey, he would mope, he would slump his head into the cup of one hand. When Pezim's stocks were dead, you could tell because his mood was black, and he'd slump his head into the cup of both hands together. When Pezim's stocks were dead, Pezim was dead too. His friends knew he was in trouble whenever he hit the couch. Sometimes he would hit the couch for weeks.

The Vancouver market quickly came to know this, and quickly came to know Glick-Pezim stocks. The VSE has a publication called the *Review*, which today is a fat, soft-cover collection of trading statistics and other securities information. In the sixties, the *Review* was a slender product given to touting stocks. In its December 1964 issue, there is a glowing report on a company called Delta Electronics, which had started trading on the VSE that November. Delta, said the *Review*, was a space-age performer, then went on to tout the company's cable-television equipment, its success in Canada and abroad (though the company had net income that year of just $75,000 and its success was far from proved), and its strong management, headed by one Sydney Wellum of Oakville, Ontario.

On its application for the VSE listing, the company names not only Sydney Wellum, but Earl Glick as vice-president and director; Bill Coldoff, secretary-treasurer and director; and Murray Pezim, stockbroker and Delta director. The underwriter was Jenkin Evans. The company's head offices were the Glick offices on Bay Street. Delta was just one of ten, one of twenty, one of thirty Glick-Pezim stocks over the years. It seemed a good idea, one of those companies of which Pezim says, "it could have been the biggest thing ever." Perhaps. But it was cash-flat and never succeeded in sealing the hoped-for cable-service contracts. Glick and Pezim took their leave, Delta re-emerged as Triple Crown Electronics, and the company went nowhere.

The final resting place of these myriad companies wasn't the point for Glick et al. It was the money made in the early days. And Vancouver turned out to be almost as accommodating as Toronto had been before the Windfall scandal.

The president of the VSE in the sixties was John (Jack) Van Luven. Initially, he put considerable effort into communicating a "well-regulated" market message. But he couldn't deny that the mining explosion in 1964 and 1965 created supervisory problems that the exchange and the securities regulators couldn't control. In late 1965, he issued a press release warning investors that they should "not let speculative fever overrule their good judgment."

He added that the volume surge in mining stocks was based "largely on the results of two or three drill cores and that many of these active issues are, at this stage, strictly speculative."

Some of the VSE's members also started raising concerns about stock practices. An important issue was the primary distribution of shares, a problem that the TSE knew very well. Toronto had for years struggled with the issue of how to maintain a well-regulated market for informed investors – when these same investors were being sold stock straight off the exchange floor, unencumbered by prospectuses, free of any attention to due diligence.

But the Vancouver governors were loath to shed the venture-capital image. They did lower the limit on the underwriting of treasury shares to 600,000 from one million. They insisted that brokers identify customers by name, a move aimed at discouraging fictitious trades or wash trades, whereby one investor washes shares into and out of a variety of accounts to lend an appearance of active trading. The requirements for working capital of VSE-listed companies was more than doubled, to $50,000.

In the summer of 1963, the VSE president had been empowered by the board to suspend trading in a single stock or all the stocks in a trading session. The president closed an entire session only once – when the market went kablooey at the time of John F. Kennedy's death in November of that year. The power to suspend a single company would logically be used when, say, a penny mine showed heavy trading and handsome price increases on the basis of nothing at all.

The two mining areas that had the most feverish activity in late 1964 through 1965 were Pine Point and Valley Copper. Pine Point, on the south shore of Great Slave Lake in the Northwest Territories, was a spectacular zinc discovery. Prospectors staked any claims anywhere near the ore body – and yet another boom in what would prove to be worthless stocks was born. Pine Point was followed by Valley Copper near Kamloops. Both would come to be of particular importance to Pezim and Glick.

The Earl was running his show back in Toronto. Pezim was running his show out of the Hotel Georgia. It is perhaps natural that fissures in their relationship would start to appear.

Vancouver suited Pezim. He was liked. His brash attitude wasn't seen as offensive, as off-side. Pezim realized he could become a big man in this small town. He started to gab about how he hated the East, its establishment, its attitude. This would later become his standard shtick to the media. His ego had ballooned to a colossal size. Maybe he didn't need The Earl any longer.

In February 1964, a company called Rolling Hills Copper applied for a VSE listing. On its application form the company names Earl Glick, financier, as president, and Murray Pezim, stockbroker, as vice-president and director. Rolling Hills consisted of numerous mining claims, properties that tied primarily onto the Valley Copper area near Kamloops.

Inexplicably, in later filing statements, Pezim was bumped down to the position of corporate secretary treasurer. Glick remained as president and someone named Robert Campbell made a first appearance as vice-president. In December 1965, the company announced the staking of 108 claims in the Pine Point area of the Northwest Territories.

In January 1966, something happened. Rumours flew throughout Howe Street about the potential of a Rolling Hills mineral find at Thubun Lake, 150 kilometres east of Pine Point. Glick and Pezim were both in Toronto at the time. Rolling Hills stock rose to $3.05 a share from $1.40 over the course of a week. On January 18 the exchange traded 4.5 million shares.

Pezim and Glick flew to Vancouver. Pezim called VSE president Jack Van Luven and asked him to come to the Glick-Pezim suite at the Georgia. When he arrived, Pezim requested that the stock be halted. Otherwise, he predicted, Rolling Hills shares could very likely move to $6. Van Luven agreed. The B.C. Securities Commission then took the unprecedented step of flying an investigator to the Thubun property to retrieve the ore samples.

At a subsequent press conference, attended by Pezim but not Glick, Van Luven announced that the ore samples pulled at Thubun Lake contained no commercial mineralization. Pezim denied that he had personally spread reports that the ore samples appeared highly promising. Glick was on the record earlier as having qualified a Rolling Hills statement announcing "mineralization" at the site; he had pointed out that mineralization did not necessarily mean commercial viability. Pezim told reporters that Glick didn't make "an exorbitant profit" on Rolling Hills stock – maybe $60,000 or $70,000. Pezim said he himself had never bought or sold any Rolling Hills shares.

The blame for the rumour-mongering was placed at the feet of a person or persons unknown. The suspension was lifted and Rolling Hills started trading again at seventy-five cents. No charges were ever laid.

What we do know is that at the time of the Rolling Hills hype, there hadn't been a single exploration hole drilled at Thubun lake. Not one. We know that Glick disappears subsequently from the company's corporate filings, that Pezim for a time does, too, and that the one-time Pezim allies Morry Kessler and Pezim's brother-in-law Moe Langer are later reported as recipients of Rolling Hills shares.

How strange for Pezim to have taken the action he did, phoning the regulators, telling them a stock he was promoting was about to run away. Pezim now says Rolling Hills was the start of the breakup with Glick.

Glick disagrees that Rolling Hills signalled the end of the

partnership. "The relationship ended because Murray was determined to step out, to be his own man, to do his own thing. He has obviously done so with great success and distinction," he said in his letter to me.

The Rolling Hills incident marks the first time that Pezim hit the news. There he is, full face, in the business pages of the *Vancouver Sun*: double chin, huge nose, dark, baggy eyes. He was in his mid-forties. Although he was not a boozer, his lifestyle — the late hours, the high-cholesterol diet, the incessant smoking — had not treated him kindly.

Pezim makes a later reappearance in the Rolling Hills story, this time with a man named Dick Lennie, a one-time Vancouver radio executive. Through Lenwood Investments, Pezim and Lennie had a piece of Rolling Hills, which in turn nailed a piece of Valley Copper, the other focus for VSE speculation that year. Bill Coldoff and Nate Hurwitz were bought out of the partnership with Click and Pezim, who themselves divvied up the various corporate interests and then went their separate ways.

Pezim and Jenkin Evans also parted company. William Somerville, executive vice-president of the Toronto Stock Exchange, forced the decision by telling Pezim he couldn't run two towns at once. This according to Pezim, who chose Vancouver for good in 1966. Soon after, he attached himself to a brokerage called H.H. Hemsworth.

Pezim was still a broker. He worked the trading floor, too. By 1967, he was a Hemsworth partner, with a forty-five percent stake in the firm.

With The Earl out of the picture, Pezim introduced a whole new cast of characters into his life — mainly Dick Lennie, who later ran into a spate of drug trouble and who can't risk coming to Canada these days. Pezim moved out of the Georgia and into an apartment on Beach Avenue on Vancouver's waterfront.

As part of his separation agreement with Glick, he got a company called Galaxy Copper, which was transformed from a Glick-Pezim vehicle to a Pezim-Lennie stock. Galaxy had been looking for copper around Kamloops, a tie-on hopeful to the Valley Copper discovery. It was a nothing venture.

Through their holding company, Lenwood Investments, Pezim and Lennie also had a major position in Stampede Oils, with Lennie installed as vice-president and director. Pezim put Irwin Wallace — Wally, the husband of Murray's sister Frances — on the board. Lennie also brought a couple of his pals into Stampede. One was Joey Romano, a New York mobster type, who was listed as a member of the board of directors of Stampede. Another was Gino Cicci, who received 100,000 shares in the company at 50 cents for "arranging financing."

Romano and Cicci went on to infamy on the Vancouver scene after they were convicted of fraud in the late 1970s over their role in a Quebec uranium play called Seneca Developments — whose stock went to $3.85 from forty cents, though the company produced neither earnings nor commercially viable ore. Seneca was a striking example of how wide a net Vancouver stocks could cast. Investors ranged from New York Jets football players to friends of Frank Sinatra to members of the Palm Springs set. A geologist named Ken Darke was responsible for the geological reports on the property, the same Ken Darke who was found guilty of insider trading by the U.S. Securities and Exchange Commission at the time of the Texasgulf disovery.

The association with Dick Lennie clearly opened a new world to Murray Pezim. He started hitting Las Vegas once a month, where he stayed at the Hilton. He had a line of credit at most of the hotels — The Sands, Caesars, the Golden Nugget, the Hilton itself — running to $200,000. Bobby Schmidt was the head credit man at the MGM Grand; Pezim used to call him chopped liver because that's what his face reminded him of. On weekends when Pezim wasn't going home to Toronto, he'd head to Vegas.

Pezim hated the thought of a weekend without action. In Vegas, he and his buddies would even play bullshit poker, or what's now called liar's poker – betting on the serial numbers of dollar bills. Mornings he'd get a steam, facial, manicure, the works, though "no blow jobs," he says. At the tables he always, always played craps. Not enough patience for blackjack. He'd win fifty; lose fifty; walk away; come back. What was his stop-loss? That, he says, depended on his mood, the way he felt, his instinct.

There was plenty of money flowing into the Stormont house in Toronto. Bernice would receive gifts from strangers who had done well by Pezim companies. Cases of champagne; cases of Chivas. Bernice was house-proud, and photographs from those days show her against a backdrop of the kind of spindly wooden furniture and gold brocade upholstery that was in vogue. She looked flawless. Blonde hair piled high on her head, waist-hugging dresses that showed how trim she was in her mid-thirties. Bernice posing for photographers, her hands and feet placed just so, her head high, her posture erect, her smile perfectly drawn on her face.

There are pictures taken at the time of their son Michael's bar mitzvah in the mid-sixties. Murray looks better than he did in the *Vancouver Sun* mug shot accompanying the Rolling Hills article. Still slender, his unruly hair buzzed frighteningly close to the scalp, he seems young for his forty-five years. Bernice, in her ocelot shell with cream overjacket with ocelot cuffs, was clearly a fashion plate. When Murray gave a speech he called his wife a princess. The comment made Bernice nervous. No-one knew what Murray might say next.

Back in Vancouver, Pezim's big gamble was on Stampede Oils. It had entered into a "farm-out" agreement with British

American Oil. Stampede would drill for oil and gas on the Strachan field in Alberta, owned by British American, and earn a fifty percent interest in any results. Other Pezim-Lennie stocks such as Galaxy Copper, Bata Resources, and Silver Arrow Explorations were party to the Stampede agreement and would receive smaller net interests if Stampede ever struck it rich. Rolling Hills was in there too, for Pezim had used that company to buy a piece of Stampede.

It was Pezim's first big show without Glick, and the idea was to build a tight, interwoven empire, promote the hell out of the Strachan prospects, and make millions.

Initially, Stampede did well. A longtime associate of Pezim's recalls that one day an insurance salesman from Imperial Life paid a visit to Pezim's offices. He wanted to sell the promoter on an annuity of some type.

"Give me a million dollars," said the salesman. "We will take the money, invest it, and pay you $75,000 annually for the rest of your days. You will never want again for the rest of your life."

"Don't you understand?" replied Pezim. "Next year this stock is going to go to $25. And in five years it's going to go to $100." This was typical Pezim. Why cash out today when tomorrow holds the promise of a greater reward?

One spring morning in 1967, Murray Pezim awoke at his usual six a.m., perhaps feeling more full of himself than usual. It was his habit to check into Hemsworth's offices on Howe Street before heading to the exchange floor, where there were about a hundred traders gathered. On this particular morning the atmosphere was tense.

His Bata Resources was trading at $3.30, up from its $3 underwriting price. This was good. Then the sell orders started flooding in. It was the same old story. When people start selling,

Pezim usually says, fine, go ahead, take your money, leave the party, go home. When they started selling Bata, he started buying it back himself. They didn't understand, he screamed, that this was going to be the biggest, the greatest, the most fabulous enterprise ever.

He bought 300,000 shares at $3.30. The stock was slammed. Wham. He scuttled back to the trading booth.

"I'll take 100,000 Bata," he cried.

Sure, Murray, here, take it. Slam. Whump.

"I'll take another 100,000 Bata!"

He was such a hotshot, out to prove that he was smarter than everyone else. Bought 600,000 shares. Smart guy rode the stock all the way down to eighty cents. Pezim was wiped out to the tune of $6 million.

Here was Pezim, bust flat again, his actions forced by who knows what weird compulsion. Would he, could he, make a comeback?

A relation of Pezim's, casting back on Pezim's life, the good parts and the bad, once told me that Pezim would die either a millionaire or a bum. "And he's been both."

At this point, Murray Pezim was a bum for sure.

CHAPTER 7

Crack-up

urray Pezim was curled in the fetal position on Les MacConnell's couch. He was beating himself about the head. He was calling for his mother. He was anxious, depressed, upset. He was crying. The baggy eyes, the bulbous nose, had grown swollen and moist from the constant weeping. He looked the way the defrocked televangelist Jimmy Bakker looked when he finally crawled out from under his lawyer's desk, wet with emotion and deflated by fear, to face the fact that God really, really, really wasn't going to save him from a jail term.

Pezim appeared equally frightened, persecuted, paranoid. He hadn't just wiped out his own account on the Bata collapse. He had extended the working capital of H. H. Hemsworth twice over to support the stock. He feared he had bust the brokerage house. He had certainly cleaned out a few local brokers, the ones who had been left sitting with Bata paper after its fall. He thought investors were out to get him. He thought other promoters were out to get him. He thought the regulators were out to get him. He figured the whole damned Vancouver Stock Exchange was out to get him.

When they found him, he imagined, they'd squeeze him like a pig till he squealed.

Les MacConnell had never been witness to a Pezim depression before. In February, he had left Toronto for Vancouver at Pezim's urging, hoping to hitch a ride on the inside rail of Pezim companies. The two men had been friends in Toronto. MacConnell's wife had worked for Earl Glick. The MacConnell apartment had been used for trysts between Pezim and Marilyn Murray. Pezim had promised to sponsor MacConnell's broker application, which he did when MacConnell moved west. Now, just a few weeks later, the distraught little man was cracking up on his couch.

MacConnell had heard about Pezim's bouts of melancholy. They had become part of his persona. Every time he went bust, or every time the market moved against him, he would wrap himself into a tight little package and take to his bed.

At first, MacConnell thought he'd snap out of it. He waited for the bad days to pass. They didn't. Not this time. He called on Dick Lennie, Pezim's partner. What to do? Who knew? MacConnell phoned Bernice in Toronto. He handed the phone over to Murray. "Please," said the pathetic creature in his strange lisping way, "rescue me."

The years of separation, Pezim in Vancouver, Bernice in Toronto, had obviously been hard on the twenty-year marriage. But Bernice had not yet given up. In fact, at the time of this collapse, his worst ever, the Pezims had sold their lovely Stormont Avenue house. Earlier in the year, Bernice had gone house-hunting in Vancouver. Though she hadn't found anything to her liking she was nevertheless in the process of moving Cheryl, sixteen, Michael, thirteen, and Nanci, nine, and everything she owned to Vancouver. Instead, she flew to Vancouver, packed up her husband, who wasn't much of a husband at all, and boarded a plane back to Toronto. Pezim had aged. His love of the sun had produced a spattering of liver spots across his face. There was that nose. He was overweight. Many would have found him ugly. Perhaps even Bernice did.

Initially, she thought, as had MacConnell, that her husband would come around. She had seen his crack-ups before. In fact, periods of depression had pockmarked their marriage. Bernice was used to being ignored when her husband was flying high. She was used to the way he'd whimper for her support when the market, the proxy for his life, turned traitor.

Back in Toronto, Bernice moved her all-but-bankrupt family into a crummy little one-bedroom apartment on Raglan Avenue, owned by the DelZottos, who had become millionaire real-estate developers. Bernice put her Limoges china into storage. Cheryl, Michael, and Nanci crowded into the one bedroom. The living room served as sleeping quarters for Bernice and Murray.

Bernice said years later how tough this period was, how difficult it was to come so far down in life. "Marriage to Murray was like being on a rollercoaster. There were times I didn't know which mink coat to wear and other times I'd go to the supermarket and I'd look to buy oranges that were two cents a dozen cheaper."

Murray wouldn't leave his bed. His depression cratered. He didn't shower or shave. His paranoia got worse. "They" were after him, he was sure of it, they being the crowd back in Vancouver who had had their pockets turned inside out on Bata.

"He got into bed and pulled the sheets over his head and wouldn't talk to anybody," recalls Bernice. "It was just terrible. I was busy closing doors to shield my kids from this terrible scene. His sister Frances came, my brother-in-law Norman came. I remember they'd get him to play cards a little and he'd fall back into bed and I'd say, 'Murray, you have to get help.' He wouldn't even talk to me. He was really disturbed."

During earlier depressions, Pezim had been prescribed

Parnate, a drug used to treat psychotic-depressive states. He would not take the drug faithfully. The despondency would pass and he would leap back into the stock market with the lust of a teenager. The whole God-damned world would once again look like one big, luscious entrepreneurial opportunity.

This time was different. Bernice realized that he needed treatment. Her first call, strangely enough, was not to a psychiatrist. Rather, she slipped off to a pay phone one day and called Stan Elkind, a dapper young lawyer who had worked on some of Pezim's business deals. Bernice believed that Murray needed reassurance that he could find legal protection against the marauders from the West who, in Pezim's mind, had assumed Godzilla-like proportions.

Elkind's parents had known Pezim's parents; his grandparents had known Pezim's grandparents. The families had been part of a tightly knit group of Romanian immigrants who had belonged to the Romanian Synagogue. When Elkind graduated from law school at the University of Toronto in 1963 he had needed a break, and Pezim had hired him on a needs-be basis to help with the company's legal work – stock-exchange listings, underwriting agreements, statements of material facts.

Elkind says that when he arrived at the Pezim apartment the broken little man didn't appear to be a basket case, though he was certainly anxious. He thought that Pezim seemed relieved to see him. This is not the way Bernice remembers it:

"When I walked in with Stan, Murray looked at me as though I had been a traitor," she says. "I had brought somebody to the house. I said 'You better speak to Stan. We can't go on like this.' I remember standing crying in the kitchen, one of those little galleys. He did unload to Stan. They were talking very low. Stan said he wanted Murray to go and see a psychiatrist so that it would be on record that Murray was seeing a psychiatrist. If there were a problem it would be said that Murray was not aware of what was going on." The Pezim defence: non compos mentis.

So Bernice took Murray to a psychiatrist. "He spoke to the doctor for about half an hour and the doctor called me in and said, 'This is a very sick man you have here.' I said, 'He can't afford to be sick. He has to go back to Vancouver.' He said, 'Asking Murray Pezim to go back and help himself in Vancouver is like asking a man without arms to paint a picture.'"

This first doctor passed Pezim along to a second psychiatrist at the Toronto General Hospital. Murray and Bernice had a joint session with him, during which Murray described how horrible life with Bernice was. He was put in hospital for a short period. He was diagnosed.

Murray Pezim was manic depressive.

Manic depression is a bipolar disorder, so called because of the mood split between mania and melancholia. In the mid-nineteenth century, two French psychiatrists independent of each other described a state of circular insanity during which patients ride a ferris wheel down through states of depression up to mania and back again, with periods of normality in between. Until the 1950s, the illness was often misdiagnosed as schizophrenia.

One person in a hundred suffers from manic-depressive illness. There is some evidence to suggest that it may be genetic, though the pattern by which one member of a family may inherit the disorder from another has not been determined. Chronic mania when left untreated can last for months, even years. Manic phases are high-energy hyperactive moods that may be marked by elevated good humour or intense irritability, often moving in stages from the former to the latter. Manics may become verbally abusive, aggressive, sexually provocative. Their speech can progress from merely rapid to, in extreme cases, carried-away clanging associations, sticking together words that sound similar but have no logical communion. "I fly, I fly, look at the sky!" is one textbook example.

Delusions are common, particularly delusions of grandiosity and wealth. When manic depressives are manic they may spend money heedlessly. They may steamroll their families into bankruptcy. Judgement is often impaired. Reality is sometimes lost. Occasionally, a manic may believe he is God or Jesus Christ.

Understandably, when a manic depressive is manic and feeling on top of the world the notion of seeking help for something that feels so good seems illogical. In highly energized, highly creative states manics can, in fact, exceed themselves. There is a notable synergy between mania and brilliance, provided the mania is contained at what the experts call the "hypomanic level." Just nicely on the edge. Just on the verge of break-up. Just enough to keep, say, a highly energized acquisitor pumping though a multi-billion-dollar deal, but not enough to have him do the whole damn deal in junk bonds.

Psychologists and historians have long speculated that Sir Isaac Newton was a manic depressive, which would explain how he could stand at his drafting table for days on end, producing the proof of his mathematical genius. He also cracked up more than once, was paranoiac, and by most accounts wasn't a very nice guy.

Phases of depression have been known to last for a year, even longer, and it is normally a state of depression, not mania, that causes a manic depressive or his family to seek medical help. Sleep becomes disturbed, energy levels are sapped. Sufferers may worry obsessively and be overcome by feelings of guilt and hopelessness. Sexual drive may diminish, appetite may lessen. The depressive may be overcome by thoughts of death, of suicide. In extreme cases, a depressive may become psychotic with delusions and hallucinations. A depressive, for example, may fear the world is out to get him. Or more specifically a group of hot lawyers, brokers and exchange regulators. Or more specifically still a group of boiling-mad Vancouver lawyers, brokers, and exchange regulators who by this time, in one man's mind, have assumed Brobdingnagian proportions.

In 1967, the treatment of manic depression was still in the developmental stages. The use of electro-convulsive therapy was popular with psychiatrists, but had a bad rap with the public. The thought of electromagnetic currents charging through uncontrollably jerking limbs was frightening and undignified, and left the unknowing with the belief that ECT patients necessarily ended up effectively lobotomized and slow-witted. What ECT does do, in effect, is cause an epileptic seizure that can snap a patient out of a severe depression. It can, and often does, cause some temporary disruption in memory. When ECT was first used, back injuries and muscle sprains were common. Today, muscle relaxants serve to paralyse patients. There are no violent convulsions, just a slight trembling of the fingers.

Over the years Pezim has had ECT treatments. Whether he received such therapy at the time of the Bata collapse is not clear. If he did receive ECT in 1967, he would have undergone violent spasms. It would have looked frightening. He would not, however, have suffered any mental impairment.

At the time Pezim was admitted to Toronto General Hospital, a little-known drug called lithium had become available on an experimental basis. While the drug had been proved not to have harmful side effects, securing a prescription meant that Bernice had to sign a waiver stating she understood the experimental nature of the medication. From that point on and for the rest of his life, Murray Pezim is supposed to take a 300-milligram capsule of lithium carbonate twice a day. It is supposed to smooth out the swings. It does not, say the experts, interfere with intellectual productivity or normal emotional responses. It has no sedative properties. The side effects are minor – a trembling of the hands, perhaps, an increase in urination. It works for about a third of the patients who take the drug.

Lithium is, nevertheless, a mood stabilizer. Many patients don't like to take the drug because it deprives them of the "high." Some try to manipulate the dosage to get a bit of a rush. Some might sense a manic phase coming on and stay off the drug altogether. Several people who have moved in the Pezim orbit insist that he has gone off his medication from time to time – when he's starting to feel the rush of an "up" period, when he's got a corporate battle on his hands. This Pezim denies.

After his stay in hospital, Pezim returned to the modest apartment, still feeling low. During this period, he sought solace from his sister Frances. His mother, Rebecca, who had been the centre of Pezim family life, had died in 1960. Since then, Murray and his siblings had drifted apart. But Pezim badly needed his elder sister's encouragement during these rocky times. She had, after all, suffered her own terrible breakdown years earlier. Had been given ECT treatments. Had never been an entirely happy person.

Pezim told her that he felt responsible for other people's losses. He confided his fear that he would never swing back up again. The man who had made his past financial successes while on past manic rides was terrified the ferris wheel had stopped forever. Frances calmed, soothed, encouraged. Frances herself had a million fears.

A more practical remedy for Pezim's frayed emotional state finally presented itself. A man named Ted Turton, a partner of a young Vancouver hotshot named Peter Brown, flew to Toronto and bought Pezim's piece of H.H. Hemsworth for $23,000. The buyout helped relieve Pezim's sense of persecution. Hemsworth eventually became Canarim, the powerhouse West Coast brokerage on which

Brown has built his reputation and his fortune.

Even then, $23,000 was carfare for Pezim. The deal was struck in consultation with the VSE and the VSE's lawyers. It is likely that Stan Elkind acted for Pezim. The immediate benefit of the financial settlement was that the Pezim family was able to move from its small digs to a four-bedroom suite on the eighth floor of the El Dorado, a high-rise apartment on Bathurst Street. Frances, her husband Irwin, and their daughter Vicki lived three floors below.

Eight months after Pezim crawled into his hole he crawled back out. Not well, just better. Those who have experienced Pezim's re-geneses say that he just hops off the couch one day, starts jiving his hands in the air, and says, "Let's get to work!" That's not the way it happened this time.

One day he woke up and decided he needed a haircut a mission that at least served to propel him out of the apartment.

"I thought there were going to be a million people waiting to see me. There was no-one there. Not a soul," he recalls.

He soon realized that it was imperative that he return to Vancouver. There were children and a wife to support. There was nothing for him in Toronto, no penny market to play. But Pezim hadn't yet found his old self. How, he wondered, would he be treated in Vancouver? Would old friends still be friends or newly minted foes? He needed support. He approached Moe Langer, the husband of his sister Rose. Langer had worked as a broker at Jenkin Evans, so he knew the business. And he certainly knew his brother-in-law. Pezim wanted Langer around for his Vancouver comeback. Langer agreed.

At the Vancouver airport, the two men were met by Jack Van Luven, the president of the Vancouver Stock Exchange. This is the kind of cosiness that chills VSE skeptics. Pezim's a guy, after all, who has never done much for the legion of investors who

149

have dropped their dollars into his bottomless pit of penny hopefuls. And yet here was the head of the VSE welcoming him back because the exchange so missed his business.

Pezim got back on his feet post-Bata thanks to a loan from an accountant named Alex Fisher. Or at least that's what Pezim says. Fisher, who like Glick lives on Toronto's moneyed Bridle Path, says he didn't know Pezim at all well and would not answer any questions. There are numerous people like Fisher in the Pezim story, people who deny any association with the man, people who get angry when enquiries are made about their involvement in Pezim history.

Whatever the means, it didn't, of course, take long before Pezim was rolling again. There were, in particular, two very different opportunities to pursue: chicken and gas.

The chicken story began with Robert Kaplan and George Tidball, the men who introduced McDonald's hamburgers to western Canada long before the words Big Mac and McDLT became part of the lexicon. The U.S. was just starting to recognize what a non-stop success Ray Kroc's fast-food empire had become. Kaplan and Tidball opened their first outlet – in fact, Canada's first McDonald's – in Richmond, British Columbia, in 1967. Soon they had ten outlets selling twenty-two-cent burgers.

Tidball went on to greater fame and fortune through his ownership of the Keg restaurant chain. Kaplan decided that if burgers could work, why not a fast-food chicken franchise? As luck would have it, there was a ready-made opportunity with a Nashville outfit called Minnie Pearl, an American chain that used the name and face of *Hee Haw*'s Minnie Pearl as its selling logo.

Minnie Pearl needed a rich bagman to carry their "dee-licious chicken" to Canadians. Kaplan made a $72,000 downpayment on the Canadian rights, and agreed to open eighty outlets. Then he went looking for the $500,000 start-up costs he figured he'd need. Tidball wasn't interested. Nevertheless, the $500,000 did appear, raised by a Howe Street promoter who was unknown to Kaplan. The conduit to the promoter was an American broker named Bruce Kosman.

Kaplan met his backers in the fall of 1968 at the Royal York Hotel in Toronto: a funny-looking character named Murray Pezim and his partner of the moment, Dick Lennie. The twosome had commitments from various investors to take up 100,000 shares in Minnie Pearl at $5 a share. The plan was to then have Pezim and Lennie's Lenwood Investments underwrite a public issue of Minnie Pearl. The shares were to go to the street at $10 apiece.

Everybody wanted to get in line for the soon-to-be-public company. And no wonder. Minnie Pearl in the U.S. had been papered out in the summer at $20 a share, and had doubled on its first day of trading. By the time Pezim and Lennie had hooked their fingers into the Canadian version, Minnie Pearl U.S. had hit a high of $63. According to the *Financial Post* reporter Alexander Ross, Wall Street invented a new verb — to Minnie Pearl — in honour of the stock's performance. A stock was said to have Minnie Pearled if it doubled on offering day. Kaplan told Ross that there was so much demand that he "couldn't walk down Howe Street without somebody stepping out of the woodwork and asking for a piece of the action."

In the same article, Pezim was introduced in this way: "Murray is Murray Pezim. You probably haven't heard of him, because Murray likes to keep his name out of the papers. But Murray is one of the most adept stock promoters in Canada, a former butcher who can sell inspirational pieces of paper the way Billy Graham sells lectures." Murray Pezim had at last met the feature-writing press.

But this was not a good-news story. By the time the

Minnie Pearl caper reached print in December 1969, the relationship between Kaplan and Pezim had turned sour and the enterprise was a bust.

From the beginning, there was substantial disagreement between the Lenwood partners and Kaplan over corporate development. Kaplan said Pezim had pressured him into using the $500,000 in the treasury not for Minnie Pearl startup costs but for other acquisitions – including a Nebraska macaroni factory. Minnie Pearl Canada instead bought a seventy-five-percent interest in a U.S. coffee-services operation called Coffee Hutch.

The directors' meeting at which the acquisition decision was made was also at the Royal York. "We held the meeting in a bedroom," a disapproving Kaplan told Ross. "Dick Lennie and Kosman were sprawled on the beds. Another director was sitting on the toilet, and followed the proceedings from there. . . . People kept wandering in and out, chatting, using the telephone, telling jokes. Hell, it was a circus, not a directors' meeting."

Kaplan was understandably worried. Minnie Pearl needed a huge infusion of cash to set up the promised eighty outlets. Pezim told him not to fret. The public issue would take care of all financial considerations. Pezim, characteristically, continued to believe that Minnie Pearl would be the greatest deal ever.

Years later, ensconced in his $2-million condominium in a DelZotto building on north Yonge Street in Toronto, Izzy Rotterman rests his $2,000 black baby-alligator loafers (a gift from Pezim) on a glass coffee table and tells a story:

"Murray had a deal with George Cohon, who was unknown, and he was just starting up this McDonald's, which was nothing. And Murray was coming out with a deal called Minnie Pearl Chicken. Minnie Pearl was the rage at that time. She was the top name. She was the Bob Hope of her day. With her scream, it was like a well-known object. Cohon and Pezim were in the same

Morris and Sarah Pezim (Morris in the silk top hat at the rear; Sarah beside him) had immigrated to Canada from Romania in 1904. Thirty years later their friends, children, and grandchildren gathered in Toronto to celebrate their golden wedding anniversary. Grandson Murray is seated in the row on the far right, sixth from the back.

Murray didn't fall in love with the army. He fell in love with Jamaica, where he was posted. He's pictured here (left) with an army buddy. Murray's brother Norman (right), a D-Day vet, was a signals officer with Le Régiment de la Chaudière.

Bernice Frankel was still a teenager when she fell in love with Murray Pezim. She would write him letters from summer camp.

Murray's sisters, Frances (left) and Rose (far right), worshipped Murray the golden boy. They're pictured here in the butcher-shop days with their parents, Rebecca and Izzy.

Grandfather Morris was called the Big Zaida, smoked four packs of Lucky Strike a day, and lived to 96. His son Izzy (right), granddaughter Rose, and great-grandson Paul.

The ever-chic Bernice
and the buzz-cut Murray
in their Toronto home
in the early sixties.

The first of the three children born to Bernice and Murray was their daughter Cheryl,
who looked like a baby Pez.

The whole family: Nanci (left), Cheryl, Murray, Michael, and Bernice (in her ocelot attire) at Michael's bar mitzvah.

Murray the comedian (right) gets Michael at manhood to take a swig. When Murray left Bernice, he left her for Marilyn Murray, secretary to Pezim's former partner Earl Glick.

Pez central in Vancouver, before the move to the deluxe headquarters on West Hastings. In the background is Harvey Gould, Pezim's faithful assistant.

After Marilyn came Susan, wife number three, who was supposed to receive $3 million from Pezim in cash and stuff for six months of conjugal bliss.

NAOMI STEVENS

The VSE kingpin Peter Brown brokers just about every deal in town, including Pezim's.

The biggest Blackbird: Ned Goodman, the deal-maker behind Corona.

KAREN PERLMUTTER

And then there was Tammy. A reformed cocaine addict, Tammy Patrick continues to drift in and out of Pezim's life.

Pezim in Paradise Valley, Arizona. The sun. The heat. The void.

building. And they traded ten percent stock of each [company]. But Murray oversold his deal. Everybody wanted to buy his stock. He realized he was giving away ten percent of the strongest deal in the world. To a jerk. An unknown jerk, with a company that nobody even knew about. So somehow or other they came to a parting of the ways. I don't have to tell you that Minnie Pearl went down the drain in a little while."

I phoned George Cohon, head of the McDonald's Canada empire, and told him the tale. He laughed. Not true, he said.

What is true is that Pezim sought shareholders and lenders, including Angelo DelZotto, for the still-private company. DelZotto agreed to undertake construction of a Minnie Pearl outlet in Toronto. Two were under construction in Vancouver. But only one Minnie Pearl opened, in a shopping mall in Burnaby, British Columbia. In October 1969, a full year after that first meeting between Pezim and Kaplan, Lenwood Investments was still telling the world that an underwriting was on its way. The following month, the company announced that its underwriting had been withdrawn. Kaplan said that market conditions – the stock indexes had fallen badly that fall – and a major corporate reorganization were the reasons for the cancellation. The Minnie Pearl partnership had run aground.

In December, Pezim and Lennie declared the voluntary bankruptcy of Minnie Pearl Canada. Subsequent reports questioned the propriety of the bankruptcy. Only one director – R.M. Brown – had been present at the directors' meeting at which the bankruptcy decision was made. (Brown, like Lennie, floated through a variety of Pezim companies in the sixties.) Minnie Pearl was a million dollars in debt when it went under. Creditors were resigned to receiving just ten cents on the dollar. At a creditors' meeting in January "it was reported that $20 worth of chicken and chicken giblets left in the company's single operating store when the company went bankrupt was given to the Salvation Army."

Twenty dollars' worth of chicken-giblet assets left over from a multimillion-dollar idea. Kaplan sold his McDonald's interest at a handsome profit. Cohon went on to become a multimillionaire. When Minnie Pearl went to the deep-fat fryer in the sky, Kaplan tallied a personal loss of $53,000. His pain and suffering weren't financial penance so much as a result of aggravation from Pezim.

Pezim claimed to have lost $400,000 – though his critics maintain his drubbing wasn't nearly so severe. Ross reported, and seems to have been the first writer ever to do so, that Pezim had the disastrous habit of believing in his own promotions.

Years later, Pezim admits – and admits it over and over again – that the Minnie Pearl fiasco was his worst investment play ever.

On the upside, post-Bata, Pezim actually hit a gas strike with Stampede Oils. Stampede drilled a 14,000-foot well on the Strachan field, eighty miles west of Red Deer, on the farm-out property from British American Oils. Pezim says he made $800,000 on Stampede when it finally came through for him.

In his bedroom in Paradise Valley, Pezim has a memento of the Stampede days, one of the very few personal possessions that he seems to have kept around. It is a silver box, engraved on the lid with the stock-ticker symbol for Stampede and whichever stocks were immediately above and immediately below Stampede. Beneath, it says "Murray Pezim – Richard Lennie, on the occasion of the first $10 trade of Stampede Oils Ltd. November 6th, 1968."

But gas fell. Oil fell. The market fell. Pezim's various oil-and-gas interests were merged into United Bata Resources. Pezim took a dump on a failed $10-million takeover of an American meat-packing operation. He took an $800,000 loss on an enterprise called Federal Farms. Pezim told the tax people that his profit on Stampede was washed out by his loss on Federal. He figured he didn't owe any tax. The people at Revenue Canada saw it differently.

154

Two years had passed since the Bata catastrophe, since the manic-depression diagnosis, since the realization that there were clinical reasons for Pezim's personal rollercoaster. It was clear that lithium, if Pezim was taking it at all, wasn't going to flatten the Pezim performance. The Bata slam had been fuelled by a manic apex. Pezim had gone manic again and again. There were no signs it would stop.

Back in Toronto, Bernice had finally had it. In early January, 1970, she visited a physician named Stanley Greben. She was depressed. Life with Pezim had always been tough, and it showed no signs of getting easier. Dr. Greben later documented his consultation with Bernice to substantiate the case she made against her husband during their subsequent divorce proceedings. The doctor wrote: "It seemed clear from her report that he went from periods of severe depression to periods of elation. During the former he talked about killing himself, he fell to the floor in a heap, he prevailed upon her to find some way of helping him. . . . During his periods of elation he had been buying stocks with what sounded like poor judgment, spending a great deal of money, and often earning a great deal of money, but carrying with him the conviction that whatever he touched would turn out very well. When his efforts did not work out he would then go into another depression."

This is what Bernice Pezim had lived with for more than two decades. In many positive ways, she got more than she bargained for out of the marriage. When Pezim was "up" and winning, he would shower her with gifts, shower his pals with gifts. (One day Pezim had phoned her from the offices of Earl Glick in Toronto. He said there was this huge rubber plant that he was going to throw out. Bernice told him to send it to her. When it arrived, there was a $100 bill Scotch-taped to each leaf.)

The sad part is that money had become Pezim's touchstone

for everything in life – for happiness, success, intimacy. He never worried his head about life's big questions – man's inhumanity to man, the search for peace, the fundamental belief in dignity and fraternity, the community of nations. Over time, he seemed to have sloughed off his ability to feel deeply, his capacity for intro-spection and self-analysis, perhaps his ability to love. He had become, bare bones, a penny-ante artist who was so good at the pennies that he was anteing that he'd end up a millionaire many times over. He'd surround himself with stooges and turn bums into kings. During the Bata fiasco and subsequent collapses, he was the biggest loser of all. Just as it says in *What Makes Sammy Run?*: "When you become a bum no one wants to be your pal, or at least no one with anything to lose."

Bernice telephoned Pezim in Vancouver to tell him she had decided to divorce him.

"I want to terminate our marriage," she said.

"Let's give it a trial separation," Pezim urged.

"That," said Bernice, "is what we've had for twenty-two and a half years."

She sued Pezim for divorce on the grounds of adultery and physical and mental cruelty. He was served with the notice of the divorce petition in November 1970, at his apartment on Beach Avenue in Vancouver. So was Marilyn Murray, who was living with him. Bernice was just about the last person to discover the rela-tionship between her husband and the minister's daughter.

Murray hadn't found the marriage easy either. "She was tough, oh, she was tough. She was always late. We'd have a wedding to go to at five. She'd be ready at eight. I couldn't take it. I was a nervous wreck. Got so that I wouldn't accept any invitations. It was hell. She goes to the bathroom, she'd be there for six hours. Very neat, very tidy woman, though. Beautiful woman. Impossible. Married for twenty-two years, and it shouldn't have lasted that long."

Years later, Pezim would tell Jewish American Princess jokes about his long-time helpmate:

"What's a JAP's favorite wine?"

(In shrill, nasal voice): "I want to go to Miami."

"How do you know when a Jewish American Princess has reached orgasm?"

"She drops her nail file."

And on and on.

When people divorce in Ontario, their records are moved to numbered bins in the courthouse at Cooksville after a five-year storage period at the Supreme Court building in downtown Toronto. It takes five days or so to have the court clerks retrieve these records, which can seem a long time when you don't know if there'll be anything substantial in there or not. Pezim's was pretty interesting. Pretty sad.

There is a picture of Marilyn and a picture of Pezim, looking much as they did, one supposes, in the late sixties, when Pezim was commuting to Toronto, living with Bernice part-time, and taking his kids to feed nuts to chipmunks at Edwards Gardens. Marilyn appears a round-faced woman with a helmet of black hair cut high on her forehead in a most peculiar manner.

There's information on the children, too. Nanci, then thirteen and a good student at Forest Hill Junior High School, is described as shy, withdrawn. Cheryl, nineteen, is a "self-sufficient, intelligent girl with a tremendous out-going personality and millions of friends." Cheryl by this time was in her first year of a general arts program at the University of Toronto. Michael, seventeen, is described as an "industrious, hard-working and soft-hearted person," a Grade 12 student at Forest Hill Collegiate. The home environment was found to be attractively and tastefully furnished. "It was apparent that the children are very close to Petitioner wife. The home is a warm and loving place where even the part-time housekeeper feels free to sing." The apartment was painted as Happy Valley, and Pezim as the black-hatted villain who infrequently rode into town.

There was no push-me pull-you over the children. Pezim was never much of a father. "Petitioner wife reports that all three children were happy about the separation though there were the normal apprehensions about the future. Nanci, because she was younger and in the house more, sensed the friction more and has become more relaxed. The children have always been with the Petitioner wife. Respondent husband asked for access and she encouraged them to go but they did not want to go a second time. Petitioner wife feels that Respondent husband never took an interest in the children and he is now trying to buy their affections."

Pezim comes off badly in the divorce petition: "An unstable and irresponsible person, respondent could not distinguish right from wrong. He became involved with other women who he would bring to the marital home when Petitioner wife was away. Respondent husband craved excitement and he was seldom at home. He suffered from mood changes that seemed to be triggered by current market conditions and in the last four years of marriage he underwent psychiatric treatment. . . . In May 1970 respondent husband left the marital home with another woman after a financial crisis."

The woman was Marilyn. The particular crisis has been lost in time. There may not have been a single catastrophe. It may have been a combination of events; it may simply have been the breaking point of so many financial crises spread over very nearly every year of the marriage.

In the end, it wouldn't really matter. In his medical reference letter on Bernice, dated June 10, 1970, Dr. Greben said this: "Mrs. Pezim told me at great length of the humiliation she suffered in particular when her husband was in an elated mood. At these times she said that he spent his time with people whom she had absolutely no respect for, who used him, and he forced her to spend her time with them, much against her wishes. . . . She described her relationship with him in this way: 'When he's down I am a mother. When he is up I am a nobody and he buys other women.'" Dr. Greben prescribed antidepressants for Bernice.

Bernice had been advised by her physician not to resume cohabitation or attempt reconciliation with her husband.

She was advised that it would be a serious mistake to continue with the marriage. It was over. The Pezim sisters, Frances and Rose, thought Bernice was wrong to pursue the divorce. They thought she'd live to regret it.

After the dissolution of the marriage, various stock-market troubles continued to plague Pezim. On the personal side, he stuck with Marilyn. On the financial side, Pezim says he lost $6 million somewhere in 1971 and finally lost control of the corporate remnants that had marked his partnership with Glick. Galaxy Copper, Silver Arrow Mines, the various operations that had formed United Bata Resources were put in liquidation early in the year. He was down to what for Pezim could be called his last nickel. It was actually something on the order of a quarter-million.

In early 1972, Pezim, quite literally, got involved in another of his knock-'em-dead ideas. He decided to stage a match between the Canadian heavyweight boxer George Chuvalo and the Great One himself, Muhammad Ali. His natural instincts also told him that a fight between George ("I've never been knocked off my feet") Chuvalo and Muhammad ("Float like a butterfly, sting like a bee") Ali called for a huge, bust-'em-up, drink-'em-up bash.

The fight was scheduled for March 14, 1972, in the Pacific Coliseum in Vancouver. Pezim pegged the attendance prices at $100 for a ringside seat, $10 for a high-altitude, nosebleed seat in

159

the still-new arena. Chuvalo and Ali had fought once before, in the spring of 1966 in Toronto when Ali was still Cassius Clay. Clay had neatly defeated Chuvalo, but the Canadian champ had remained upright. A rematch looked promising. All 17,000 seats sold out.

Chuvalo was spooked. A boxer was killed in the ring and Chuvalo refused temporarily to fight. The bout was rescheduled for May 2. Unfazed by the initial cancellation, a buoyant Pezim charged ahead with the arrangements. He invited a number of starlets, including Samantha (*The Collector*) Eggar, Edy (*Valley of the Dolls*) Williams, and Yvonne (Batgirl) Craig. He even sent an invitation to Howard Hughes, who at that time was rumoured to be holed up in the Bayshore Inn in Vancouver.

"He'll probably come in a disguise," Pezim spouted to *Sports Illustrated*, which had sent a writer to cover the fight and the surrounding spectacle. "Like in a wheelchair, or wearing a fake nose. . . . Maybe he'll come in black-face. That'd be something – Muhammad Ali is standing there with the party squirreling all around him, flapping his lip like he always does, and this tall, skinny, old, black man comes shuffling up in a tatty cotton suit and Ali tells him to get lost and the next day Hughes buys all the other boxers in the world and refuses to let any of them fight Ali." This was Murray Pezim's imagination running free.

But sales were not as good the second time around. Pezim started to worry. He had planned to throw his pre-fight party at the Bayshore. Slow ticket sales encouraged him to shift to the cheaper Hotel Georgia.

"This is where the action is," Pezim told the skeptical *Sports Illustrated* writer. "Fight headquarters – here we'll get the real atmosphere of a heavyweight fight. The hard little guys from New York with their wisecracks and their broads wrapped in ermine and mystery, the smoke-filled rooms, the trainers and cut-men getting nervous as the big moment nears . . . that kinda thing." Murray Pezim gives interviews the way Jimmy Breslin writes. He is a reporter's dream.

But the party was a disappointment. Not only did Howard Hughes not attend, neither did Ali. Chuvalo did, "sipping a ginger ale and trying to smile through his scar tissue," said the sports reporter. "His right eye, which Joe Frazier had punched deep into Chuvalo's skull, was back up front where it belonged, and the shattered cheekbones, which had had to be mended with wire mesh, were bulging like alternative noses."

Batgirl, Edy Williams, and Samantha Eggar were no-shows. Pezim had initially planned to fly them in, his ticket, but the poor sales squeezed his wallet which was, in fact, too flat to do much of anything promotion-wise, booze-wise or food-wise.

There's a picture of party-goers Pezim and his fiancée Marilyn in the sports magazine. Murray is laughing but looks strained. He wears a glaring houndstooth-check jacket. Marilyn is conservatively dressed in black, and still quite plump through the face. They are pictured with Ali's dentist and the wife of Ali's dentist. Marilyn tells the reporter that she and Murray are thinking of getting married in a boxing ring, Murray in a tux, she in a tuxedo pantsuit with frills and gold studs.

On fight night, the Pezim entourage gathered ringside, Marilyn wearing a black and white polka dot dress, Murray wearing a tux. In addition to Murray and Marilyn, there were roughly 8,798 other spectators. The Coliseum was slightly more than half full.

The fight was mannerly, though Chuvalo got in a couple of good hits. Pezim recalls the eighth round in particular:

"Chuvalo had his back to where Marilyn was sitting and Ali hit him a punch in the face. The gloves get wetter and wetter, you know, and she got splattered head to toe in blood and all this crap. She wanted to kill me. Here I'm sitting there and I know I've lost all my money. Terrible feeling."

Neither fighter was knocked down. The only participant who was KO'd was Murray Pezim. He says that he left the Coliseum with $64 to his name. Pezim was broke; the dismal weekend-long party was, by all accounts (even Pezim's), a bust.

He had been broke before, but this time there seemed no obvious avenue for recovery. There were no saviours. And Pezim still had Revenue Canada breathing down his neck over the profits in Stampede Oils. "Finally a chap by the name of Hurst, head of the collection department, said 'Murray, you're such a strong swimmer. Why do you want to swim with an anchor around your neck? Why don't you just declare bankruptcy? I've already had three investigators who have had nervous breakdowns on your case.'"

In 1972 Pezim declared personal bankruptcy. He was 50 years old.

"The day I declared bankruptcy I found a bunch of bottles, cashed them in for a nickel apiece, went to McDonald's with Marilyn. Had a meal. It was one of the greatest meals I ever had. I had no worries then. Nobody could bother me for money. They can't ask you for anything. You're all washed up. I didn't have a pretzel."

In 1973 Murray Pezim was released from bankruptcy. The release from the marriage with Bernice marked the end of his Toronto ties. Now he was wholly a Vancouver creation, and very soon he was going to let the entire world know how great a phenomenon he was.

Marilyn Murray and Murray Pezim were quietly married after the Ali-Chuvalo fight. While Bernice says she is the only wife to have married Murray for Murray, others say that she was proud to be

Mrs. Murray Pezim only when he was in the money. They say that when Murray was down, Bernice turned hard. Pezim says it is Marilyn who hung in during the toughest times. Certainly, the financial straits after the Ali-Chuvalo fight bear that out.

But the fact is, marriage two turned out to be strangely reminiscent of marriage one. Years after the relationship between Murray and Marilyn had fizzled, on that hot March day in 1990, Marilyn Murray, black and white from head to toe, told me that in the difficult days when the market wasn't moving right, Pezim would bed down with cowboy and Indian movies and become uncommunicative. At other times, when he had good news to tell, he told it to Gus McPhail or Art Clemiss. "I gotta tell them this," Pezim would say in passing, eager to gab on the telephone with his buddies, not his wife.

"You could be lonely in your own place," Marilyn said.

For Bernice Pezim, there was a time in the early seventies after the divorce when she was strapped for cash. Pezim gave her generous support, but there wasn't always money to send. Bernice had educations to pay for. Cheryl was in university. Michael would soon be there, too. If she needed cash quickly, there was a cousin of Pezim's who would relieve her of her jewellery. She remembers a diamond set − earrings, brooch, bracelet − which she believed to be worth $20,000 and for which she received $5,000.

If she was less pressed for time she would take some of her pretty pieces to Birks to be sold there. She sold her wedding ring. Today Bernice receives about $12,000 a month from Pezim, of a $15,000-a-month agreement. (Revenue Canada is supposed to get the difference.) Marilyn divorced Pezim after eleven years of marriage for a $1-million settlement. There would then be the mega-settlement to his third wife Susan and the maintenance of Tammy Patrick.

Sitting in her uptown Toronto condominium, bought for

her by Murray, Bernice reflects on life with Pezim, on what makes Murray Murray, on why he seems to keep beating himself about the head even when he's not depressed.

"When you and I make a mistake," she says, "we let the path govern us and we say 'I made that mistake. I mustn't do that again.' Murray has the facility to draw down a blind and close out the badness, and he doesn't have the bad things to work with any more."

Seemingly from nowhere, she mentions the autobiography of J. Paul Getty. "He said that although he felt he was a great financial success he felt his life was a failure. He never had a love relationship with a wife and none of his children love him."

Do you think, I ask, that Pezim feels that way?

"I think he thinks everybody loves him."

CHAPTER 8

Beat the House

P eter MacLachlan Brown was first drawn to the sagging mess that was Murray Pezim in 1968. As Brown tells it, when Pezim scurried and scuttled this way and that across the floor of the Vancouver Stock Exchange, hoping beyond hope to beat the house on Bata Resources, the performance was as much for Brown's benefit as it was to try to save his own skin. Pezim, says Brown, was out to prove how adept he was at playing Stop. Playing Stop was never Pezim's métier.

Brown had returned to Vancouver that year from Montreal, where he had worked as a bond salesman for Greenshields, in the days long before Greenshields merged with Richardson Securities and formed the brokerage house we know today. Brown was a private-school product, a snot-nosed kid in Pezim's vocabulary. Vancouver-raised, he had been educated at St. George's before an unsuccessful stint at the University of British Columbia. Brown was the type of Peck's Bad Boy who wouldn't hit his stride until he unearthed what excited him. For Brown – bewitchingly smart, wily, and an unpleasant adversary – it was money and it was stock.

At the time of the Bata spectacle, Brown was just twenty-six. Pezim was more than twenty years his senior. The contrast between the uneducated Jewish kid whose family had pulled itself up out of nowhere and the establishment progeny who, by all appearances, never had to scratch for a living, was pronounced. Yet, from the time of Bata, on through the seventies, and even today, the two men have found themselves repeatedly aligned.

Pezim and Brown each found in the other something of value. The collegiate-looking Brown would watch the way Pez would riffle through his trading stats, his cigarette resting loosely between his index and middle fingers, periodically moistening the tip of his middle digit to move the paper along, all the while running the numbers through his brain for a final computation. Pezim was brilliant with numbers. He was also more often than not the most capable person around at promoting stocks. There was a third feature. Brown saw Pezim as a deal junkie who couldn't care less about money.

Brown, on the other hand, cares a great deal about monetary rewards. When Pezim resurfaced from bankruptcy in 1973, Brown had fifteen percent of Canarim Investment, the successor firm to H.H. Hemsworth. Harold Hemsworth himself had thirty-one percent, and Ted Turton, who had bought out Pezim's position in the firm in 1967, had fifty-four percent. The chief function of a firm such as Canarim was and is to underwrite initial public share offerings, to underwrite subsequent issues, and to sell stock. For a guy like Brown to get rich on an exchange such as Vancouver's, he needs to manage the kind of share offerings the VSE loves – that is to say, small stuff, primarily small resources stuff.

But the same market slump that had swept away $6 million of Pezim's paper wealth two years previously was still hurting VSE-oriented firms such as Canarim. The exchange had had a spectacular run from the late sixties until the oil-and-gas boom went bust in the early seventies, taking Pezim with it. A lot of people around Vancouver in those days would have bet that the man who had come to be known as The Pez would never again become the reigning promoter on Howe Street. The odds were that Pezim would crawl into some two-bit hole, never to be seen or heard from again.

The market downturn fed into the recession that began in the latter part of 1974. It can be argued, in fact, that the exchange would have had a tough time staying solvent in the early seventies had it not been for the closed-door policies of the reputedly more respectable exchanges. The fact was, the mine-financing requirements on the Toronto, Montreal, and other North American exchanges were just too tough for the junior companies, a situation that perfectly suited the VSE.

The Toronto Stock Exchange was still intent on convincing investors that its intentions were to act in the public interest as a responsible self-regulatory body. The message was clearly meant to emphasize that the Toronto market was purely investment grade – established companies with a history of earnings. It wasn't true of all TSE companies, of course, but outwardly the exchange gave the impression that speculators, stock pushers, junior specialists, people like Pezim, were best left in the West. There would be talk, now and again, of creating a stand-alone junior-resource market or loosening the requirements for stock listings. But it would be years before the Toronto regulators would move in that direction. That suited the VSE just fine, too.

But there was, nevertheless, a change coming. Jack Van Luven, the VSE president who had met Pezim at Vancouver airport in 1968 to welcome him back to the rock 'n' roll exchange, had been dumped in 1971. Van Luven was seen as representative of the old guard, which had allowed loose regulation and disorganization to tarnish the reputation of the exchange. Now a new generation of aggressive, soon-to-be-powerful participants emerged. They wanted to build on Vancouver's reputation as Canada's pre-eminent resource exchange. They wanted to attract much more international money from Europe and the U.S. The most aggressive, the most successful, certainly the most resilient of these was Peter Brown.

Through the late sixties, the West Coast regulators had inched toward providing better protection for the province's estimated two hundred thousand small investors. In 1967 the province passed a new Securities Act, closely modelled on the Ontario version introduced in 1966. The act increased the requirements for financial disclosure and placed more stringent controls on stock promoters. To discourage improper insider-trading practices, insiders had to report stock transactions within ten days of the end of the month in which the trades took place.

Before the new act came into effect, the Securities Commission had a woefully inadequate staff of seven; it was big news when it expanded its roster of audit accountants from one to three. With the introduction of the more stringent regulations, Bill Irwin, then the Superintendent of Brokers and an alumnus of the Ontario Securities Commission, doubled the Commission's staff to fifteen – but this was at a time when the OSC itself had a stable of ninety. Irwin's offices were swamped with prospectuses for mining promotions eager to catch the bull market that would close out the decade. The SOB was caught between an increased demand for prospectus-processing and compliance with the more rigorous requirements of the new securities act.

In 1972, the B.C. Securities Commission attempted a further tightening on mining promotions by stipulating that each company must have one corporate director with a minimum of five years' practical experience in the mining industry. But the B.C. regulators would forever be caught in a Catch-22: the province's resource-based economy by its very nature necessitated the raising of high-risk junior venture capital. Too strict a regulatory market could shut out the junior exploration companies. In the seventies, the listings of junior resource companies at times made up ninety percent of all Vancouver listings. British Columbia couldn't afford to ignore the economic imperative of supporting speculative companies. By 1978, mining accounted for roughly five percent of the gross provincial product, making it the second-largest (after forestry) goods-producing industry. One provincial study showed that sixty-two percent of British Columbia's mineral discoveries were made by junior operators, not the blue-chip mining houses.

On the other hand, the public impression was that VSE investors were dupes, and that the markets were being run for the benefit of the underwriters, promoters, brokers, and insiders.

In the summer of 1974, Canarim Investment co-managed a share offering in a company called B.X. Development along with Gus McPhail's Continental Securities and the third big house in Vancouver, Carlisle, Douglas. B.X. had started out as a Pezim penny called Trojan Consolidated Mines. Its assets consisted of a smattering of mining and oil-and-gas claims, none of which at the time of the issue could boast commercial ore or recoverable oil and gas reserves. In fact, B.X. had ceased exploration work on some of the claims held.

The proceeds from the offering were to be used to explore the copper-silver potential on a property in Arizona on which the company had secured a ninety-nine-year lease. Pezim was president and director and listed his occupation as a financier employed by Zareba Investments, his private holding company. Art Clemiss was a director and listed his occupation as business executive. The company fulfilled the requirement of the B.C. Securities Commission by having a mining engineer join the board. An accountant named Bob Liverant appears as the firm's auditor.

B.X. had pledged shares in the successful Valley Copper Mines near Kamloops as security for repayment of a quarter-million-dollar loan to the Canadian Imperial Bank of Commerce and a $35,000 loan to the Royal Bank. In the summer of 1974, at the time of the underwriting, B.X. was in arrears on interest charges. The banks were putting the pressure on to seize the shares of Valley Copper.

Izzy Rotterman used to pop over to Vancouver from Toronto from time to time, sniffing around the Pezim properties. He likes to think of himself as a master paper-pusher, and he says it was because of his efforts to raise capital for B.X. that the company was able to pay its debt.

He recalls sitting in the Vancouver offices of Davidson Partners, the brokerage house. Pezim was sitting with his head in his hands, looking deflated, because B.X. was his big chance for a comeback and the banks were about to blow it for him.

"I took my jacket off. I bought 20,000 shares. I started to call a few people across Canada. In a few days, they had enough stock sales they were able to pay the bank. Murray says to Art, 'We're partners. The three of us.'"

B.X. Development had another stock promoter, a licensed registered representative named Ross McGroarty who in 1974 was a broker with A. E. Osler & Co. in Toronto. Over the course of a year, McGroarty sold B.X. stock to about a hundred clients, for a total investment of 700,000 shares, or one third of the company's share capital.

In late 1974 the VSE critics, the ones who believed that the exchange was an inside game rigged in favour of inside players, got the proof they were looking for. A report by the law-enforcement unit established by the still-green New Democratic Party government of Dave Barrett alleged that profits from a $500-million drug trade were being laundered through the exchange.

The report charged that criminals working through the exchange were manipulating between twenty and thirty percent of VSE stocks. Promoters and directors of such companies were intent on defrauding the public, said the investigators, not on creating viable businesses.

The Barrett government never released any substantiation to back up the report. The law-enforcers and stock-exchange officials complained about the lack of hard evidence to support the statistics. The public, of course, wanted to know which stocks, by name, were in that fraudulent twenty to thirty percentage group.

The report served as a retelling of an old story. The criminal promoters, it said, activated shell companies or arranged new company underwritings. The stock would then be distributed among insiders and friendly outsiders to lend the appearance of proper public distribution. The manipulators would work to give a misleading appearance of stock activity, buying and selling among themselves, the same wash-trading techniques that had spurred innumerable stocks on the Toronto exchange in the days before the Windfall scandal. With the stock moving upward on the basis of false trades predicated on false rumours, the manipulators would reel in the shares carefully placed in friendly hands, then sell the stock at a higher price to the public. The insiders would blow off all their stock and walk. The new investors would watch their investment, devoid of any market activity to keep the price buoyant, sink like a stone.

The burden of investor protection lay with the RCMP, local police, and the superintendent of brokers. The British Columbia regulators, at least in part because of this report, decided that they had to take greater initiative in cleaning up securities malpractice in the province. The provincial government approached the RCMP in 1975, and a new watchdog, the Market Manipulation Group, a section within the commercial-fraud division, was formed. The man in charge was Sergeant Rupert Bullock, who had been with the Horsemen for fifteen years, most recently with the commercial-crime division. He had eight people working under him.

One of the first actions of the securities SWAT team was to install a trading terminal to undertake surveillance of VSE trading. Bullock made no bones about the fact that a couple of high-profile investigations of high-style VSE players would be the logical way to shake down the shady side of the market. Like the regulators in the East, the westerners favored big-money targets.

Meanwhile, in Toronto, TSE vice-president William Somerville, the same man who had encouraged Pezim to confine his activities to Vancouver after Windfall when Pezim was working both towns for Jenkin Evans, had hired a former police inspector and newspaper investigative reporter named Kesley Merry as a TSE intelligence officer. Merry's mandate, he told the *Financial Times of Canada*, was to gather information on individuals who "have been or in our opinion are capable of breaking securities rules." The *Times* dubbed Merry the TSE's "super snooper."

In May 1975, B.X. Development purchased the Paul Lime plant in Douglas, Arizona, for $2.2 million (U.S.) from the trustee for its bankrupt parent, Home Stake Production Co., which had led its investors into spectacularly fraudulent tax shelters. B.X. had sold its piece of Valley Copper to Cominco, and used the proceeds to help pay the $1-million cash requirement that was part of the deal. B.X. was to pay the remaining $1.2 million on instalments of $50,000 a month, a cost it planned to meet from cash flow from the lime plant, which produced lime for pharmaceuticals, feed additives, waste-filtration products, and other chemicals for markets in Arizona and New Mexico. Under its previous owners, Paul Lime had been a money-loser.

Through the fall of that year Pezim promoted a series of

ten-cent resource companies in addition to B.X. Development. Working out of an office on West Georgia Street, he touted Charleston Resources, Cutlass Exploration, Gentry Oil & Gas, and a number of other small mining companies. He would gab and shout and cajole, mostly over the phone, telling investors either to get in or to get out.

"What's taking you so long? The time to buy is now!"

"Come on, you putz. Leave the place."

Ba-ba-ba-ba-ba-ba-ba. The hands motioning. The cigarette trailing smoke. The food shovelling in.

Pezim granted options to friends and touted stocks to favoured brokers and allies. This has always been his practice. And over time, it has made him many enemies – that legion of stooges who never benefited from his companies or who claimed that he promised them options or other favours and then reneged.

In 1975, one of these stooges turned stoolie. He made contact with the RCMP and claimed that Pezim was unquestionably a stock manipulator, a cheat, and that the market-manipulation people would do well to scrutinize his current promotions.

This was all Bullock's squad was waiting for. Corporal Darryl McConnell was put in charge of the investigation. In October, he took the radical step of wire-tapping Pezim's telephone lines at home and work and planting bugs in his office. Over the course of three-and-a-half months, the RCMP taped five thousand phone calls from Pezim's phones; four thousand of them were market-related.

On January 28, 1976, at 9:30 a.m., the RCMP, Vancouver city police, and officials of the Superintendent of Brokers Office raided Pezim's office on West Georgia, seizing documentation on B.X. Development, Geo-Dyne Resources, Charleston Resources, Manox Petroleum, United Fortune Channel Mines, and Cutlass Exploration. The search party also seized documentation on

Pezim's investment company, Zareba Investments, as well as on Licon Management, the private investment company of his friend and partner Art Clemiss, who had control of Charleston. The focus of the investigation was on alleged manipulation of B.X. shares. The squad swept hundreds of files from Pezim's office.

The RCMP conducted simultaneous raids on the offices of other brokerages in Vancouver, Toronto, and Winnipeg, seizing the trading records of investors known or presumed to be trading in the stocks in question. Astonishingly, the raids were not conducted in conjunction with the VSE, and trading in the stocks in question was not halted.

As word of the raids made its way around Howe Street, the still free-trading shares went into free fall. B.X., the most substantial stock of the lot, fell $1 to $1.25. The rest, the pennies, fell by pennies. In total, six hundred thousand shares were sold. The market value loss in B.X. was $2.2 million. Overall, the loss for the companies named in the probe amounted to close to $3 million.

That same day, Pezim talked to a reporter with the Vancouver *Province* about his frustration. The RCMP had conducted a raid, he complained, but had not laid any charges.

"I don't know how to defeat them," he said plaintively. "I'd almost have to swear they short my stocks." Pezim went on. "They came with a search warrant and served my office, my apartment, and several brokers. Yet there were no charges. I don't control markets. My stocks are the freest in the market. They trade in volume so people can always find a buyer when they want to sell or find a seller when they want to buy. You should have heard the phone calls from shareholders today. It was pathetic."

In the *Vancouver Sun* he said, "We don't wash stocks and we don't fabricate markets. I'm a big boy. I can take it."

The press coverage also made the point that Pezim and his

companies were responsible for up to twenty-five percent of the VSE's trading volume on any given day. It could well be, said the *Sun*, that the very future of the exchange could depend on "how Pezim makes out and what is revealed in this legal drama of his."

The market-manipulation guys mulled. They sifted. They screened. There were hundreds of files, mountains of documentation. In pre-trial testimony, investigators explained that they even went so far as to turn their spying eyes to a Toronto hotel room where Murray and Marilyn Pezim stayed. What, wondered the courts, did the Mounties do when Mrs. Pezim started to undress? They looked the other way, they said.

As Pezim waited, the VSE slumbered. He grew depressed. By the summer, he had wound down his collection of penny stocks, dispensing control to friends and associates. He handed most of them to Barry Mann, a close friend who also happened to be on the board of B.X. Development.

Was Pezim merely creating an illusion of distance between himself and his companies? Certainly the regulators weren't forcing him to divest. Was Pezim feeling persecuted? Undoubtedly. With no companies to promote, with no riches to sustain him, Pezim packed his wife and his bags and moved to Arizona. It was late June, 1976. No-one goes willingly to Arizona in the summer.

The city of Douglas, Arizona, sits smack on the Mexican border, just south of Chiricahua Park, three hundred kilometres southeast of Phoenix in Cochese County. The city had started primarily as a copper town, but also had gypsum mines and limestone quarries.

The acquisition of the Paul Lime plant in 1975 had brought with it a hacienda-style house just north of Douglas. Pezim had no intention of becoming an operations man, a hands-on manager in a limestone plant. The fact was, he was borderline broke and the Douglas situation offered a mortgage-free setup.

It was hot, which was good, but it was dull. No social life. No friends. Douglas had just one restaurant. Marilyn wasn't much of a cook. Most evenings, Murray threw something on the barbecue. They longed for visitors. The plant was within walking distance, so close, in fact, that wiping the hacienda free of the fine white dust that settled there daily could have provided someone with a full-time job. A few ducks skittered about a small pond. The ducks and the pond were meant to evoke a pastoral aesthetic, but the mise-en-scène was disturbed by the nearby graveyard, where some of the mine workers, many of them Mexican immigrants who had travelled north from Aqua Prieta, Cananea, and other points south, ended their journey.

Though it was devoid of social amenities, Pezim came to love Arizona – for the heat, the sun, the casual lifestyle. He regretted only that there were no direct flights between Vancouver and Phoenix. In Arizona he found peace. He camped out. He waited.

Meanwhile, in Toronto, the regulators had quickly suspended Ross McGroarty's broker's licence after the raids. Pezim had a bad reputation in the East. The eastern brokerage establishment couldn't figure that any Pezim stock was intended to be anything other than a Pezim scam. If a Pezim stock did prove to be viable it was deemed a fluke. So McGroarty hadn't done himself any favours by being such an active participant in B.X. Development stock. McGroarty says that Kesley Merry, the TSE's super snooper, interviewed him half a dozen times. Merry believed that something smelled. McGroarty had pushed an enormous volume of B.X. shares on his clients.

"Ross," said Merry to McGroarty, "you've been in the business for a long period of time. You've got a clean record. Now's your chance to change your story."

An Ontario Securities Commission hearing into McGroarty's

conduct alleged he used false documents to place stock in various accounts, that he used high-pressure selling techniques, and made recommendations based on spurious research. In fact, McGroarty had placed orders without client approval. Harry Bray, then the vice-chairman of the Ontario Securities Commission, wrote in the commission's assessment that McGroarty "is not a fit and proper person to hold registration as a securities salesman."

Nonetheless, McGroarty's ten clean years in the business worked in his favour. Seven months after his suspension he was allowed to reregister as a broker. Fifteen years after the event, McGroarty's eyes grow moist when he talks about his persecution.

"I hadn't done anything wrong," McGroarty says today. "Well, certainly not of the severity to play with my life for seven months."

Pezim, ensconced in his Arizona hideaway, fought back through the press. No-one remembered the good he had done, he would wail to the Vancouver media. The Strachan gas discovery, its 14,000-foot test. Denison Mines. What were the Vancouver regulators trying to do? Turn the VSE into another Toronto exchange, another Montreal exchange?

"I'll put my heart and soul into B.X.," he told the *Vancouver Sun*. "But they're going to be hearing from me in Vancouver. I'll be back. But it'll be different things. I've got to come back with a clean cloud over my head. I'm not a kid with a halo, but I've done some good things."

If Pezim was staying out of Vancouver, he wasn't staying entirely clear of promoting B.X. In September, 1976, he travelled to New York where he met a promoter named Martin Orenzoff at the offices of a broker-dealer. Orenzoff subsequently sued Pezim for nonreceipt of stock options, options that Orenzoff said he was promised in exchange for promoting B.X. The suit went nowhere, but the case serves as an example of how

Pezim dealt himself into and out of friendships and contacts.

Charges were finally laid against Murray Pezim, Art Clemiss, Izzy Rotterman, and Larry Page, a lawyer who had become a B.X. director, in January, 1977. The allegations pertained only to B.X. Development.

Pezim et al. were charged with conspiracy to defraud the company of 350,000 shares, conspiracy to defraud the shareholders of the same 350,000 shares, and conspiracy to commit theft of the shares. Robert Liverant, the accountant, and Pezim, Clemiss, and Rotterman were charged with conspiracy to defraud the company of $50,000. The $50,000 was allegedly fraudulently paid by B.X. to Shillingford Investments, a private company whose principals were Pezim, Clemiss, and Rotterman.

The 350,000 shares were received by Pezim through his Zareba Investments, by Clemiss through his private investment company Licon, and by Rotterman personally. The shares had, in fact, been B.X. treasury shares, issued as part of a 500,000-share block to a party involved in the sale of the Paul Lime plant to B.X. According to the defendants, the shares came back to them in exchange for promotional work that would enhance the value of the 150,000 shares left with the seller.

As previous cases had proved, and as subsequent cases to this day would prove, it's well-nigh impossible to make market-manipulation charges stick in court. Judges don't understand markets. Juries don't understand markets. It's not, says Bullock, like laying out a smash-and-grab theft case. By laying fraud instead of market-manipulation charges, the Bullock team thought they had a good chance of success.

"I would venture to say in any of these operations you don't know how far the connections go," says Bullock, "Money shifts back and forth between the groups."

Pezim wasn't the only supposed VSE miscreant that Bullock and his team had in their sights. They also went after Joey Romano and Gino Cicci, the same duo who had cropped up during Pezim's involvement with Stampede Oils in the Dick Lennie days. Romano and Cicci were nabbed over the fraudulent promotion and manipulation of Seneca Developments, the Quebec uranium play. Both were convicted.

In the summer of 1977 lawyers for the defendants worked to quash the charges against Pezim and his cronies. Then they tried to have the wiretap evidence ruled inadmissible, an application that was turned down. In the pretrial days, the RCMP's McConnell, who held a degree in accounting, came under scrutiny for his misunderstanding of financial reports for the Paul Lime operation. McConnell was doubly cursed: not only had he muddled the figures, he couldn't document his allegation that Pezim had touted inflated earnings for the company. False representation was one of the allegations used to seek court authorization for the wiretaps. Without evidence of the stock touting, the Pezim lawyers argued, the wiretaps themselves were fraudulently obtained. McConnell, seen by the force as a diligent investigator, maintained in a pretrial hearing that the B.X. books were cooked. He said that conversations overheard in Pezim's offices reinforced his allegations.

Sentences like this one were read into the record:

"Mr. Pezim will fuck that lime plant into bankruptcy."

And this one:

"Isn't it wonderful when you get a Jew, an Irishman, and a mafioso together?"

(There were, in fact, two Jews – Rotterman and Pezim – and one Irishman – Clemiss – and if there were any mafiosi no-one proved it.)

On another occasion McConnell said he overheard a

conversation concerning $50,000 that had to be accounted for because they "didn't want to go to jail for $50,000."

In late June, 1977, the trial began before Provincial Court Judge Les Bewley. The Jews and the Irishman made an odd court mix. Clemiss, quiet, withdrawn, hating the limelight. Probably hating Rotterman, since the cheesy promoter wasn't Clemiss's style.

Rotterman's spectacularly crass sense of humour wasn't to Clemiss's liking. Not even Pezim could be happy about watching Rotterman make the motions of masturbation in the witness box in order to rile Crown counsel. Rotterman was given to telling everyone on the opposition benches to go fuck themselves. His co-defendants quickly figured out that Rotterman wasn't doing them any favours. No doubt, he told them to fuck themselves, too. (Today, Rotterman is a fat little grey-haired guy who drives a bright red Miata and doesn't look as if he'd be really big on table manners. He is the father of a daughter who loves him. He is the husband of an invalid wife whom he visits daily in hospital.)

The trial was excruciatingly long, with several adjournments. Pezim stayed put in Arizona when he could. He moaned about the press coverage, about being smeared on a daily basis. If Ross McGroarty thought his seven-month-long scrutiny was an endless purgatory, Pezim's fight over B.X. Development, which lasted for very close to four years, should have been an unrelieved hell.

Not so. Insider-trading reports for the period show that Pezim was merrily buying and selling B.X. shares. Over the course of two months in the spring of 1977, Pezim and Clemiss made a quarter-million-dollar paper profit on share sales. They went mad for press releases, hiring McGroarty to handle PR for the firm out of Toronto and Los Angeles. McGroarty called his public-relations firm the Wall Street Financial Corp. So wonderfully establishment and big-time.

In November 1979, Pezim, Rotterman, Clemiss, Page, and

Liverant were exonerated. By that time, Rupert Bullock had left the RCMP and become, ironically, the province's superintendent of brokers. Bullock says that when the SOB appointment was announced, Pezim telephoned to congratulate him. The two men, not surprisingly, went on to have numerous dealings over the years, battling over Pezim's escrowed shares in one company or his stream of directorships in others.

After the trial, Pezim and Clemiss shut Rotterman out of their partnership. Thereafter, Rotterman came in on deals only when it suited Pezim's purposes. Pezim would tell another court at another time over another case that Rotterman was a terrible nag.

Pezim chose instead a strong alliance with Art Clemiss, who bought a house in Arizona and who for ever after has remained within trading distance of all Pezim deals. He has become, according to a former member of the Pezim entourage, a millionaire fifty times over. Taxes paid.

Invigorated after being cleared of wrongdoing in the B.X. case, Pezim set about reinserting himself into the Vancouver market. Just one month after the judgement, the Vancouver Stock Exchange published its year-end *Review*, including a two-and-a-half page glossy treatment of B.X. Development. Likely a result of the promotional machine of Ross McGroarty, the article, extolling the virtues of this squeaky-clean enterprise, refers to one Murray Pezim, chairman of the board, who has used his "financial expertise to the benefit of the company."

The piece also touted the success of the Paul Lime acquisition in Arizona. "It was Mr. Pezim's negotiation of the financing as coordinated with stock prices and equity financing which made the acquisition and subsequent expansion possible. He has committed to extend his efforts on behalf of the company to further lime production increases and expanded oil and gas industry projects."

If Pezim had any such intention to proclaim any sort of

181

commitment, it would have been because for a brief moment he paused to study where to turn next. In December 1979, B.X. hit a monthly high of $7.20, down from the year's high of $9.10. But Pezim was desperate to get out. The taint of the fraud charges hung over B.X. like a bad smell.

The following year, the stock hit $24.50 on the strength of a takeover by Brent Petroleum, a Calgary-based oil and gas explorer run by a man named Walter Ruck. Brent hit the news when a Merrill Lynch broker in Calgary was charged with fraudulently running up the stock while piling away huge blocks of stock. He went to jail.

As B.X. was transmuted into Brent, Pezim went from an active to a passive investor. Eventually, he wound himself down and out of Brent altogether. It was time for him to find the next big chance, the next Pezim incarnation.

In 1977, long before the court exoneration, Murray and Marilyn had moved out of the lime-dust-encased hacienda in Douglas to an L-model home on Valley Vista Drive in Scottsdale, Arizona. The houses in the area are unassuming, uninspired, and somewhat cramped: two steps out the kitchen door and it's into the pool. This is what is known as an adult community. The residents don't raise children; they raise cacti.

Right next door to where Murray and Marilyn once lived is the home of a tall, grey-haired man named Elliott Roosevelt, the son of Franklin Delano Roosevelt. Just up the street, Murray's brother Norman and his wife Helen — a hobbyist painter — live out their retirement. They moved there at Murray's urging in 1979. Murray probably told himself that he was helping his older brother by hiring him on as a secretary and assistant, but it's likely that Murray wanted to have Norman around as a support — though he would never admit it.

Today Norman Pezim is shrunken and a terrible driver. Someone should really take that brown Cadillac Brougham d'Elégance – the one that says "Norman Pezim" on the glove compartment – away from him. Other Scottsdale drivers shake their heads as they try to out-manoeuvre his curb-to-curb, slow and smooth driving style. Norman's a nice guy. He'd love to meet Elliott Roosevelt, but just as he approaches the Roosevelt house, the tall grey man moves quickly indoors.

Norman spends much of his time sitting at his brother's Arizona offices, packaging corporate documents, sending them hither and yon by Federal Express. Norman is the strongest link that Murray has to the past, the Toronto days in the 1920s. Norman, once a dashing military officer, now seems more like a doddering aunt. When Murray Pezim looks at Norman Pezim he worries that he too will soon go dithery. He is hoping that the company of many young women will forestall the inevitable.

By the time Norman and Helen arrived in Scottsdale, Murray's second marriage was already foundering. He saw other women. When Murray's children visited from Toronto, their father would cook the roast; their stepmother would lay out the napkins.

Murray has little to say about his time with Marilyn, about the time spent with any of his women. "Marilyn came from a very poor family, you know, her father was a minister," says Pezim. "She was a real disappointment, you know. Turned into a very cold person. . . . I wouldn't share business with Marilyn. She wouldn't understand it. . . . Business is my first love, no question."

And women in general? "Um, hmm. Someone to sleep with."

Did you want to marry Marilyn? "I guess so. I don't recall."

Isn't it a big decision? "Not to me."

As 1979 wore on, Pezim moved back to Vancouver, back to the apartment on Beach Avenue, at least for the summer drilling season. Marilyn spent most of her time in Arizona.

Once he was reinstated in his role of Godfather of the VSE, Pezim's renewed personal mission was to reinforce the understanding that he was the biggest, the best, the ballsiest promoter in town. There were a number of ways to accomplish this. The first was the woman thing – always have a blonde around, always impress the competition and any onlookers. Always have a cause, a way to get your name in the news even when the market is dry. Charitable events are good, and Pezim became a prime mark for these.

Pezim loves a celebrity roast. He threw a big bash round about 1979 for the seventy-seventh birthday of Judge Angelo Branca. Branca's familiarity with the VSE and mining promoters went back to the thirties, when he defended a mine superintendent on charges of stock fraud and of "salting" mineral assays. Salting assay results is merely an attempt to top up the mineral content of ore samples, making worthless ore look gold-rich. Branca got his client off on the salting charge but couldn't do anything about the eighteen-month sentence for stock fraud.

In 1979, the judge appeared on the CBC television series *Connections*, an exposé of organized crime in Canada. Branca later told his biographer that he thought he was being interviewed for a piece on ethics and the judiciary, which he was, in a way. He was displeased to see the *Connections* people make reference to his social connection with Joe Romano, the same Romano the Bullock squad nailed in the Seneca fraud case.

"Joe Romano co-exists easily with the respected levels of B.C. society," said the program. "The friends and business associates are from a wide spectrum of legitimate occupations."

Pezim brought his comedic connections to the Branca roast. What would the likes of Red Buttons, Joey Bishop, or Jan Murray do without such invitations? The Branca roast raised $100,000 for a children's camp.

Around the same time, Joe Cohen, the Vancouver-based brother of the Winnipeg-based Cohens, the guys who have the rights to market Sony products in Canada, had cancer of the bladder. So Pezim threw a four-day party in Cohen's honour and raised $1 million for the Vancouver General Hospital. Bob Hope was there. It was a big bash, a Pezim success. Not like the Ali-Chuvalo disappointment. Cohen first met Pezim in the offices of Gus McPhail. Cohen was walking around Howe Street looking for donations for one cause or another. Pezim says Cohen raises money for every charity in the bloody world. Pezim does too. Cohen today seems remarkably well. He says Pezim is the easiest mark for a worthwhile cause.

A mark is only worth spotting when he's in the money. In the late seventies, gold became the new pursuit in the stock market.

In 1971, gold had at last been freed from any monetary backing. Governments, including the Canadian government, decided that individual investors could be bullion buyers. Over the decade, enthusiasm for holding gold as a hedge against bad politics, bad economics, bad stocks, increased. The gold bugs became gold-hoarders.

By the late seventies, gold had built up a head of steam. It went from $175 an ounce in 1976 to more than $700 by the decade's end, a 1,400 percent increase since gold was freed up in 1971. By January 1980, when the price met $850 (U.S.), it seemed as if the world had gone kablooey.

One theory held that the Middle East was converting inflation-losing dollars into gold, thus shortening supply and heightening demand. Certainly, inflation seemed to have caused the start of the runup; investors sought gold as a hedge against devaluing currencies. But no-one could have predicted the attempted coup in Saudi Arabia – or did they? – and the temporary departure of

185

King Khalid for Switzerland. The Saudi reserves fell "unexplainedly," according to one press report, by $7.5 billion. I'll take a crack at explaining it: I bet Khalid and his entourage took it with them.

The reaction to the gold shortage and increased demand was predictable. Pawnbrokers told stories of customers bringing in gold crowns. There were line-ups at Deak's, the money changers, of people wanting to swap old gold for cash. Eager buyers, meanwhile, snapped up Napoleons, Krugerrands, any gold coins.

But with precious metals, as with stocks, the herd charges in at the right time psychologically, which is absolutely the wrong time for making money. Gold turned down, falling $135 in a single day in February.

The fall in the gold price didn't matter to Pezim and others like him. The break in the price in 1980 started a whole new ball game for gold-mining companies. Even at $500 an ounce, the prospects were awfully appealing. Even at $400 an ounce. Some of the gold in this country is mined for cash costs as low as $175 an ounce.

The 1980s saw the emergence of a new breed of gold-miner. No longer were they geological experts. They were financiers, hedging experts who would sell their gold forward in order to peg future sales at prices set in the present. These forward sales, while criticized by those who believed the gold game was built on high risk and high reward, allowed the new executives to introduce conservative strategies that appealed to a more prudent investor who liked the idea of a security blanket to protect against falling prices. These same executives championed gold loans – that is, borrowing gold that is immediately converted to cash, which in turn is put into mine development and repaid, at a minuscule rate of interest, from future gold production.

This new gold industry was light years from the base-metals

industry that had formed the bedrock of Ontario's economy. It was a time of unprecedented exploration, spurred by healthy tax incentives. Large financial institutions, pension funds, and mutual funds all took a new look at gold equities – solid stocks, with proved track records, of course.

But as has always been the case, the real fun was in the junior players, the small companies with a few mining claims. The same kind of companies that had made investors speculate wildly through the days of Denison and Texasgulf and had made some people very rich.

With this new optimism for gold there came an undistinguished mining company that more than any other became the junior-gold success story of the decade. The company was International Corona Resources. The story it took to investors involved a long-ignored spread of Precambrian rock called Hemlo in northern Ontario. Throughout the eighties, this company found itself mired in a prolonged court battle over the most valuable prize in Canadian litigation history.

The man behind the story was that itchy kid named Murray Pezim, who once was good at algorithms and shelling meat and very little else. The fight would ultimately take the promoter back to Toronto. Pezim was now sixty, but he was still careering around the stock market like a punch-drunk fighter. True to form, he once again managed to pull himself to his feet when everyone thought he was down for good.

CHAPTER 9

Hemlo

I n Murray Pezim's Paradise Valley refrigerator – one of those mammoth, double-sided, graze-through numbers – there are oval milk chocolates, perhaps two inches long and an inch wide. Each is wrapped in gold foil that clings snugly to the chocolate landscape of Pezim's face. It is not a bad likeness, really, considering the difficulties there must be in creating a mini-mould of someone's puss. Pezim has the confectionery custom-made in Vancouver. It is a tinsel conceit. He likes the way he looks in gold.

There are other gold-pitch trinkets dotted throughout the world of Murray Pezim: T-shirts and coffee mugs with "PezGold" and "Nose for Gold" stencilled on them, tins of top-quality British Columbia salmon with labels bearing a sketch of Pezim and the words, "The Pez Nose Gold," and other clever slogans.

Pezim is obsessed with gold. It is, in fact, the single pursuit that has worked for him. He is smart enough to know the value of capitalizing on one's strongest asset. Gold, for Pezim, has good marketing value. Gold, for Pezim, started with Hemlo. In fact, if one were to search for the reason The Pez is the phenomenon that he is, how The Pez has been able to manufacture himself into a living legend, one would look no further than Hemlo.

Something must first be said. I've never entirely believed the Hemlo tale, start to finish. It's rather like those cheesy headlines that rage across the tabloids at supermarket checkout counters. We know that Elvis is really and truly dead and therefore don't believe the various Elvis sightings in Gdansk, or wherever, and the matter of the baby-stealing aliens goes a bit far, but some of that other stuff has the slight scent of the credible. The Kennedy assassination, for example. The tabs tell us that the official explanation of who killed Kennedy just doesn't stand up to their kind of scrutiny. Or the death of Marilyn Monroe. The tabs chose murder over suicide. Hemlo's like that. An itchy story that gets under the skin and rubs the wrong way. Something's not right here. Something's not right here. If only the *National Enquirer* would take the time to tell us the truth.

Hemlo is a gold-mining yarn, a magical story about an uninspiring tract of land that cuts under the Trans-Canada Highway on the north shore of Lake Superior, thirty-five kilometres east of Marathon, 450 kilometres along the rail line east of Thunder Bay.

How this motherlode of gold was staked, sold, and mined has been packaged into a narrative that boldly paints heroes and villains, princes and paupers, a semi-establishment Goliath and a very tenacious David. Discovering the truth behind the mythology has been made all the more difficult by the fact that the Supreme Court of Canada has closed the book on the country's most prolonged piece of litigation.

David and Goliath fought an eight-year brawl over the richest of the Hemlo mines. The Williams Mine at the outset had nine million ounces of gold. There's still six and a half million ounces left, which, at the 1991 price of about $400 an ounce, makes the treasure worth $2.6 billion. Hopes are that the mine's wealth will extend beyond that. By August 1989, when the Supreme Court handed the mine over to a once-scrappy gold-miner called Corona, the David in the fable, the story of Hemlo had become sanitized, codified within Canadian mining history and, for my money, a tall tale.

The story began in December, 1979, near a former railway station called Hemlo. No one called the area Hemlo then. Most referred to it as Manitouwadge.

Winter in the northern Ontario bush is uncompromising: The snow piles crotch-high, the temperature falls to forty degrees below zero, frigid enough to make the nose hairs crystallize. It is in weather such as this that prospectors do what comes naturally: they slap on snowshoes and spend hellishly long hours traversing wretched terrain in a self-flagellation exercise called claims-staking.

To this end, two prospectors entered the Manitouwadge bush at Christmastime, 1979. One was Don McKinnon, a small, bookish man of fifty with wire-framed glasses and a quiet demeanour, the type one might cast as a peevish, peaked accountant who slides to and from a day job with a sad lunch packed in a tattered satchel. The other was John Larche, fifty-two, a Johnny Canuck type, a big man with big hands and a reputation for being an extremely able staker, but who nevertheless seems slightly slow off the mark.

The Manitouwadge area had been staked and restaked, appraised and rejected through years of Canadian mining history. This is not at all uncommon. The mining business has been built on one man's realization of the riches overlooked by another. Geological reports can sit gathering dust for years, for decades, forever, ignored as mineral markets wax and wane. Claims can be drilled and abandoned, ore potential disregarded.

The accepted story is that McKinnon went staking with an old-time prospector named Eddie O'Neill. O'Neill fell ill and returned to his home base of Timmins. McKinnon continued, staking solo.

He eventually ran into Larche, who had been contracted to stake seventeen claims in the area for a small geological-consulting firm. McKinnon told Larche he had already staked twelve of the seventeen. Larche took his word for it. Unable to fulfil his staking contract, Larche moved on to stake adjacent territory, claims that McKinnon hadn't realized were available.

Given that each man now had something the other coveted, and given their mutual interest in the plentiful claims remaining in the same territory, the two extended mitts, shook hands, and agreed to split whatever proceeds came of their staking efforts. Together, they went on to stake thousands of Hemlo-area claims.

The objective of the prospector is, of course, to sell the claims he has staked. Which is just what McKinnon then set out to do in the spring of 1980, stumping his and Larche's offerings around Toronto's financial district, armed with maps and geological reports, hoping to arouse some interest from senior mining companies, local financiers, promoters, any old Joe. Judging from the yawning lack of interest the prospective buyers showed for McKinnon's claims, it looked for a while as if he and Larche might have wasted their time.

On a winter's afternoon in Timmins, a day just as frigid as those Christmastime prospecting days in 1979, I had a conversation with Eddie O'Neill, the grizzled old-time prospector who was out staking in the early Hemlo days. O'Neill is, more properly, Edward B. O'Neill. "The B is for bullshitter," he said, matter-of-factly. Eddie, during his long career, had taken up the habit of "salting" ore samples, topping up the rock with extra bits of gold or whatever mineral was in vogue, thus making the sample seem more appealing to potential buyers when Eddie went to sell the claims. This may account for the nickname. O'Neill later told me that the B. actually stood for Bonaventure. The Timmins crowd, when they talk about Eddie O'Neill, refer to him as Dirty Deal O'Neill.

Eddie O'Neill features in the Hemlo story. He has spent a lifetime prospecting, and he knew the rules of the game. So it was Eddie who explained to me just how the process works: "You start staking a claim by first pinpointing a focus point. You establish the Number One post at the northeast corner. You go from there approximately 1,320 feet south and establish a Number Two post. You go from the Number Two post, blazing lines as you go, to establish a Number Three post west of the Number Two post. You blaze a line north 1,320 feet approximately to the Number Four post, then back to the Number One post to make a complete square."

To each of the four posts, the prospector affixes a metal tag issued by the local licensing office, signing his name and writing the date on the Number One post.

As he moved through his claims-staking explanation, sitting in a warm and snug seafood restaurant in Timmins (owned, incidentally, by a couple of women reputed to have made a fortune gambling on mining stocks), Eddie O'Neill's lot didn't sound like such a bad one. But as we moved outside into the Arctic blast, and as his car ran out of gas, and as he had to borrow $20 to buy half a tankful so he could get home to the basement of his daughter's house where he lived, it was hard to see where the fun came in, where the glory could be found, and how there could ever be riches.

In truth, men and the few women who call themselves prospectors rarely become wealthy. But there is freedom and independence. And the dream. The prospector's dream is to claim ground that contains mineral wealth, sell off the claims for cash, company shares, and maybe even a net-smelter royalty (a return from the eventual mineral production of a mine).

There is a corollary to the hardships of prospecting. Given the appalling economics, the difficult physical circumstances, and the tendency to heavy booze consumption, what are the chances that this can be an ethical trade based solely on the value of a man's word? Slim, very slim.

I once read an unpublished account of two prospectors breaking into the cabin of another. The job of the outside man was called "Keeping Six"; the job of the inside man was to rifle the maps of the competition. If anyone approached, the outside man was to yell "Six" as a warning (which brings to mind Damon Runyon and the Oh May Gag and Murray Pezim's early years as a bit of a scoundrel). Prospectors who got wind of a consulting-firm's claims contract have been known to rush into staking in advance of the contracted stakers and back-date claims to make them their own. Or worse.

"One time I staked two hundred claims in Ungava [in northern Quebec] and I was never there," a prospector told a private eye I know. "I was a young punk in those days. We were sitting in the Bellevue Hotel and they gave me a hundred bucks to fill out the recording sheet."

Eddie O'Neill's version of what happened in the northern Ontario bush in December 1979 is too variable and muddled to be taken at face value. Indeed, every statement that issues from O'Neill needs to be carefully sifted for its tiny nuggets of truth. He once told me he thought the Ayatollah Khomeini, at the time still the ailing ruler of Iran, was really Howard Hughes. Much as I warmed to the thought, it was clear that such pronouncements did little to heighten Eddie's credibility.

He told me that he went staking in late 1979 all right, but not with McKinnon, as McKinnon later claimed. He said he was on his own and when he fell ill, he gave McKinnon some tags to register claims on his behalf at the mining-recorder's office in Timmins. However it happened, O'Neill's tags ended up on the initial twelve Hemlo claims staked by McKinnon that snowy December. The same claims would one day factor into the courtroom tribulations of Hemlo. For a brief moment, Eddie O'Neill thought that his small part in the gold rush might bring him that long-hoped-for payoff.

But Eddie O'Neill came away dirt-poor. "There's two breeds in the same business," he told me. "One is a prospector, who always gets screwed out of the business. The other's a contract staker; for two bits he'll sell out your grandmother."

In this instance, O'Neill's aphorism was wrong. Don McKinnon, prospector, became a multimillionaire.

While Don McKinnon was on Bay Street trying to flog the Hemlo claims, Murray Pezim was in Vancouver getting manicured. After the B.X. Development case, after his long persecution, Pezim had again risen to penny princedom through his raucous stock promotions. Brent Petroleum, which had taken over B.X. Development, had made him a rich man – on paper at least. Maybe $20 million worth of rich as Brent moved to $24.50 a share compared with B.X.'s high of $9 the previous year.

He was feeling flush, so flush, in fact, that he remarried Marilyn, even though the marriage was more or less dead. This ceremony was conducted with far more flash than those first nuptials back in 1972 when the bankrupt Pezim was licking his wounds after the Ali-Chuvalo match. For their second marriage, Murray and Marilyn appeared before two hundred people in the Hyatt Regency Hotel in Vancouver. Marilyn's father, the minister, officiated. The best man was Joe Cohen, the Vancouver businessman, brother of the Winnipeg Cohens, the men who built Gendis into a multimillion-dollar empire through the marketing of Sony products.

In 1980, the watchwords on the Vancouver Stock Exchange were oil and gas. The Alberta boom had fuelled the rise of hundreds of stocks. Pezim's contributions – Jet-Star Resources, Banner Resources, Rabbit Oil and Gas (named for Peter "The Rabbit" Brown), Berle Oil (after Milton Berle, cross-dressing comedian and Pezim friend), Youngman Oil and Gas (after Henny "Take my wife . . . please" Youngman), and a number of other creations – went along for the ride. At the centre of Pezim's group of companies was Pez Resources. The energy boom had boosted it out of the penny-stock classification: Pez Resources shares had moved from loose change to $7, to $8, to $9, and on.

Pezim followed his usual practice, distributing exploration claims among his various companies, then going to market with the standard disclaimer about the speculative nature of the shares. None of the claims could boast proved mineral reserves. The companies would, of course, buy pieces of one another, creating paper trails and trading euphoria that fluttered daily through the Vancouver Stock Exchange. Critics would raise the usual outcries about arm's-length transactions and the need for tighter securities regulation.

Pezim loved to shuffle around the stock-exchange trading floor. He would spew his enthusiasm for this stock, that gadget, perhaps tossing plastic Pez-embossed lighters, or samples of his Brushaway promotion (travel-sized toothbrushes with preapplied toothpaste). Pezim was the perfect pitchman. Drove the exchange officials mad. The media loved him and his indiscriminate exploits. When someone somewhere in the Pezim entourage discovered a wine called Château Pez, the man himself bought up every bottle. What could be more perfectly Pezzpromotional?

He was having fun, but he had zero credibility. The odour

196

of the B.X. Development investigation still followed him on his brokerage rounds, as did lingering suspicions of the part he had played in the perplexing Rolling Hills venture with Earl Glick. He had a faithful following, but his only success was the Strachan discovery a decade earlier, when the drilling for sulphur turned up a certifiable gas find.

Pezim was dubbed the Godfather of the Vancouver Stock Exchange. He took this as a compliment. In the east, meanwhile, particularly in Toronto, Pezim was a joke. No amount of charity work – and Pezim undertook a lot of it – was going to change that impression.

Despite his low credibility quotient, Pezim's offices were action central for anyone looking for junior-resource funding through the VSE – prospectors praying for payday and cashless promoters jockeyed with the two-bit comedians and the charity hopefuls for time with The Pez.

Don McKinnon knew of Pezim from the woolly Texasgulf days back in the early sixties. In the summer of 1980, McKinnon went to Steven Snelgrove, a broker in Midland Doherty's Timmins office, a hangout for the local junior-mine junkies. Snelgrove told him he had the financing connections to help McKinnon deal his Hemlo claims. Snelgrove contacted Doug Collingwood, a Vancouver promoter who had an office in the same building as Pezim. Collingwood, like just about everyone else in Vancouver, was more interested in oil-and-gas deals at the time, but took the geological reports to Pezim, who was also interested in oil and gas but, as everyone knew, would look at anything.

Nell Marie Dragovan, a one-time freelance writer, was another Vancouver promoter with an interest in oil. She had a company shell, an asset-empty concern called Corona Resources that had a VSE listing and had drilled a couple of dry oil wells.

197

One of the people in Dragovan's circuit looking for oil deals on her behalf was Les MacConnell, the same Les MacConnell who had watched Pezim flail through the manic-depressive phase after the Bata Resources disaster. MacConnell by this time was a successful broker working for Ted Turton and Peter Brown at Canarim Investment, the securities house.

As MacConnell recalls events, Snelgrove came to Vancouver and showed Pezim the Hemlo-area reports prepared by a geologist named Thomas Skimming. Pezim then contacted MacConnell, who had on another occasion introduced Pezim to Dragovan. She agreed, on Pezim's recommendation, to buy the Hemlo claims for her Corona Resources that summer of 1980.

"I thought it was going to be an oil deal in Texas," says MacConnell of Corona's initial intent under Dragovan. "Instead it was a gold property in Ontario."

"Leslie," said Pezim to MacConnell, "You're gonna love it."

In *Fleecing the Lamb*, a 1987 book examining the Vancouver Stock Exchange, Alison Griffiths and David Cruise say that it was Collingwood and Dragovan who brought Hemlo to Pezim's attention, but that he wasn't interested. "By the time they badgered him into getting involved, there were already sixty-five holes drilled with decent results."

"Bullshit," screams Pezim, sitting at his kitchen table in Arizona, drinking an orange soda and telling the Hemlo tale for the umpteenth time. "Out-and-out lie. Doug Collingwood? Where the hell does he stick his nose in it? I was the one who got the property. I got it from Steven Snelgrove. Arranged the whole thing. I needed to have a shell. Nell happened to have a shell. I said, 'Nell, put it in here and I'll get the financing.'"

MacConnell and Art Clemiss and the other members of the Pezim circle started buying Corona stock. But it was Dragovan who really started Corona rolling with a personal investment of

$40,000. In the summer of 1980, the Corona claims held no greater appeal to Pezim than any of the other sixty-odd penny companies he had on the go.

In January 1981, the drilling of Hemlo commenced under the guidance of a thirty-seven-year-old geologist named David Bell. Through the ensuing months, Pezim personally bought and sold Corona stock. But it was Dragovan who was running the company. And it was Dragovan who was overseeing Bell's drilling program.

Hemlo turned hot in May. David Bell hit a fabulous streak of gold in the seventy-sixth diamond-drill hole. The drill core showed ten-and-a-half feet of 0.209, which meant that if the rest of the ore body was as rich, the Corona property unquestionably had found itself a gold mine. "Point two" is high-grade gold, representing 0.2 ounces of gold for every ton of rock. Ore bodies can be economically mined at "Point one" and even less.

Pezim says today that Hole 76 wasn't that big a deal, that one hole does not a mine make. He points out that thirty or more drill holes beyond the discovery would have to be assessed before the company was certain it had an honest-to-goodness gold mine and not just an anomalous streak of ore. The assay certificate, confirming the mineralization results, was obtained on May 16. Two days later, Pezim's offices had a press release prepared. Ten days after that, the assay information was released to the public.

But Hole 76 had huge potential. Any geologist who has gazed at a piece of gold-host rock, turning it this way and that in the sun, staring at how the gold lustre doesn't dull or diminish regardless of the angle of observation, who knows the immutability of gold, its power, knows that that first proof of the viability of Hemlo was the biggest deal the Canadian gold-mining community had seen since a couple of prospectors stumbled onto the Golden Stairway in 1909. The Stairway, in the Porcupine Lake region near

Timmins, Ontario, still ranks as the country's largest gold-mining discovery. The Dome Mine alone, one of the prizes of the Porcupine, has produced fourteen million ounces of gold and is still producing today. In the thirties, during its heyday, it mined two million ounces over the course of the decade. All-in, the Porcupine mines have turned out more than fifty million ounces of gold.

Understandably, Pezim was chuffed. And surprised. Until Hole 76, he had stayed at a corporate remove from the company. Certainly, he had been trading Corona shares. In December 1980 he bought 40,000 shares. In January he sold them. Buy and sell. Buy and sell. Pezim moved paper often without rhyme or reason, taking losses here, winnings there. Before Hole 76, in early 1981, Corona was a ninety-five-cent stock.

By the end of April, Pezim had a modest 140,000 shares. But after Hole 76, Pezim quickly became a Corona director. He needed a bigger position in the company. It had three million shares sitting in escrow, tied up like the founders' shares that had so often made the Pezim-Glick mining deals of the fifties so lucrative. Escrowed shares are, essentially, shares held in trust by the corporation's treasury. Common in the mining business, particularly the penny-mining business, such shares are housed in the treasury until a company can prove to the securities authorities that it has carried out a satisfactory amount of exploration work on the property. Only then will the regulators allow such shares to be traded on an exchange. In this way, the regulators try to protect the investing public from scam practitioners who will pump up a stock, walk away with investor dollars, and never explore anything at all.

Corona's escrowed stock could be released only at the behest of the superintendent of brokers. The SOB at the time was Rupert Bullock, the same Rupert Bullock who had tried to run Pezim aground over B.X. Development. Pezim's proposal was to release the escrowed shares, which were tied to a couple of dry oil wells, the same wells that Dragovan had drilled before anyone had ever heard of Hemlo.

Pezim's application to revive the escrowed stock was turned down. The stock was cancelled. His proposal was rather like a bad bubblegum-card trade: one Eric Lindros rookie card for one John Kordic. The SOB ruled the fair market value of the shares exceeded the fair market value of the Hemlo claims. Pezim, still craving shares, needed an underwriting. He phoned the brokers. Gus McPhail at Continental Carlisle underwrote 600,000 shares. Pezim personally received 100,000 Corona shares for his part in taking McKinnon's claims into Corona. By August 1981, Pez Resources held 1.4 million Corona shares.

At the same time that David Bell was studying the first hopeful core results for Corona, subsequent to the press release on Hole 76, he had a meeting with Dennis Sheehan, chief geologist for a company then called Little Long Lac Gold Mines. There was nothing unusual in their meeting, nor in their discussions.

While the business of claims-staking can lean toward high espionage, mining companies immersed in the exploration stages of a property frequently feel each other out about the possibility of a joint venture in which they share the costs of future exploration and then the exorbitant cost of taking a mine into production. Ultimately, they will share the payoff. During the course of these meetings, Sheehan was made privy to much of David Bell's work. The two men studied the drill core drawn, examined maps, discussed how best to proceed.

Sheehan was a well-respected geologist on the Canadian mining scene. Little Long Lac was a company that in the early fifties had come to be controlled by a Toronto securities dealer named Jack Allen. At the time, Little Long Lac had in its possession the deteriorating Little Long Lac mine near Geraldton,

Ontario, and a smattering of gold-mining prospects. Jack Allen had subsequently amalgamated these companies, and had handed the corporation over to his son, Peter, in 1976, when he was thirty-five. Peter Allen was a smart engineer with a good education and a love of classical music. When he inherited his father's company, gold was $100 an ounce and the ore at the company's mines was fast depleting.

Fortunately for Peter, he also inherited Dennis Sheehan, the head of the company's exploration department and a man who had already established Little Long Lac's reputation for being a mine-finder rather than a mine-buyer. In the mid-seventies, Sheehan had discovered the company's key properties, the Bousquet and the Doyon. The mines, both in the Bousquet Township of western Quebec, near Val-d'Or, were brought into production in 1980.

It was Chris Pegg, Little Long Lac's exploration manager in Kirkland Lake, who told Sheehan that the Hemlo area warranted a close look. Corona was already there, and other claims staked by McKinnon and Larche would become what is known today as the Golden Giant mine, owned by Noranda, the mining giant. In fact, the Hemlo area's potential was not for two gold mines, but for three. While Little Long Lac was interested in forming a partnership with Corona on Corona's own property, it was the third property, a group of patented mining claims staked decades before by an American radiologist named Jack Williams, that both Lac and Corona wanted to buy for themselves. Williams had spent his summers in the thirties and the forties prospecting the northern Ontario bush. He died in the fifties, leaving the claims to his wife Lola.

Don McKinnon had tried to buy the Williams claims before the disovery of Hole 76 in May. It made sense to go after Claim Block E, the eleven Williams claims running north from Highway 17 to the power line, hugging the contours of Moose

Lake. It made sense because every other postage-stamp piece of Hemlo had been swarmed by prospectors trying to tag on the properties that Larche and McKinnon themselves had staked. Trouble was, McKinnon had a hard time locating Lola Williams. But finally, in June 1981, he did. At around the same time, Williams also received an offer from another gold-mining company: Little Long Lac Gold Mines.

That same month, Pezim, Bell, and Dragovan held what the securities industry calls a dog-and-pony show for Corona Resources at the Hyatt Regency Hotel in Vancouver. They followed the typical dog-and-pony ritual: they invited every mining analyst and every broker on the street, put together a nice information package on David Bell's exploration property, and tried to convince a skeptical audience that this time, unlike the five hundred times before, it was the real McCoy.

David Bell may be an excellent geologist, but he is not a motivational speaker. Nor was he known to the mining community. The dog-and-pony was mostly dog. The brokers didn't believe the fairy tale. Years later, a private investigator interviewed George Cross, the author of an investment newsletter who had written press releases and annual reports for Pezim, and therefore knew the story well. "There was nobody willing to listen," he said of the Corona promotion. "Jesus, every broker on the street sold their stock the next morning. The price of the stock dropped way down because everybody thought it was another Murray Pezim scam."

Corona stock, which the earlier Pez touting had pumped to nearly $8, fell almost a dollar. To make matters worse, the *Northern Miner*, the weekly bible for the mining industry, printed an editorial that said, in essence, that the Hemlo story was more fable than fact. Similarly, John Ing, a gold-mining analyst with Pitfield Mackay Ross in Toronto, issued a research report that suggested Hemlo and the Corona story was just another moose-pasture deal.

Who could blame the skeptics? Who could believe that there was a gold mine sitting right there along the Trans-Canada? With all the smart geologists stomping the territory, how could such mineral potential have been overlooked?

The summer of 1981 was as hot, steamy, and smelly as Toronto ever gets. Brokerages were besieged by promoters clutching rock samples. I spoke with an analyst who remembers that year well. He was new to the business, working for a small, independent brokerage that specialized in junior-mine financing. He recalls one stock promoter in particular who presented himself, rock in hand, and said simply of his Hemlo sample, "This is gold."

"No, it's not," said the analyst, a geologist. "What this is is pyrite."

Fool's gold. That's what Hemlo was to Bay Street, a fanciful story from the Disney studios. Anonymous fliers started arriving at securities firms claiming that Corona was nothing but air. The cynics said that the only reason Corona made it to Hole 76, long after most exploration projects are abandoned, was that Pezim needed a stock, any stock, to keep his various interconnected companies, each of which by now had pieces of Corona, pumping up, up, up.

In late July, the other side of the Hemlo story, the Williams side, turned bad for Pezim. The widow herself phoned Don McKinnon, saying she was turning down his offer of $100,000 cash, to be paid over three years, and a net smelter royalty of three percent. Lola Williams didn't know at that point that she was dealing with Corona. From her perspective she saw a man named McKinnon and a company called Hemglo Resources, which McKinnon had formed with Larche and two Toronto backers. McKinnon later said that although Hemglo was the corporate name he used when dealing with Williams, he had intended all along to sell the property in turn to Corona. Williams told McKinnon that day in July that she had decided to accept the offer from Little Long Lac Gold Mines.

Pezim was incensed. Corona decided to try to get the widow to change her mind, this time making the approach directly, without McKinnon as middleman. While Lac was prepared to offer more cash, its net smelter royalty offer was only half Corona's. Corona's efforts were wasted. In August, Lola Williams formally signed her eleven patches of land over to Little Long Lac.

Murray Pezim, sitting in his office in the Toronto Dominion tower in downtown Vancouver, got the bad news. Toronto had won, the big bad East had won, the Establishment had won. Days later, Dennis Sheehan ambled into Pezim's office, still interested in developing a working relationship with Corona on Corona's claims.

"First thing I want is that you give back what you stole from me," sputtered Pezim to Sheehan.

Furthermore, Pezim said he wanted Sheehan to accompany him to the Vancouver Stock Exchange to make a public announcement that he was giving the Williams property "back" – even though Pezim had never had it in the first place. Sheehan, not surprisingly, demurred. When Pezim describes the scene today, he says he lunged for Sheehan's throat, grabbed his tie, all the while swearing into the man's face. High drama.

Vancouver by this time had come to love Corona. The tireless public relations for the Hemlo area paid off, and the stock moved to $20 from $8 on the VSE during August 1981. One brokerage thought the stock so risky that it eliminated margin buying, that is, buying the stock on credit, with a percentage down and the balance of the stock price loaned through the brokerage itself. (If a stock is deemed to be high-risk, what a brokerage doesn't need is high-risk players in over-leveraged accounts unable to cover their margins if and when the price of the stock falls.)

Gold looked good, talked good, sold good. Gold became Pezim's shtick. There had been a bounce in the world price from

$530 to $850 (US) an ounce in January 1980. By the time of the excitement of David Bell's drilling program, gold was wandering between $550 and $650, still handsome prices. Handsome enough to make gold-producers outperform other mining companies in an economy that was moving into a recession.

There was a flurry of Hemlo activity much like the excitement generated by the Texasgulf find. The new generation of northern dealmakers were latter-day Earl Glicks and Murray Pezims. They called themselves broker-dealers, but they were in essence spruced-up boiler-room operations that cold-called unsuspecting investors and loaded and reloaded their customers into any old tag-on mining prospect, keeping sixty-five cents in commission for every dollar of mine-financing raised. They would continue to promote "Hemlo area" stocks for years to come.

The popularity of gold-stock stumping gave rise to what became known as gold shows, annual fêtes that featured evangelical gold bugs, corporate executives, and investment-newsletter authors, all gathered together to flog this or that gold stock, or simply bullion. Big-money investors – pension funds, investment counsellors – travelled to New York or New Orleans or San Francisco to listen to corporate spiels and tales of gold-mining opportunities.

Pezim liked to hold his own shows. He held a dog-and-pony for Ventora Resources in Las Vegas. Milton Berle was there. Ventora was ostensibly a Nevada gold play. In reality, it was a pile of dirt. "Short me a thousand Ventora," said one investor to his broker after the Pezim-Berle performance. To short is to borrow from a brokerage a stock at current prices. The investor sells at the market price and waits for the stock to fall. When it does – and to make short selling profitable the share price must fall – the investor buys the stock at the lower price, replaces the stock he has borrowed, and pockets the profits. To short was to bet against Pezim.

But shorting a Pezim stock wasn't as easy as being able to

establish that the fundamental value of the stock wasn't there. Pezim's detractors would bitch that he would position his players in a stock (forming what is known to some in the stock trade as the jerk circle) and keep the stock trading at enormous volumes that in turn would keep the stock price up. When Pezim's allies turned against him, that's when Pezim's stocks would crumble and Pezim himself would lose.

And Pezim was playing some tricks of his own. George Cross, when interviewed about Hemlo years later, said that Pezim was masterly. "Every time a new press release came out, Murray would be out yelling at everybody to buy the stuff. Then he would jam the stock through the market. They [the other investors] would find out it was him selling the stock and get pissed off."

Pezim has never denied his role as a "market-maker." He once explained his function to a courtroom this way: "The New York Exchange, they have specialists that specialize in buying and selling the stock in order to maintain an orderly market. But in Vancouver the brokers there are not market-makers. . . . My function would be one to make a market and maintain an orderly market. And what I mean by that, if there is a large block comes in to be bought, I might sell it, and if a large block comes in to be sold, I might buy it."

By September, Corona had completed more than fifty thousand feet of drilling. Two drills were working flat out, and the company had defined two "zones" or specified areas of minable ore. Pezim announced that the company would be splitting its shares, which were then above $20, on a four-for-one basis. Every existing Corona share would create another three. While the share price would also be split to reflect the paper change, the increase in the potential number of shares to the marketplace had Pezappeal – the greater the number of shares, the greater the number of potential investors.

Bringing down the share price would also serve to draw new buyers, Hemlo-watchers who thought they might like to invest in the Hemlo stock play but who would rather invest at $5 a crack than at $20.

The Hemlo furor coincided with changes at the Vancouver Stock Exchange. On October 23, 1981, the VSE floor traders left for the last time the paper-strewn floor of their Howe Street head-quarters and headed into martini heaven. It was a Friday and, as always, the VSE ceased trading at 1:30 in the afternoon, half an hour after the 4:00 p.m. close in Toronto. The following Monday, the same traders piled into the VSE's new and much more spacious grounds in a high-rise tower on Granville Street.

It was the end of the Howe Street era. It was a time of change in other ways. In 1979, $104 million worth of stock was underwritten on the exchange, and that was considered a very good year. A total of $600 million worth of shares changed hands. In 1980 total financings reached $220 million, and $4.4 billion worth of shares were traded. Vancouver had never seen business like this.

That same month, Murray Pezim called his lawyers. He wasn't going to let Little Long Lac get away with taking the Williams property. Before the month was out, Corona had launched a lawsuit seeking $100 million in damages for "stealing" the Williams property.

Before the year was out, Corona traded 8.5 million shares. Pez Resources traded an incredible twenty-one million shares on the year for a total share value of $61 million. Pezim was the hottest promoter in town. Pezim *was* the VSE.

Economists monitor the health of the nation through price indices, real-estate sales, unemployment numbers, interest rates, and other indicators. Journalists are more inclined to measure economic health by the relative availability of positive business stories. Stockies measure the health of the economy by the ebbs and flows of capital markets. In 1982, there was a lot of ebbing. Gold collapsed to a low of $297 an ounce in the summer of 1982. On the stock market, volumes remained strong, but share values were slashed by half. The economy headed for the crapper.

As the Vancouver market deflated, so too did Pezim's paper wealth. Throughout the summer, he and Art Clemiss had stacked a bunch of Hemlo-area claims into penny-stock promotions: Mackenzie Energy, Rideau Resources, Grant Exploration, Northern Eagle Mines, and others. He called this sweeping of claims into his various penny stocks Operation Pezamerica, and changed the name of Pez Resources to Pezamerica Resources.

By the fall, brokers were making margin calls, forcing Pezim to pay up on those stocks for which he had made only a partial payment. That was only part of his problem. He was also worried about the financing of Corona. The business of transforming a scrubby tract into a producing mine is a long, expensive process that extends far beyond stock promotion. David Bell's exploration work was still in the feasibility phase, assessing the economic viability of the project. The company would have to determine the per-ounce production costs of the operation and the overall reserves on the property before any decision could be made. That would take money. To take a mine into production could take hundreds of millions of dollars.

And Pezim wasn't getting any younger. He was sixty years of age and nothing in his experience had prepared him for the difficulties involved in establishing a project the size of this one. Raising a few million dollars on the stock exchange was one thing. Raising a couple of hundred million dollars to set up a mine was something else again. For that kind of sum, conventional lenders like banks must be involved. But Pezim didn't hold a lot of sway with bankers.

In truth, raising that kind of money doesn't fall within the expertise of any promoter. The more normal course is for the junior company to lure a major mining company into a joint-venture project, as had been Corona's intention early that summer when the company first met with Little Long Lac's Dennis Sheehan.

Pezim was desperate for a partnership, any partnership. He tried his longtime friend Stephen Roman of Denison Mines in Toronto. He talked with Hudson Bay Mining and Smelting. He talked to the people at Placer Mines. He met with John May and John Hallbauer of Teck Corp., a Vancouver-based mining company primarily in the base-metals business. That meeting led to one with Teck's leader, Dr. Norman Keevil, whose nickname, at the time, was Evil Keevil. He well knew how tough it is to overcome the doubting Thomases in an investment community. But by 1982, Teck had had a number of successes, including the Afton copper mine, five kilometres west of Kamloops, B.C. Coincidentally, the Trans-Canada also ran through the Afton property. Almost two kilometres of it had had to be rerouted in 1977.

Teck and Pezim struck a deal on Hemlo. Teck bought 200,000 shares of Corona at $5 a share. For its million-dollar investment – and an obligation to continue funding the exploration program – it got a fifty-five percent interest in the property and the right to take into production what would become the David Bell mine. For Teck, it turned out to be a fabulous deal. For Pezim and Corona, the association provided cash and credibility.

Pezim felt like a new man. For the first time he had a partner with certifiable money. Hemlo was real and that made Pezim real – in the West. So he thought he might as well make himself a big deal in Toronto, too. He checked into the recently refurbished King Edward Hotel in downtown Toronto and staged an impromptu family reunion. Rose and Frances were urged to come on over to the hotel and bring their families. They feared they would find themselves in the midst of a three-ring circus for Pezim hangers-on, which, in fact, is what they did find. Nevertheless, Rose's son Bruce made the effort, with his two children in tow.

"Love your face, kid," said Pezim to Bruce's seven-year-old daughter. "Here's a hundred bucks."

Would success spoil Murray Pezim? Not on your life.

One wag in the Vancouver brokerage community started what he called a "Box Score" on Pezim. In 1983, Pezim was listed as a director of sixty-seven companies and was either an adviser or a substantial shareholder of eleven others, for a box score of seventy-eight.

It was a phenomenally successful year for the exchange: 3.1 billion shares traded, surpassing the combined total of Montreal and Toronto. Pezim and Peter Brown made hay over how the VSE was shoving it to the East; how Hemlo was going to prove that the mining game was played as well, if not better, in the West. Canada's venture-capital capital, said Pezim and Brown to reporters, was now unquestionably Vancouver.

When the CBC television network sent its crew west, east, and north to film the Hemlo saga, they recorded Peter Brown saying that "there was no joy" for the first eighteen months of the Corona promotion, that "nobody believed Murray Pezim in Vancouver had found Canada's most important gold camp in the heart of the Toronto mining community. They just couldn't face it."

Pezim, in close-up, fills the camera. "I think what really egged me on — I was taking such a beating in the East."

There is footage of Pezim getting a rub-down from Mr. Poland, his personal masseur and one of the innumerable tag-ons who have sucked on the Pezim payroll over the years.

"I'll whip up a whole country," Pezim crowed.

He was riding high. Everyone in town knew he was in the chips. Anyone who needed a buck would try to make it past the Pezim group of flacks to Pezim himself.

One of these was Susan Hanson. Tall, blonde, and twenty-nine, she had first met Pezim at a charity lunch at a North Vancouver hotel. Later, her sister Julia had had dinner with Pezim one evening. Susan and Les MacConnell had joined them and made the gathering a foursome.

Susan and a friend named Kelly had started a balloon-a-gram company, Kelly Sue Balloon Experience, despatching hapless out-of-work types to sing a few lines of "Happy Birthday" before handing over a balloon gift. But by February 1983, the enterprise was strapped for cash. Julia came up with the bright idea of getting Susan to talk to Murray, Mr. Venture Capital himself. Susan tried, but couldn't get through. Then Susan had a bright idea of her own. Knowing of Murray's fondness for the company of young women, Susan and Kelly dressed up as Playboy bunnies and arrived at Pezim's office.

Susan, looking back, says that Kelly was the real crowd-pleaser: "They were all drooling over my girlfriend," says Susan of the men in Pezim's office. "She's got big, huge boobs and great long legs."

This Pezim confirms: "I was interested in her girlfriend Kelly, who had great bazooms."

Pezim, according to Susan, never came through with any money for the balloon business, and Susan went off and joined a circus for a time, where she dressed as a clown and sold balloons. Kelly, left in charge of the Vancouver enterprise, took off for Vegas at one point with Pezim, along with a couple of his flacks and hangers-on. They were shacked up there when Marilyn made a surprise appearance, leaving the Pezim entourage to scramble, whisking away pantihose, an ironing board.

To this day, Susan regards Murray's relationship with Kelly as a betrayal – despite the fact that Murray was still married to Marilyn and Susan didn't have any legitimate claim on him. Susan says that Pezim bought Kelly a 1967 Mustang convertible for $8,000 that Susan maintains was a hunk of junk.

When she returned from the circus she says she found what was left of the Kelly Sue Balloon Experience – invoices, ledgers – in a cardboard box on her front stoop. She phoned Pezim. She kept phoning him and kept getting the brushoff. In October 1983, she presented herself on his doorstep. From that day forward, she says, they were inseparable.

Which is not the same as saying Pezim was faithful. The Corona excitement seemed to coincide with a growing need within Murray Pezim to prove himself young and invincible.

When Vancouver hosted the Grey Cup on November 27, 1983, he and Susan had a box at the Coliseum. The night before the game, Pezim and Sam Rosen, a longtime helper, found themselves in an elevator at the Hyatt Hotel with a group of young women, including a barefoot Pearl Whalley. Reflecting on that first meeting, Pezim says Pearl looked worn, bedraggled. Pearl says she had been helping out with the B.C. Lions cheerleaders.

"I knew the lady who was their chor-e-o-graph-er," explains Pearl today, with an emphasis on the "graph."

"Choreographer," says Pezim, pronouncing it correctly.

"Yes. I would help them out with their makeup and all that kind of stuff."

When Pezim and Susan et al. gathered at the game the following evening, Pearl was there, too. "This Pearl person," as Susan calls her.

"Murray started pushing us together," says Susan of Pearl. "She was low-class, brassy."

Susan explains that from the outset of their relationship, Pezim had begun work on remaking her. She had two children, then aged seven and fourteen, who did not live with her. She also

213

had a problem with booze. So here she was at the Grey Cup, in the early stages of being remade into Pezim's idea of a socialite, when in walks Pearl, who to Susan's eyes needed a lot of fixing up. The Toronto Argonauts defeated the B.C. Lions by a score of eighteen to seventeen that day. Through the evening Pezim inexplicably kept trying to push Pearl and Susan together. He likes his women friends to be friends among themselves.

The day after the Grey Cup, Pezim talked Susan into joining Pearl, or Pearl into joining Susan, in helping out in a charity event. It involved pushing Murray in a bed race down a street in downtown Vancouver. Susan was livid. Murray, she says, lost no time in becoming intimate with Pearl.

As Pezim's eye for women wandered this way and that, so too did his eye for corporate encounters of a more enlivening kind. In 1983 he had a good chunk of Hemlo, but the Hemlo excitement didn't keep his juices pumping for very long. He was distracted, and the annual report for Pezamerica Resources that year shows just how far he could roam.

It is, at first glance, a straightforward thirteen-page document. Pezim's report to the shareholders outlines the importance of Pezamerica's 1.7 million shares in Corona Resources and the future plans for Hemlo. It described Corona's Hemlo operation with Teck, which was moving smartly toward production and was clearly a handsome moneymaker for both companies. Corona had become International Corona Resources in 1982, as Pez Resources had become Pezamerica Resources. The names had grown bigger, grander.

Then, suddenly, the report from Pezamerica's chairman of the board veers off track. The company, Pezim continues, has "diversified its operations," a phrase that should strike fear into the heart of any investor, considering past diversifications such as the Minnie Pearl chicken disaster. He then goes on to explain that Pezamerica has purchased a two-thirds interest in Swensen's Ice Cream Co. of Canada. As if that weren't depressing enough news, he then goes on to introduce one of the company's "most exciting ventures ever," Pezzazz Greetings from the Stars.

Pezamerica, the annual report explained, had worldwide rights to market taped greetings from "notable stars" – such personages as Slappy White, Red Buttons, Buddy Hackett, and Milton Berle. Bizarrely, Lynn Redgrave had allowed her name to be added to the roster. Henry Winkler's name is crossed out with a black marker from all copies of the annual report. The Fonz must have changed his mind (if he had ever agreed to this ludicrous notion in the first place).

These celebrities would produce a line of six tapes, devoted to Birthdays, Anniversaries, Marriage, Graduation, Cheer Up, and What is Love. Buddy Hackett, for example, discourses on the subject of Marriage. The flip side of the tape was left blank, so that customers could record a personalized greeting.

"Cash flow from the operation should be extremely substantial and management believes that the market potential of the Greeting Cassettes should have international appeal," according to the annual report.

The board of directors included the usual cast of characters: Murray Pezim and Art Clemiss, Izzy Rotterman, Les MacConnell, Bob Liverant from the Paul Lime plant excursion, and Larry Pezim, the son of Norman, Murray's brother. A Vancouver stockbroker, Larry did what none of Pezim's own children was interested in doing. He went to work for Murray.

Extraordinarily, while Corona's deal with Teck was worthy of just one page in the report, a full two pages were devoted to Pezzazz Greetings. "It is estimated in its first month of production Pezzazz will produce around 1.5-million cassettes and that within a year over thirty-million cassettes will be produced."

As Pezim's promotional attention span wandered here, there, and everywhere, Corona's need for capital grew. In December 1983, the company was approached by an obscure Toronto outfit called Royex Gold Mining, a subsidiary of Campbell Resources. Campbell had looked at, and had rejected, the Hemlo camp in the heyday of Hemlo exploration. Now, Royex and the man behind Royex – a one-time institutional money manager named Ned Goodman – decided to take a second look.

Goodman had grown up in NDG, or Notre Dame de Grâce, a middle-class neighbourhood in Montreal. He studied geology at McGill, then got his MBA at the University of Toronto. After graduation, he hooked up with an investment manager named Austin Beutel and together they worked as a money-management team for Edper, the investment arm of the Edward and Peter Bronfman conglomerate. In 1967, Goodman and Beutel left to form their own money-management firm, and built a $7-billion portfolio. But Goodman had sideline interests, particularly gold-mining.

In the late seventies, Goodman and a Toronto brokerage-house president named Myron Gottlieb had got themselves onto the board of Campbell Resources. Through a proxy battle in 1979, they won control of the company, which had interests in uranium, coal, asbestos, and gold. It had never been a stellar performer. Goodman and Gottlieb wanted to see Campbell make some swift moves into oil and gas. With Royex, they hoped to create a credible gold-miner.

In December 1983, Goodman and Tim Hoare, a mines expert with the London brokerage Alexanders Laing & Cruickshank, entered into negotiations with Corona. Hoare had come to know Goodman when he directed British investors into Royex's Cullaton Lake Gold Mines. Together, Goodman and Hoare created a corporate agreement that would see Royex put $6.5 million into

Corona's treasury and put 900,000 Corona shares into Royex, representing 8.2 percent of the company.

The agreement provided that the eight-member Corona board be constituted of four Pezim nominees and four Royex nominees. Goodman considered Corona's management team, led by Pezim, to be less than satisfactory; the board arrangement provided a mechanism through which he could keep his investment in check. The deal closed in January, 1984.

Pezim likes other people's money. He doesn't like corporate invaders. The following June, Pezim's Pezamerica made a takeover bid for Corona, offering two Pezamerica shares for every Corona share. Pezim personally had twenty-six percent of the shares of Pezamerica. After the share swap, Pezamerica had increased its stake in Corona to 6.5 million shares, fifty-seven percent of the 11.5 million shares outstanding. Pezim was in control.

Along the way Pezim had convinced his allies – Art Clemiss, Izzy Rotterman, Les MacConnell, and Nell Dragovan – to tender their Corona shares for the Pezamerica equivalent. The Pezim strategy had two results: Ned Goodman was kept at a distance from Corona, and Pezim's friends ended up with a company of wacko interests instead of simply Hemlo.

In August 1984, a research report issued from the offices of Midland Doherty on the subject of Pezamerica noted that though it is engaged mainly in exploration, "it may pursue other businesses not specifically described as 'resource oriented.' In fact, its newest and latest involvement in Pezzazz Productions has promise to become one of the brightest stars in its firmament." Heavens.

But Pezim was already headed for trouble. Shares in his corporate collective started to slide on the VSE. Pezim was spread thin and highly margined. He announced his intention to wind his way out of fifty-five of the seventy-five companies he controlled. He fired Mr. Poland, his masseur. He cut back on office space.

217

In October, junior resource listings on the VSE collapsed, including the Pezim companies. By mid-October, Pezamerica shares, which had hit $8, started to crater, finally collapsing at $3. Pezim's own Pezamerica position had been bought on margin as high as $7. Brokers started calling, telling him to cover his margin. He couldn't. Ensconced in his lair on the fifteenth floor of the stock-exchange tower, Pezim once again moaned that the world had turned enemy. It happened very quickly, just as it had with Bata Resources. Please, said Pezim to his friends, help me.

"I needed money. The pressure from brokers. Couldn't get it from my partners. You're only talking a couple million dollars," he recalled years later.

MacConnell, Dragovan, Clemiss, and Rotterman huddled. They would have to come up with about $7 million to rescue Pezim. But they had more personal concerns. Here they were in a company called Pezamerica and Pezim's wild gyrations were spinning his companies out of control. He was manic. If they stuck with him, there was no telling where they would end up. There was another alternative. Ned Goodman.

The friends chose to leave Pezim to founder. The way the powerful eastern money men tell it today, it was these people who finally squeezed Pezim. Conversely, there are Pezim people who believe the promoter was the victim of a masterly shorting campaign orchestrated by Goodman himself.

On October 18, Pezim left his office and paid a visit to the office of Canarim Investment's Peter Brown seven floors above. Tim Hoare, representing Goodman's interests, was waiting. Goodman purchased 1.4 million Pezamerica shares at $3.50 a share from Pezim. Pezim's payoff was $5 million.

Before this meeting, a holding company called PezCor had been established to hold the Corona interests of both the Goodman side and the Corona side. In October, Pezim agreed that the

PezCor board would consist of six Royex nominees and only two of his own choosing. In the end, Royex had control of PezCor, which had sixty-two percent of Corona. In addition, Pezim signed a voting-trust agreement giving Royex voting control over any shares Pezim held or would come to hold in Corona, either personally or through any of his companies. The voting trust had an expiry date of January 31, 1986.

Goodman struck deals with the one-time Pezim supporters. Rotterman took cash for his Pezamerica shares; Clemiss, Dragovan and MacConnell converted their Pezamerica holdings back to Corona holdings.

The deal closed October 25. "I paid off all the brokers," says Pezim today. "Told them good-bye. Good luck. Fuck you. I'm not too fond of brokers, you know. I think they're a bunch of whores. They want to be holier than thou but they want to do all the business. It's fine for the major firms to talk about Vancouver, and what a bad exchange it is. But they've got their hands out there for the commissions pretty darned good. They'll take all the money they can."

Pezim curled in the fetal position again. He didn't care if he died. Les MacConnell checked him into St. Paul's Hospital in Vancouver. He spent the night in the psychiatric ward. Then he went home to the Beach Avenue apartment.

He felt his friends and family were traitors. "Marilyn didn't do a damn thing. She didn't care if I died."

In fact, she had been spending most of her time in Phoenix. But Susan visited him during this bad time. She says his apartment was like a morgue. Sometimes Pezim would lie by the heating registers under the apartment's picture windows to stay warm.

"The air was so thick. Murray would lie in bed. Cry. He would say he's scared. His biggest fear was ending up on skid road with no friends."

219

Marilyn eventually stepped in and shipped him to a psychiatric hospital in Scottsdale. For Murray there were electroshock therapy treatments and group-counselling sessions. He knew he was sick and needed help.

Peter Brown, meanwhile, spoke to the press on Pezim's behalf. He said that while it was true that Pezim had been creamed on Pezamerica, he estimated that he was still worth $9 million in "hard assets" – $2 million in cash, a $2-million home, and between $4.5 million and $5 million in share holdings.

"I think Murray will be back and kicking," Brown told the *Toronto Star*.

Brown, Tim Hoare, and Ned Goodman moved onto the Pezamerica board. The new ownership arrangement wove together Campbell, Royex, Pezamerica, Pezcor, and Corona. The bottom line was that Corona belonged to Royex.

The crack-up was Pezim's worst ever. His problems extended far beyond losing control of Corona. He was booted off the board of a company called Tri-Basin Resources after using Tri-Basin's treasury to buy up Corona shares before the October collapse. He was being sued by suppliers over unpaid invoices relating to Swensen's ice cream.

Documents registered with the Supreme Court of British Columbia show evidence of the thwarted efforts of the plaintiffs to uproot the defendant from his Arizona hideaway.

In Pezim's defence are medical testimonies. One is a letter written on October 25, 1984, from a doctor named Mervyn Lakin, of Paradise Valley: "Mr. Pezim has been a patient of mine for many years," it says. "He has recently needed to have intensified medical care due to a severe depression reaction."

Another letter, dated in early December, from a Scottsdale doctor, said that because of Pezim's depressed state, he could not make himself available for the court proceedings on the Swensen's case. "I am presently treating Murray Pezim for a mood disorder, bipolar type. . . . In my medical opinion he must not do any travelling at this time so we can stabilize his condition. As his response to medication thus far has been unstable, I am unable to predict when he will be well enough to return to Vancouver."

The plaintiffs tried various means to determine whether Pezim was really incapacitated. One phoned his Paradise Valley home, representing himself to Pezim's secretary as Joe Cohen, the friend who had been his best man at his second marriage to Marilyn. When Pezim came to the phone, the complainant said in an affidavit, he didn't sound that sick.

But those who know Pezim well say this collapse was catastrophic, worse than the Bata debacle. While it's possible that Pezim could have used his manic-depressive diagnosis as a dark-alley escape from irate investors and creditors, and while on some days he may have appeared at peace, in control, he was a defeated little man.

Before October, Corona had upped the stakes in the lawsuit. Instead of seeking $100 million in damages, Corona decided to go for the mine instead. By the time Pezim shut off the lights, crawled into bed, and pulled up the covers, Little Long Lac and Corona were well into preparations to fight for the mine in court. It took months before Pezim was back on his feet. The $5-million payoff from Goodman was small consolation. When the two companies finally met in court, Pezim was still hurting.

In February 1985, Ned Goodman announced one of many amalgamations that he would come to devise in his Corona endeavours. In its simplest terms, Royex ended up with a wholly owned subsidiary called PezCorona, which had sixty percent of Corona itself. Goodman chaired the meeting at which the amalgamation was confirmed. Pezim stayed in Arizona.

In June, Goodman took Royex out from under Campbell

Resources. Pezzazz Productions was petitioned into bankruptcy. The company's interest in Swensen's ice cream was written off. In July, International Corona was listed for trading on the Toronto Stock Exchange. The company, or so the eastern men in charge hoped, had shaken its shady VSE beginnings.

But there was a hitch. The Royex-Campbell split accomplished what corporate reorganizations often do. It made life confusing. Corona issued new shares as part of the deal. The share increase diluted every shareholder's piece of the pie. In the end, Corona ended up taking control of Royex and Royex, in turn, saw its interest in Corona watered down to thirty-eight percent, which is a long way from fifty and thereby a long way from airtight control.

That same summer, Little Long Lac Gold Mines changed its name to Lac Minerals. As Corona set to battle Lac in court, a still-deflated Murray Pezim met with Alan Lenczner, a tough litigation lawyer with McCarthy & McCarthy. Lenczner had inherited the Corona case from Doug Laidlaw, a respected lawyer who had been killed in a highway traffic accident. Laidlaw had been Lenczner's mentor and had been leading the Corona argument with another lawyer, Ron Slaght, as co-counsel. After Laidlaw's death, Lenczner and Slaght formed a partnership and went after Lac.

When Lenczner was introduced to Pezim, the promoter's ego was blowing hard. "Don't worry about me. I'll kill the cocksuckers. I can handle anything they throw at me."

The funny thing was that after the ego-blow, Pezim settled down, straightened the cuffs on his monogrammed shirt, and was suddenly transmogrified into an insecure kid applying for his first job, hoping like hell he said the right thing.

Lenczner would ask a question. Pezim would stare back, querying without speaking. What, wondered Pezim, was he supposed to say? He looked at Slaght, at the Vancouver lawyer Larry Page, hitching his eyebrows, waiting for some signal, like two fingers down from the baseball catcher. He probably didn't remember the facts, long since buried among the detritus of a hundred other Pezim mining ventures.

Pezim's courtroom presence was essential for only a small part of the Corona argument. But it was imperative that he state unequivocally that he had instructed Don McKinnon, the prospector, to acquire specifically for Corona the eleven patented mining claims owned by the widow Lola Williams. Just as crucial was that Don McKinnon come across as credible when he asserted that had he been successful in purchasing the claims, they would certainly have been passed on to Corona.

Corona had a two-edged case to argue. First, it alleged that Lac acted on confidential geological information when it went after the Williams claims – because of those early meetings between the geologists David Bell of Corona and Dennis Sheehan of Little Long Lac shortly after Hole 76. Second, Lac, said Corona, had an obligation to deal in good faith. It was a question, argued the Corona lawyers, of fiduciary duty, which simply means you don't break your word where money's concerned.

When Pezim's day in court came, it was Slaght, the more reserved of the two lawyers, who led the examination. Pezim gave a rundown on his business history beginning in 1935, the poor years, the war years. In 1951, he said, he was working as a butcher when a very tragic event happened.

"Somebody came into our shop. He was a broker by the name of Max Guthrie. I worked in a butcher shop that was in a very poor neighbourhood, and he ordered three centre-cut loin steaks. I felt he got some money because nobody ever bought those out there, and he talked me into buying some stock. And the evolution was in six weeks, I lost all my money."

Can you tell us, asked Slaght, what your role is as a promoter?

223

"Well," said Pezim, "I'll start this way and I'll tell you what a good promoter is. A good promoter is one who must believe in what he's doing; he must have absolute faith; he must have a good layman's knowledge of the product he is going to deal in; he must surround himself with the best engineers, accountants, lawyers, consultants that he can. He must have credibility with brokers – that is an absolute must – in order to raise capital.

"You must remember that risk capital, in my view, is more important to a country like Canada than investment capital. Anyone can sit around and buy and sell bonds, but you don't develop a country like Canada and we wouldn't find mines or create anything without risk capital. It is a tough job because it is the toughest kind of money to find. You must have that credibility with brokers. You must believe and you must be a leader of sorts. You must be able to laugh, by the way."

All the Corona witnesses said all the right things. Nell Dragovan even cried when she talked of the dastardly Lac and its underhanded tactics.

On March 7, 1986, a Friday, Mr. Justice Richard Holland of the Supreme Court of Ontario rendered his judgement: The property, he ruled, was legally Corona's. Lac, which had borne the expense of building a mine on the property, was awarded $154 million in damages.

The stock market had had the jitters waiting for the news that Friday. Pezim told a newspaper reporter that he threw up twice waiting for the decision. On Monday, when the stocks resumed trading, Corona opened at $25, up from $11 and change before the weekend. Lac sank by very nearly $18 to $23.

It was the end of Round One. It was also the end of Round Two of Pezim's marriage battles. Later that same month, divorce proceedings commenced between Murray and Marilyn Pezim.

CHAPTER 10

The Male Climacteric

Murray Pezim rose from a king-sized bed in a $1,200-a-night room in the Baur au Lac hotel in Zürich. Susan Hanson remained snuggled under the sheets. Pezim walked to the mirror, took a few deep breaths of Swiss air, and said what he usually says when he is about to take on the world:

"Ya-ba-da-ba-doo."

Other times, he says: "I'm the greatest."

It's his way of getting psyched up.

It was February, 1987, and Pezim was playing with his pills. He doesn't admit to this, but Susan maintains that he was. When Pezim goes off his lithium, he can hope to achieve a manic high, which gives him the energy to push stock tirelessly. It was imperative that Pezim be able to do just that. He had another fight on his hands. He was sixty-five years of age. His energies were not what they once were. Lithium serves to inhibit the emotional peaks and valleys of manic depression. That's exactly what he didn't want. He needed to create a scene.

Susan, by this time, was working in the Pezim offices, fielding phone calls, serving as Pezim's faithful assistant. She had recently passed the Canadian Securities Course, which is a requirement for anyone who wants to be a registered representative – that is, a stockbroker. Just about everyone, including Pezim, was surprised that Susan had had the tenacity to stick with it. By the time of the Zürich trip, Susan Hanson was Susan Hanson, stockbroker.

This was not the only sign of self-improvement in Susan's life. At Pezim's urging, she had had her nose bobbed – not that there had been anything wrong with it in the first place. It had been one of those unexceptional noses with a little ball at the tip. Pezim had promised her a Lincoln Continental if she had it deballed. Right after the surgery, she had made her way to the car lot, bandages and all, to pick out her shiny new Lincoln. Susan had told everyone that Murray Pezim was buying her this great car. Then he reneged.

Pezim followed the nose assault with a breast campaign. He figured Susan, at thirty-three, needed hers tightened a tad. And then there were her teeth. Susan should wear braces, Pezim said. He felt they needed straightening. He also wanted Susan to lose weight. And learn to dress in a manner befitting the consort of Murray Pezim.

Nose jobs, teeth jobs, boob jobs, starvation dieting are standard operating procedure for women who become involved with Pezim, says Susan. Marilyn, when she first met Murray, had a plump, somewhat matronly figure. During her years as Marilyn Pezim she had trimmed down to an anorectic size six. Had her nose done. And other restructuring.

All this remodelling pressure was difficult to bear. Pezim, to put it gently, has a largish nose of his own. He is not the fittest of creatures. He loves shovelling in the food, with no regard to nutrition. (In the Swensen's ice cream days, he would keep tubs of the stuff in the fridge, along with The Pez chocolates.)

Together the remodelled Susan and the indefatigable Murray had travelled to Europe. Pezim was in one of his red rages. Months before, he had proposed to the board of International Corona Resources that he be restored as the company's chairman, a proper role, he felt, for the self-described founder of Hemlo.

Pezim had resigned the chairmanship in the spring of 1985 to make way for Peter Steen, a South African mining engineer who had worked for Anglo American in Zambia for twelve years. Steen had moved to Canada in 1968 and in May 1985 had been successfully courted by Goodman. The Steen appointment had been struck at a Corona directors' meeting at Pezim's Paradise Valley home, under the portico, just outside the kitchen, while Pezim was still convalescing from his collapse the previous fall. Steen was now Corona's chairman and chief executive officer. From the start, he made it clear that he didn't want Murray Pezim anywhere near the operating side of the company.

Pezim and Ned Goodman shared the title of vice-chairman of Corona. But by the fall of 1986, Pezim was eager to align himself more tightly with Hemlo, to wear the Hemlo crown. The gold camp's David Bell mine, which Corona shared with Teck, and the Williams mine, which had been awarded to Corona, were both in production. The Golden Giant Mine, owned by Noranda, was also up and running. In short, Hemlo was driving the northern Ontario mining economy.

Lac Minerals, meanwhile, had appealed the court decision in which it had lost the Williams mine. Bay Street analysts were advising investors to hedge any Corona investment with a Lac investment. Few were willing to take a gamble on the final judicial outcome on the mine's ownership.

In the months following the first court ruling in March, Corona had increased its interest in the David Bell mine to fifty percent, making the company an equal partner with Teck. When

1986 drew to a close, Ned Goodman's Royex had thirty-eight percent of Corona as well as controlling interests in three other mines. Corona had fifty percent of the Bell mine and forty-nine percent of Royex. Stock-market experts had made decoding Corona a new sport.

At a Corona board meeting in mid-December, 1986, Pezim had said again that he wanted to reassume the chairman's chair. He wouldn't interfere, he said, wouldn't try to run anything. But he did want more involvement than he was being offered.

Pezim's principal undertaking had become a company called Galveston Resources. With it, he was more or less starting from scratch once again – looking for gold in the Hemlo area, in Quebec, in the Northwest Territories, in northern Saskatchewan. Galveston didn't have much to show for itself, but it did hold 261,000 shares of Corona and 970,000 warrants of a company called PezCorona Gold. The warrants could be converted into Corona shares at an exercise price of $7 a share.

He would be happier, he told Goodman, if he were elevated in the company that he had, after all, created. Goodman knew that Steen would resign if Pezim were promoted. Steen never much cared for the Pezim persona, the crassness, the running off at the mouth to the press. Goodman knew too that all sorts of institutional investors would balk at any closer corporate alignment with the penny pitchman from the West.

Goodman's goal was to turn Corona from a Howe Street hit to a Bay Street triumph. The company had become a well-known entity in the East. But at the same time, it was a newcomer that didn't have the establishment patina of, say, an Inco, or a Falconbridge, or an established gold-mining operation such as Dome Mines.

At the end of January, 1987, Pezim was sprung from the voting-trust agreement, the one that handed voting control of his Pezamerica-Corona interests to Royex, the one that he had signed when he had been creamed by the margin calls in the stock-market collapse of October 1984. On Sunday, February 1, Goodman told Pezim that his chairmanship idea was a no-go.

Pezim was peeved. He had already planned the European trip, hoping to arouse investor interest in Galveston. He had also planned to undertake a little promotion on behalf of Corona itself. He had approached Steen. He said he needed a pile of Corona annual reports – forty would do – to help him tout Corona and thereby Galveston.

Steen had turned him down. In the midst of the court tussle, this was all he needed, Steen thought, this little sprout gabbing around Europe about a company he no longer ran.

Pezim told the Vancouver *Province* that after Steen said he didn't want him representing Corona overseas, he went back to his Toronto hotel room, packed his bags, jumped on a plane, and "threw up five times on the way back to Vancouver," thereby reinforcing Steen's concerns about the ill-considered messages that Pezim was given to sending through the press.

So Pezim flew to Switzerland and took Susan the stockbroker with him. He didn't have the Corona reports, but he didn't really need them. All he needed was his mouth, a few phone lines, and media access.

Once Pezim was safely tucked away in the Baur au Lac, Goodman, through Royex, orchestrated the purchase for $52 million of thirty-six percent of a mining company called Lacana. With access to Lacana came access to the $30 million held in Lacana's treasury.

Corona still had a forty-nine-percent interest in Royex; but Royex had just a thirty-eight-percent piece of Corona. Goodman liked this ring-of-fire style of interownership. It was an effective means of keeping potential acquisitors at bay. But it wasn't any security against the unpredictable Pezim's taking a run at Corona.

The Lacana acquisition could be made without the knowledge of Pezim. Although he was involved in Corona, which controlled Royex, he had no direct involvement with Royex itself. Nevertheless, Peter Steen made a courtesy call to Art Clemiss and Larry Page, both allies of Pezim, and told them of the purchase. Would they, asked Steen of Clemiss and Page, pass on the news to Pezim in Europe?

Pezim and Susan had reached Paris by the time he heard of the Lacana acquisition. Pezim surmised that the $30 million would be used by Royex to purchase Corona shares, thereby going from thirty-eight percent to fifty percent and gaining control of the company. That would give Goodman the clout he needed to say goodbye to him forever, while at the same time stopping the danger of takeover attempts once and for all.

Pezim panicked. He was going to buy shares on the open market, he said. He was going to regain control of Corona, he yelled. He had money behind him. Big money. European investors, bagmen who would come through for him. He phoned Goodman at home, but the two didn't connect. He phoned Paul Carroll, Ned Goodman's longtime personal lawyer. He yelled, he screamed, he heaped abuse. He did the same when he tracked down Peter Steen.

After the Lacana news broke, the *Vancouver Sun* reached Pezim in full transoceanic braggadocio. "I want Corona back, I want the West to have it," Pezim told the newspaper. "I felt they hurt me when they took it from me. They treated me very shabbily. I intend to take more from the East. . . . They are my enemies. Steen should be working underground, in a mine."

Responded Steen: "I have always treated him with the utmost courtesy."

The Pezim threat was more than mere bluster. In 1985, when Ned Goodman had been rejigging the Corona-Royex association with racehorse speed, he had at one juncture created the Pez-Corona warrants. The idea had been to please the Pezamerica share-holders: as they saw their share holdings wound this way and that and eventually into Royex, they would at least get one warrant for every four Pezamerica shares. Every warrant could be converted into a common share of Corona itself.

With the warrants that Pezim had access to through his various corporations, particularly Galveston, he technically had the might to battle Goodman. If Pezim were to exercise his warrants and take Corona shares in their stead, Royex's hold on Corona would be diluted to twenty-five percent from thirty-eight.

But Corona shares were then trading in excess of $35 and the company had an enormous volume of twenty-three million shares outstanding. The market capitalization of the company was approximately $800 million. Even with the warrants — and it wasn't at all clear how Pezim could find the cash to exercise them — he would have to pay a prohibitively high price for Corona shares in order to get fifty percent of the company.

Murray and Susan flew home from Europe almost immediately. Pezim embarked on a public-relations campaign. He lured Canarim's Peter Brown and Herb Doman, the chairman of Doman Industries, onto Galveston's board. Then he enlisted the support of Jimmy Pattison, who also signed onto Galveston's board. A few days later, Pezim met with Goodman in Toronto. Goodman brought Paul Carroll. Pezim brought Art Clemiss and Larry Page.

"What are you going to do with Lacana?" demanded Pezim of Goodman.

"What would you do?" asked Goodman.

"You're going to buy Corona shares, that's what you're going to do," said Pezim, who drowned his cigarette in a cup of coffee and blew out of the room.

Later, Goodman said in a court affidavit that during the course of the thirty-minute meeting, Pezim "showed a range of emotions from professed affection towards myself to complete hatred and uncontrollable anger."

The Goodman group was concerned enough about the danger Pezim presented to take immediate action. At the Corona annual meeting in mid-February, Art Clemiss and Larry Page were dumped from the board of Corona. Two management nominees, that is to say individuals hand-picked by Goodman, took their places.

Pezim attended the meeting. "That's my baby up there," he blathered, jabbing in the direction of the dais, his hands darting about in agitation. Then he stormed out, announcing that, "Like MacArthur says, 'I shall return.'" Which is, in fact, what General Douglas MacArthur did say when he left the Philippines in the face of the Japanese onslaught.

After the meeting, Pezim spoke briefly to Steen: "Give me back my fucking company." Then he held a press conference, reaffirming his intention to buy Corona stock on the open market. He said he could round up six-million Corona shares. He later said eight million.

At a board meeting immediately following the annual meeting, it was proposed that Goodman take the chairman's job. Pezim fumed. Peter Brown, who had brokered the corporate relationship between Pezim and Goodman in the first place and who was also on the board of Galveston, stepped in. He proposed that Pezim and Goodman remain as vice-chairmen pending futher discussion. For the moment, this was enough to placate the besieged Pezim. But he continued to be a loose cannon − off the wall, unpredictable, uncontrollable. He was talking to the media when he shouldn't.

The Goodman group scrummed. They decided to shut him

out. At a subsequent board meeting, Pezim was removed as vice-chairman. He was also removed from the executive committee. That left a four-man, decision-making control group of Goodman, Paul Carroll, Peter Steen, and Tim Hoare.

Pezim's lawyers went to work. In late February, in the Supreme Court of Ontario, Pezim filed an affidavit in which he announced his intention to launch a proxy battle for control of Corona. He sought to remove Carroll, Goodman, Hoare, Lord Shaughnessy, and Norman Anderson from the board. (Shaughnessy and Anderson were the two management nominees.) Carroll, Goodman, and Hoare, said the submission, were exercising the power of their directorships, "in a manner that is oppressive or unfairly disregards the interests of the Applicants." That is to say, Pezim.

In addition, Pezim wanted Page and Clemiss returned to their slots. He sought to set aside any purchase agreements between the Corona web of companies that had taken place after mid-December, 1986, a move that singled out the Lacana purchase.

Steen was among those who filed affidavits in response.

"I found him friendly and amusing," said Steen of his initial impressions of Murray Pezim. The charm soon wore thin, he said. When Steen took over operations, Corona had few internal controls, little organization. And there were those ventures of Pezim's. Pezzazz Greetings From The Stars. Swensen's ice cream. The typically disastrous dabblings of Murray Pezim. It was Steen who cleaned house.

"I set about shedding Corona of these ventures so that the company could concentrate on its real attributes and become a senior mining concern."

Steen said he had been frustrated by repeated efforts on the part of Pezim to undermine his authority as the official representative for Corona. He documented deals that could have died because of Pezim's interference. He detailed an instance in

233

which Pezim had tried to sell himself out of a company at a considerable profit, disregarding the minority shareholders he professed to be considerate of.

He told of how he had found himself on the board of Galveston Petroleums (the predecessor of Galveston Resources), but had been disturbed that no board meetings were held. He said he showed up at Galveston's offices once, and after a period of time when very little had happened, made his way to the nearest elevator. There he encountered the office manager, waving a sheaf of papers to be signed by Steen. The papers voted Steen off the board seat he had been persuaded to assume. He signed. He was, he says, quite happy to do so.

Goodman, Steen, et al. continued to be unhappy that Pezim was playing out the power struggle before the press. After all, the Williams mine decision was still under appeal, and the true worth of Corona remained uncertain.

The ties that bound Pezim's opponents were tight. Carroll had been Goodman's personal lawyer for fifteen years; Goodman and Gottlieb were loyal partners and friends from the Campbell days; Goodman and Hoare had remained close, even though Goodman's Cullaton Lake gold project, which Hoare had directed overseas investors into, had been mothballed; and Goodman and Steen were close because Goodman had handpicked Steen for Corona. Goodman was the common denominator.

The five men had begun referring to themselves as the Blackbirds, a reference to an early Goodman mining venture called Blackbird Resources. They were as close as the cosiest of men's-club members, and while each tolerated Pezim to differing degrees, they hung together in their determination never to allow him to run amok over their territory.

Pezim, meanwhile, was nervous, and it showed – in a trembling of the hands, in his rapid-fire speech. He cornered Peter

Steen one day at a New York gold conference and emphasized that the actions he had taken were not to be construed as displeasure with Steen directly. When he got control, he said, he wanted Steen to move to Vancouver and run the company from there.

Up and down; up and down. Nervous, then insecure. Defeated, then unbeatable.

The Blackbirds were powerful, but they were not omnipotent. Goodman said at the time that he wasn't discounting the threat that Pezim represented. "Everybody seems to think he's just a mosquito on the wall," he told me in April, 1987. "But we're not dealing with a pathetic little man."

Pezim, meanwhile told the *Wall Street Journal* that Goodman was his "sworn enemy. I'm going to dig up everything I can on him. I'm a street fighter."

The object of the exercise, Goodman told me, "was to eliminate the scourge of Murray Pezim and his friends."

In mid-March, Royex announced that it too would go for control of Corona, though it didn't explain how it would do so – except to say that it was speaking with certain institutional-investment dealers. It outlined another Goodman shuffle involving Royex and Royex affiliates, wherein one affiliate, a company called Mascot, would be sold to another affiliate, the recently purchased Lacana. The deal would spring $150 million from Lacana's bountiful treasury.

John Ing, the mining analyst, had by this time come onside with the Hemlo story and had moved from Pitfield to be president of the Toronto brokerage Maison Placements. He called the manoeuvre "Pez repellent." Pezim, meanwhile, pronounced it the "biggest rape in history."

The take-over battle for Corona was growing richer by the day. On March 11, Corona's shares closed at $41.50 on the Toronto Stock Exchange.

Goodman spelled out his intentions at the beginning of April. Royex proposed a purchase package consisting of two convertible preferred shares, one Royex warrant and $4 cash in exchange for each Corona share. Royex was looking for a total of four million shares to bring it up to a fifty percent control position.

Analysts grumbled about the paper swap, saying that its complexity made it difficult to assess. Conversion packages were offered to holders of Corona warrants: one consisted of a 1.75 convertible preferred retractable zero coupon preferred-share series B with a nominal value of $35 and a five-year $7.50 Royex share-purchase warrant.

Pezim told *The Globe and Mail* he would have to get out his dictionary before commenting on the terms of the offer, which was set to close in the third week of April.

By closing day, Goodman had acquired enough shares to give Royex control of Corona. Pezim was cornered. He hadn't been able to assemble the troops of money men to support his takeover battle. He had no choice but to give up on the fight for Corona, the company he called "his baby," the one he had vowed would never be taken from him.

Goodman threw a crumb Pezim's way: Larry Page returned to the Corona board and the executive committee. Pezim again signed a voting-trust agreement, which in effect meant handing over voting control of his own Corona shares and those held by his companies, including Galveston. Goodman didn't want any more Pez-inspired trouble. If Pezim wanted to stay anywhere near the Corona orbit – and thereby the Hemlo orbit – he probably had no choice but to sign.

It was a pathetic conclusion to a noble beginning. Pezim said he was happy to put the internal squabbles to rest.

He looked like a loser. He was a loser.

In October 1987, Lac's appeal was dismissed. The courts

again said that the best piece of Hemlo, the Williams mine, belonged to Corona, which belonged to Royex, which more or less belonged to Goodman.

Pezim could celebrate all he wanted, raise a glass of champagne here and there, shout about how good the victory felt. But the fact is, it couldn't have felt very good. The victory wasn't his. Nor was it final. Days after hearing the Ontario court's decision, Lac announced it was taking the case to the Supreme Court of Canada.

Murray Pezim proposed to Susan Hanson in November, 1987, at the Hyatt Regency Hotel in Vancouver. The stock crowd had gathered to honour The Promoter of the Year, an annual award within the closely knit VSE community. That year the title went to Pezim.

On this evening, Susan was sitting at the head table, wearing strapless velvet, her shoulder-length blonde hair pulled back, some lovely jewellery nuzzling her neck. She had been wearing a five-carat diamond ring for months, a bauble that Murray had tossed to her one day as if it were some Cracker Jack prize. She was booze-free, slender, and had very nice teeth. She hadn't done anything about the breasts yet.

Pezim rose to speak. He told the crowd how tickled he was, at the age of very nearly sixty-six, to have his work finally recognized. As with most such tributes, the timing was off. Pezim should have been fêted in his Hemlo heyday. There were younger, more aggressive promoters about town. Pezim went so far as to admit that he was no longer Number One, no longer the Godfather of the Vancouver Stock Exchange.

Pezim's thank-you speech was vintage Pezim – Rabelaisian, occasionally tasteless. Susan recalls that he was just about to tell one of his "shit jokes" (as in, "What have you got when you've got three lawyers up to their necks in shit? Not enough shit.")

when Pezim turned toward her, told the crowd that there was something that everyone was very curious about, then asked Susan if she would marry him. She said yes.

This kind of grandstanding is right up Murray's alley. He loves to show off in front of his friends and would-be friends. When he tossed Susan the ring in the first place it was in front of a room full of hangers-on, who smiled, laughed, applauded. When he gave her a Blackglama mink it was because some friend had bought a similar gift for the woman in his life. It is important to Pezim that he be seen to be equal, then be seen to be better. The Promoter of the Year dinner afforded him the chance of proposing in front of a crowd of several hundred people, a crowd that included Larry Page and Peter Brown and Ned Goodman.

After the brouhaha over Corona, after the defeat by Goodman, Pezim had lain low in his Vancouver office. The month before the roast, however, he had at last re-emerged with a new story to tell. A company called Prime Capital Corp. had been created by Corona in Toronto but would be run out of Vancouver with Pezim as chairman. Corona would have thirty-three percent of Prime. Prime, in turn, would round up appealing junior resource prospects, using Pezim as Pezim is used best, as a lure to the promoters, the stakers, the mining men with something to sell. The setup put Corona in a position to pick its way through those prospects that seemed the most promising. This time, however, Pezim wasn't allowed to go solo. John Ivany was hired from Noranda to work as Prime's president. Nevertheless, Pezim was reinflated by Prime.

I met Murray Pezim for the first time soon after the Promoter of the Year dinner. He was careering about the very unsophisticated offices of Maison Placements in downtown Toronto, chain-smoking, waving those lovely hands, as he explained with what appeared to be real enthusiasm the gist of Prime. The arrangement perfectly suited Pezim as it perfectly suited the controlling powers in the East. Pezim could sign up any mining outfit that took his fancy. Corona would only option the pieces it liked. The control position allowed the Toronto crowd to keep a tight rein on Pezim. There would be no amphibious aircraft, no ice-cream enterprises, no fried-chicken outlets. If Pezim wanted to get crazy again, he'd have to do it under a different corporate banner.

The presence of Ivany added much-needed ballast to the selling of the venture. Pezim might have received the promotional award in Vancouver, but in the East he remained the most visible example of the lunatic fringe. In addition to Ivany, the Prime operation drew Jimmy Pattison to its board, along with the predictable cast of Ned Goodman, Myron Gottlieb, and a newcomer to inside operations, Maison Placements' John Ing, who had helped conceive the idea of Prime.

Goodman, meanwhile, was telling the press that his Royex-Corona creation was the foundation for the Consolidated Gold Fields of the future. Consolidated is the British blue-chip mining house that has a powerful hold on South African gold production. Suggesting that Corona would one day be a Consolidated Gold Fields was like suggesting that Ned Goodman would one day be the Queen of England.

Goodman was not having an easy time attracting institutional investors, analysts, or even ordinary investors. They complained about the complexity of his deal-making, which, they charged, was too much paper-shuffling and not enough substance; they said the company had too many losing pieces in oil and gas and other companies that detracted from the Hemlo appeal; they particularly disliked Goodman's multiple voting-share structure, which gave the Blackbirds voting control of Corona though they held a relatively small number of shares.

Pezim, of course, fed off the distress as if it were mother's milk. He griped about Goodman to his friends, then to the media, then pleaded that reporters take care not to get him into trouble with his nemesis, his Nedness.

After the Promoter of the Year dinner, Susan and Murray started to plan the wedding. As Susan tells it, she wanted a modest ceremony in Vegas; Pezim wanted a Vegas road show. They couldn't agree about the simplest aspects of what had turned into an extravaganza. Was it Susan's fault that it hadn't occurred to her to invite Henny Youngman?

The guest list grew to four hundred. Susan says Murray wanted a thousand close friends – politicians, brokers, power-brokers, comedians. He even sent an invitation to Neil de Gelder, the superintendent of brokers, a cool, smart lawyer in his thirties who wanted to make his mark by cleaning up the VSE. When he and other lucky recipients opened their invitations, pieces of confetti fluttered onto desk tops, Bass Weejuns, and brokerage-house floors.

There was much to do. Pezim was fat and feasting on junk food, working killing hours trying to get Prime on the go. Susan decided that remaking Pezim was essential. What Susan wanted was a faster, fitter Murray. It was for his own good, she would say. Her mother, Drena, was installed in the Pezim offices as a kind of diet cop; she monitored his consumption and periodically served up little trays of vegetable sticks and fruit.

I recall sitting one day beside Pezim when he still had his offices in the stock-exchange tower. His desk was cluttered (this was before the move to the luxe West Hastings headquarters where today he has his sweeping control-central Corefam desk) with the usual press releases and trading stats and news reports and gadgetry. On the desk was a cartoon of Pezim in his office, which said, "The Pez Sez: I'm bullish on marriage." On a nearby table sat a few prettily wrapped wedding presents. In the corner of the room was a stationary bicycle, bought for Murray by Susan, inspiration to get his heart rate up and his weight down.

The scene seemed hugely incongruous. When Drena walked in, bearing her glass luncheon plate with its array of rabbit food, a sad little offering to a man who lives for cholesterol, I found myself pitying Pezim. Being made over at his age seemed painfully unnecessary. Drena is an attractive woman who seemed much younger than the man she was serving. Were it not for the fact that I had seen a picture of the bride-to-be, I might have made the blunder of asking him whether this woman was Susan.

Much money was spent in aid of connubial bliss. There was the construction of an enormous new house in Point Grey, at an early estimated cost of $5 million. Pezim gave Susan a spanking-new white Corvette, which very likely made up for the Lincoln Continental that never appeared after the nose job. There were more diamonds. And a condo at the fashionable Whistler ski resort, which also seemed incongruous, in view of Pezim's hatred of the cold.

There were, too, the usual pre-wedding social obligations to meet. The stripper who visited the Pezim offices. The stag the night of the Mike Tyson – Michael Spinks fight at Richard's on Richards, a popular broker hangout. The more restrained party at the Belmont Avenue home of Peter Brown. Pezim says that ninety-nine percent of his friends advised him not to get married.

On July 9, 1988, the inner circle of the chosen four hundred gathered on a yacht called the Hotei in Vancouver Harbour. There was Murray at the makeshift altar, waiting for his soon-to-be third wife. The band played "Here Comes the Bride". Then they played it again. And again. Someone passed Murray a card from Susan. It said that she needed more time to ponder the commitment she was about to make.

Susan says today that she played the prank because she was stressed out from planning a wedding that was far more lavish than the one she had envisaged. She says she remembers standing in the shower a few days before the wedding trying to figure out ways to "get back at" her fiancé for all the distress he had caused her. She thought it was funny, this little joke of hers.

Murray thought otherwise. A woman who knows him better than most had, in fact, forewarned him of Susan's intentions. She watched his face as he stood there, stuck, having to play to someone else's performance, waiting for Susan to arrive. Pezim was embarrassed. The observer believes that the marriage, to all intents and purposes, ended right there.

Finally, a helicopter hovered into view carrying the bride. She was later than even she had planned. Dresses flew up. Hanson descended onto the deck.

The ceremony was performed by the Reverend Valerie Reay, a United Church minister from Pemberton, B.C., and mother of a young woman named Tammy Patrick. Tammy had met Pezim on the stock circuit when she had worked as a broker. Tammy and Susan became friends. Indeed, after her mother performed her nuptial duties, Tammy herself gave a speech to the happy couple.

The occasion received mixed reviews.

Jimmy Pattison was so cheesed off by the delay in the ceremony that he hijacked the helicopter back to Vancouver as soon as the vows had been exchanged.

Susan had a falling-out with her matron of honour. They didn't speak the entire evening – and haven't spoken since.

Henny Youngman, an irrepressibly bad comic, did his standard five-minute turn. "You know why Jewish husbands die before their wives? Because they want to." Ba dum.

Michael Pezim, son of Murray, was best man. He told the

crowd that he hadn't been around for his father's first wedding and hadn't been invited to the second. Now here he was, best man, in the celebrations for marriage number three. Perhaps next time he could be master of ceremonies?

At the reception that evening, Susan gave her guests a $200-a-plate dinner. Yet, as they milled about and chatted, many of those so-called friends were saying behind her back that the marriage wouldn't last twenty-four hours.

Susan Hanson had defied the odds, the endless stream of Pezim nymphets, to become Susan Pezim. What she didn't know then, but what she swears now is beyond dispute, is that Tammy and Murray had slept together before that wretched day in July.

After the marriage there was much to do. Breast surgery. Setting up housekeeping. The newlyweds moved into a house in West Vancouver while they awaited the completion of their palatial Point Grey home. Susan flew around the globe searching for the right fabrics, the perfect decorative touches, for her massive interior-decorating mission.

Pezim, meanwhile, was trying to arrange an underwriting for Prime shares; he hoped for a listing on both the TSE and the VSE. This became his main concern. Business, after all, was business, and this was big business. Wives are just wives, small currency in Pezim's world. Like children. Like any form of true intimacy.

That same summer, Ned Goodman threw one of those lavish buffet parties where high-powered associates, comrades who deserve a bit of a pat, and a pack of media types get together to schmooze. This one was held at Stop 33, atop the Sutton Place Hotel, a room that offers a panorama of downtown Toronto.

The official reason for the festivities was to celebrate the amalgamation of Royex and Lacana and International Corona and Mascot and Galveston into one neat package called Corona. The unofficial reason for the festivities was that it would help provide much-needed reassurance to the institutional investors and other influential money-managers who were twitchy over Goodman's complex corporate structure and deal-making style. The new company, with Goodman as chairman and Steen as chief executive, presented a laser show with dry-ice effects. The bartenders served the then-fashionable Mexican beer called Corona Extra, which seemed terribly clever.

Murray Pezim was there, wandering around, hands clasped behind his back, ignored for much of the evening.

At one point, Goodman went to the podium, to offer the requisite words of greeting. He raised a glass to various corporate accomplishments. He toasted Peter Steen. He didn't toast Murray Pezim. What he did say was that the party was not meant to be an eastern version of Murray Pezim's wedding.

It was a joke. To Ned Goodman Murray Pezim is often a joke.

In August 1988, Lac applied to the Supreme Court of Ontario to begin the Hemlo fight all over again. Meanwhile, its appeal on the initial decision, which had granted the Williams mine to Corona, had yet to be heard by the Supreme Court of Canada. Now Lac was arguing that it had new evidence that would prove that key testimony at the first trial had been false. Lac supporters, all those investors who never believed the story Corona told in court, started to hope against hope that victory might be theirs. In September 1988, the sparring partners once again went to court.

Lac's case this time centred on evidence unearthed by a private investigator named Bruce Dunne, who clearly had a long history of private-eye work. One had only to look at him to see that this was so: Six-foot-three, 225 pounds, Dunne carried himself like a sad sack of a man who had to spend too many long nights in bad motels drinking rank coffee.

Dunne had done plenty of corporate gumshoe work. He had

dug up material on the Belzbergs at a time when Sam Belzberg, the hostile raider from Vancouver, was making an unwelcome takeover grab for Bache Securities of New York. Dunne had also put together a file on Peter Munk and his gold-mining company, American Barrick Resources, when Munk showed some interest in going after Consolidated Gold Fields, the gold-mining giant.

Dunne had been working on the Hemlo mystery since 1985. Lac had hired Kroll Associates, a high-powered New York private-investigation firm, to come up with evidence that would help their case against Corona. Kroll specialized in corporate work – takeovers, leveraged buyouts, that kind of situation.

The firm's founder, Jules Kroll, had walked smartly into the power-play arena that marked corporate America in the eighties. When I met him in his Manhattan offices in 1988, the former assistant district attorney was sucking a fat, juicy cigar. His suspenders were black with green polka dots; his tie was blue, decorated with white stars, green stripes, and red donkeys. Kroll at the time was busy tracking money, specifically the money squirrelled away by the deposed Philippines dictator Ferdinand Marcos. He didn't much like being interviewed. But he consented because he wanted to make one thing very clear: there was nothing Mickey Mouse about Kroll Associates, nothing Mickey Mouse about the people they hired.

Kroll had put Bill Kish, the company's senior investigator, on the Lac case. Kish in turn had hired Bruce Dunne. It was for Kish that Dunne had worked the Belzberg case, the Munk case. Kish liked what Dunne could do.

Dunne went to Timmins and started from ground zero. What was this Hemlo story and who was telling the truth? There were claims-staking records to be searched, witnesses to be interviewed. When, finally, he found Eddie B. ("The B's for Bullshitter") O'Neill, Dunne became convinced that the story put forward by Corona, Lac's adversaries, was, simply, bullshit.

It was Dunne who, with O'Neill's lead, discovered a staking discrepancy in the early days of Hemlo, when Don McKinnon, the prospector, had gone into the bush and struck the gentlemen's agreement with his fellow prospector John Larche, thus sealing what may have been the most profitable prospecting arrangement in Canadian mining history.

It was Dunne who came up with evidence that O'Neill's name was on the first twelve Hemlo claims that McKinnon had said were his.

Lac has never clearly explained why it didn't use any of the Kroll gatherings in its earlier litigation against Corona. In fact, Dunne says he was released from his Lac contract in 1987 and took the evidence he had gathered to a little company called Scintilore Explorations. Scintilore thought it had a case against Larche and McKinnon. It maintained that when Larche went staking in the bush that woolly winter of 1979 he had been instructed to stake those initial seventeen claims for a company called Geoex, and that Geoex was the contractor working for Scintilore. Scintilore's position was that the confusion over the O'Neill claims proved that when McKinnon told Larche he had already staked twelve of the seventeen claims, he, in truth, hadn't.

What has also never been satisfactorily explained is why Lac subsequently changed its mind and decided to use Dunne's evidence after all. Lac brought new lawyers in on the case. The staking discrepancy, the lawyers said, could put McKinnon's earlier testimony into serious question. When Round One began in the early courtroom days, in 1985, McKinnon had testified that it was he who started the Hemlo staking. Yet Dunne's evidence showed that the initial twelve Hemlo claims were registered not in McKinnon's name but in Eddie O'Neill's. That, said Lac, should have been enough to convince any court that McKinnon's testimony was perjured, or at the very least misleading.

If McKinnon was wrong on the actual Hemlo staking, who was to say that he was telling the truth when he testified that he went after the patented claims of Lola Williams while he was acting as an agent for Corona?

On a sunny day in October, as Bruce Dunne made his approach to the downtown Toronto courtroom, he shielded his face from a news photographer. It isn't good business for a private eye to have his mug splashed across the daily newspapers. It makes it tough to work undercover. Nevertheless, when Dunne slapped his hammy hand across his face, it created the wrong impression: it looked for all the world as if Lac, in hiring a private eye, had been involved in something underhanded, covert.

Dunne got his head kicked in on the stand. The business of the staking discrepancy got buried by discussions of the tactics Dunne had used in obtaining information. Invoices to Kroll had been tampered with, the name of Lac replaced with Scintilore's. Who was really paying the private investigator's bills? Scintilore? Lac? Dunne testified the tampering was merely an effort to correct past errors. He admitted he had lent his secretary $25,000 to buy shares in Scintilore. There had been the purchase of a guard dog to protect the girlfriend of one of the people who had assisted Dunne in his evidence-gathering. The guard dog, which was billed to Kroll three times over, responded only to commands given in French. Peter Allen, the head of Lac, was code-named Poppa.

There were other seemingly dirty tricks. Mr. Justice Richard Holland, the judge who had rendered the first decision on the Williams case in March 1986, had been tailed. His daughter had also been tailed. Dunne had sent an anonymous letter to the Ontario Provincial Police, alleging that Don McKinnon had stolen some recording documents from the mine recorder's office. The Cayman

Islands home of Nell Dragovan's one-time boyfriend was searched. All of which had cost Lac about $8 million in investigation fees.

In truth, Dunne's exploits were side issues. People on the Corona side had used investigators, too, so there was no question of their taking the moral high ground. It was the sheer tenacity of Alan Lenczner and Ron Slaght and the weakness of the Lac side – which produced ill-prepared witnesses in the first go-round and ill-equipped legal counsel in the second – that determined the final state of play.

In the October application, Alan Lenczner was his smooth, dapper, terrifying self. He is the kind of lawyer who knows when not to be nice to witnesses. Slaght is softer in presentation, but just as sharp. Together the team from McCarthy & McCarthy tore the Lac application apart. Lenczner played to the courtroom spectators. He made jokes. He would turn to the audience and raise an incredulous eyebrow as the various admissions about the Lac investigations came pouring out.

By the time Don McKinnon made his way to the witness stand, the true substance of the application had been long lost. Why did he forge his claims-staking, using O'Neill's tags and O'Neill's name on some of the claims?

Happens all the time, said McKinnon. "It's a decoy to keep away competitors." Mining recording offices "have their little spies," he said. It was better not to let any other prospectors figure out just what Don McKinnon was up to.

Mr. Justice Coulter Osborne accepted this explanation. In his decision in mid-October, he excoriated Dunne and his devious tactics. Then he tossed the Lac case aside. There would be no new trial. Corona had won again.

Pezim fumed about the despicable practices of the private eye. Trailing the judge, for Pete's sake. Trailing the judge's daughter. Shameless. It was all very reminiscent of the days of B.X.

Development and the phone tapping and the spying and the time when British Columbia investigators watched Marilyn Pezim disrobe in the couple's hotel room.

In the course of his investigation, Dunne worked up a dossier on Pezim. Attempts were made to link Pezim to the Mafia, to money-laundering. But there was no proof. "Pezim is well known in the brokerage community for promoting various stocks and then selling shares from the company's treasury in order to raise money," said Dunne's report. "This is what brokers on the Vancouver Stock Exchange refer to as a 'Pezim scam.' In the case of Corona Resources, sources indicate that the promotion and stock issuance were fully intended to be another Pezim scam. There was never any intention of discovering gold."

To the Vancouver stock-market watcher George Cross, Dunne said, "Start at the beginning. I heard you knew everything about this if anyone did."

Said Cross: "Jesus, if anyone ever knew everything, everybody would probably go to jail."

By the time Lac's application was dismissed, anyone who had watched the Hemlo tale from its inception understood that fact and fiction had been blended together so seamlessly that the truth about Hemlo would never be told.

The early days in the bush, the confusion over claims, would remain muddled. The whole issue of confidentiality, whether Lac acted improperly in going after the Williams property, is questionable in a business such as this. If Dennis Sheehan knew none of the potential of Hemlo before David Bell told him, then he wasn't a very good geologist. Sheehan was, in fact, a superb geologist. The notion of fiduciary duty? Alan Lenczner once told me that throughout the first trial he used to phone Ron Slaght every morning and say, "How are we arguing this again?"

To my mind, the largest questions are these. Did Murray

Pezim keep drilling Hemlo because he thought he could smell gold or because he was merely interested in pumping another stock play? The second is whether Don McKinnon would have bought that Williams property for himself and his partners or for Pezim's company.

No sooner had Lenczner and Slaght won that round than they found themselves in Ottawa, arguing before five Supreme Court of Canada judges who had assembled to hear the final Lac appeal. The lawyers explained one last time why Lac had behaved badly, how it had broken the bounds of fiduciary responsibility, how it had proposed a deal and had then grabbed the property.

Pezim, at this point, seemed uninterested in the case. In fact, he seemed lost. Ned Goodman, meanwhile, was upbeat, though his stock lolled between a disappointing $7 and a barely tolerable $9. Bay Street laid the blame for the seemingly depressed share price on something called the Ned Factor. The multiple-voting shares. The Byzantine deal-making. That, they said, was the Ned Factor.

Goodman had Corona, but little glory. Pezim had Prime, but it was young and hadn't yet found a winner.

Pezim also had a marriage that was going to hell.

It ended during the week between Christmas and New Year's, the week when Murray Pezim celebrates his birthday. Pezim usually likes to spend his birthday, which falls on December 29, in Paradise Valley. But for his sixty-seventh celebration, he thought Hawaii might be nice.

Susan had other plans. She thought it would be fun to have a party at the couple's condo at Whistler. After all, Peter Brown, Larry Page, and others in the Pezim circle spend their holidays at the popular ski resort, a three-hour drive up the B.C. coast from Vancouver. Besides, there's nothing going on at the VSE during that last week of the year.

Pezim hated the idea, but finally caved in. Forty or fifty people showed up at the condo. Many had driven up for the party from Vancouver, among them Nell Dragovan and her husband Chet Idziszek. Tammy Patrick was there. Pearl Whalley, too. Susan believes the party itself went well, that Murray had a great time.

Pezim has a different assessment: "I went up there and froze my balls off."

The day after the party, Susan went skiing. Murray went for a walk with Tammy Patrick and her mother Valerie, the minister, who occasionally led the service for the Whistler congregation, and who had presided over Murray and Susan's nuptials scant months before. Susan didn't think Tammy was interested in her husband. She says that at some point during the week, Tammy turned to her and asked, "How can you sleep with that old man?"

From Pezim's perspective, the marriage was crumbling. Susan was tough, uncompromising, militant. The way she would snap his cigarettes in two (a gesture that she found amusing but Pezim didn't). Tammy, on the other hand, was young, soft, pliant.

New Year's Eve, in the late afternoon, Susan, Tammy, and Pearl, all naked, were in the hot tub at the condo drinking champagne. Pezim arrived and joined them. That evening was one of those rare occasions on which he got drunk.

Early in the new year, the Pezims returned to Vancouver. Murray announced to Susan that he was checking into the Four Seasons Hotel until the Point Grey house was completed. Susan visited him there one afternoon and they made love. Susan says Murray had a habit of bitching at her for not being more interested in sex. She was trying to make amends. Then again, she adds, Murray couldn't always get it up.

That night Pezim told the *Vancouver Sun* columnist Denny Boyd that the marriage was kaput.

The next day, Susan was tooling around Vancouver. She

251

phoned Pezim's office from her car phone, checking in, as was her habit. Someone at Pez central conveyed the bombshell that had appeared in Boyd's column. She tried getting through to the man she had thought was still her husband. She was rerouted to one or another of Pezim's assistants. She phoned the paper, maintained that the marriage was alive and well. She complained that Denny Boyd had made her out to be "the worst gold-digging bitch on the face of the earth."

That afternoon she got together with friends. They drank. By the time she was able to reach Murray, Susan was smashed.

"You son of a bitch," she said to him.

"She knew it was coming," says Pezim today. "She said she didn't know, but she knew it was coming."

The next morning, the lawyers cut off her credit cards, her access to Pezim's bank accounts.

The press had a field day documenting the fact that in return for six months of married bliss, the very briefly Mrs. Pezim would receive a $3-million package, including $1 million in cash.

Pezim swore to the media that he would never remarry. He will now admit that he was already seeing Tammy when the marriage collapsed. "At that time I had been with her intimately, okay? Not like on a regular basis. I always had a lot of fun with Tammy."

What is it with Pezim and his women, I wanted to know.

"I love women," he told me. "Do you know, I love cuddling with women? Just hugging them and holding them. They're so soft and tender."

But why does he always gravitate toward this particular type?

"I seem always to pick girls from the other side of the tracks," he said. "I didn't fall in love with them. I tried to change them, improve them."

And they're so young.

"I think young women keep me young. I know physically they keep me young. I can get it up with a young girl. Some of the old gals, I can't get it up with them."

The Murray Pezim roast, sponsored by a group of British Columbia policemen and firemen, was held on Friday, March 31, 1989. This was pure Pezim. A real roast, done up in an imitative Friar's style, complete with a dais and a museum of comedians that included Pezim's cronies Henny Youngman, Milton Berle, and Red Buttons, as well as Joan Rivers and Don Rickles and more.

Pezim was once again in bachelor mode, though he was technically married still. In attendance for the roast were Bernice Pezim, Susan Pezim, Tammy Patrick, and Pearl Whalley.

Two days earlier, Murray's sister Frances had died in Toronto of Parkinson's disease. Her daughter Vicki had immediately phoned her uncle Norman in Arizona to give him the bad news. She needed to make funeral arrangements. She assumed that Norman and Murray would both need to make travel plans to come to Toronto.

"My uncle Norman seemed mildly upset," says Vicki. "He seemed more upset about the roast. He said to me it couldn't have happened at a worse time. I told them I would be accommodating to them. If they wanted Thursday, fine. If they wanted to make it Friday morning, fine. Half an hour later, I got a call back to say he had spoken to my uncle Murray. My uncle Murray said he would like her 'held over' to Sunday. I explained my mother was not the Pope. In Jewish you get buried immediately."

The funeral was held on Friday for the woman who had consoled Murray in his first big crack-up, who had shared with him her own torment when she had had her own breakdown, envisaging little men crawling out of the walls, who had worshipped both her brothers. Norman attended the funeral. Murray attended the roast.

It was a cosmic event in the life of Murray Pezim. Rickles, Youngman, Rivers, Buttons. The lesser comedic talents of Norm Crosby and Jan Murray. An audience peppered with the Vancouver establishment: Jack Poole, then the head of the troubled real-estate developer BCED; Eleni Skalbania, wife of the then financially troubled real-estate flipper Nelson; Joe Cohen, who thus far had escaped any financial woes, which made him very unlike the rest of the Vancouver upper crust.

Milton Berle offered tired bits of Canadian content, about his own introduction having been as sincere as "Margaret Trudeau saying 'ouch' on her honeymoon" – a joke a mere ten years out of date.

He said his performance would be short, "and if you believe that you'll also believe there'll be a Svend Robinson Jr." – a joke that was out of date from its inception.

Henny Youngman told the joke that wouldn't die. "Why do Jewish guys die before their wives? Because they want to."

Joan Rivers said the more appropriate purpose of the roast would have been to pay tribute to Pezim's three wives: "St. Bernice, St. Marilyn, and St. Susan, or the white Robin Givens," referring to the similarly compensated ex-spouse of the heavyweight boxing champion Mike Tyson.

The roast was dreary. As damp as could be. When it was over, Pezim invited Bernice to have a coffee, an offer she accepted. But when they arrived at the curb outside the hotel, Susan was waiting beside a rented Rolls-Royce, draped in sable that flowed down to her ankles.

Susan had attended because she was interested in reuniting with Pezim. Murray was distracted. He wanted to talk to Bernice, but was interested in fondling Tammy, who was also on hand. A puzzled Bernice wondered who this Pearl person was, who had joined the group at curbside. And there they stood in the gathering rain, this curious collection of women, Pezim's nuclear family, the Pez brigade.

Bernice remembers the evening well. "Susan looked at my raincoat," she recalls. "Then she turned to Murray and said, 'Look at Bernice. She's dressed so poor. Why don't you buy my sable for her? I'll give it to you for $40,000.'"

With that, Murray, Susan, Tammy, and Pearl clambered into the car.

Bernice hung back. "Murray's sitting in the front seat and I'm standing there and one of them says, 'There's no room in here for anybody else.' When I looked at Murray sitting there with these three chippies, I thought this is exactly what his mother said he was going to end up with."

For a time, Pezim himself thought otherwise. On a trip to Toronto that summer, he invited Bernice over to the Four Seasons, where he was staying. He said he wanted to get back together. To get married again.

He expressed these intentions to Ned Goodman, Alan Lenczner, John Ing, and his brother Norman, all of whom apparently agreed that remarrying Bernice might be a heck of an idea, a salvation of sorts. Bernice saw some charm in it, too.

"He had this big house in Vancouver," she says. "He wanted someone who would be a lady and a hostess for him. I've seen that house and I thought how nice it would be to have a place for the six grandchildren. I began to think that maybe I would give it a chance."

Bernice went so far as to buy a cocktail dress and other clothing to wear at the parties that would surely be part of the wedding festivities.

She remembers that any thoughts of remarriage ran aground in August. It was the month in which Pezim was reborn. There was first the Supreme Court of Canada decision on August 11 ruling

255

that Corona had formally and finally won ownership of the Williams mine. Then, too, there was new excitement on the Vancouver Stock Exchange as the Eskay Creek gold find started to show potential.

By mid-August, Pezim was being credited for single-handedly reviving the flagging fortunes of the VSE. The exchange that month repeatedly hit record share-trading volumes: thirty-five million shares one day, then forty million, then a phenomenal fifty-three million shares. Fourteen of the top twenty volume traders were Pezim's. That month, he had fifty companies sitting in Prime Resources, including control of Calpine Resources, which held fifty percent of the key Eskay property.

Pezim had never flown so high. There was a flurry of Prime press releases on the Eskay results, most spectacularly on high-grade gold holes drilled by Calpine. Options were meted out, then repriced. Deals were struck. There was so much excitement that the office of the superintendent of brokers started to pay very close attention.

One day, Bernice Pezim happened to be flipping through a newspaper in her uptown Toronto condominium. There she came upon a story about her one-time husband and potential husband-to-be, announcing his intention to wed one Tammy Patrick: "Tammy Reformed Cocaine Addict. I think that was her last name. Reformed Cocaine Addict. I was hurt. My first feeling was a feeling of relief. That God had done me a favour, because how could I live with this man?"

The toothy Tammy, blonde, blue-eyed, mid-twenties, had indeed been a cocaine addict. Had admitted as much to the press at the time she had aligned herself with Pezim. In fact, Pezim had shipped her down to Arizona to stay with Susan after the Susan-Murray match had fizzled. It was Susan who introduced Tammy to Cocaine Anonymous.

"It's changed my life," Tammy said of her support group, in an interview in the *Vancouver Sun*. "I don't need to have alcohol or cocaine to enjoy myself any more."

She went on to explain that the cleansing process had been assisted by spiritual pursuits – including an amulet-making business she had embarked on.

"It has a lot to do with New Age philosophy. It's that we all have the power within ourselves to heal ourselves, not just physical ailments but also mental."

Tammy told the reporter that as soon as Pezim's mansion was complete she would be moving in, though not solo. There were Mark Gastineau, the former football player, and Brigitte Neilsen, the actress, both of whom planned to move in and call the Pezim palace home. "We're all very close friends," Tammy explained.

Gastineau, six foot six, 280 pounds, was in the process of transmuting himself from football player to boxer. There was even talk about his going up against Mike Tyson, until it became clear that Mark was as wuzzy in the ring as Neilsen was on the movie screen. Nevertheless, Gastineau and thereby Neilsen had stayed with the Pezim circus because Pezim had come up with another idea. In September, 1989, he bought the B.C. Lions football club.

Were it not for the sense of national pride that the Canadian Football League instils, at least in some of us, one would be inclined to view an investment in a CFL team about as favourably as, say, a fast-food chicken franchise or musical taped greeting cards. To buy the Lions, Pezim had pledged the net smelter royalty he has through Corona as collateral against a $2-million line of credit extended by Central Capital, the Toronto trust conglomerate. The approval went through Peter Cole, then head of Central, a friend of Ned Goodman's and a CFL fan.

And so in the fall of 1989 Pezim had in hand Tammy

Patrick, Mark Gastineau, Brigitte Neilsen, and a lumbering foot-ball club. Still to make an appearance was Doug Flutie, Heisman Trophy winner at Boston College in 1984 and a quarterback made famous by his Hail Mary pass.

The stock exposure, the sports exposure, the love-nest exposure, the entertainment-personality exposure. All of it had made Murray Pezim's life wilder, flashier, more outrageous than ever. Feeling full of himself, he readily, even eagerly, accepted an invitation to speak in Toronto at a United Jewish Appeal fund-raiser. Pezim's avowed dislike of the East does not extend so far that he won't take up an offer to do a star turn when called upon.

When he rose before the UJA, Pezim told a few jokes, typical Pezim-type jokes, like the one about the man who decides to have a hundred-dollar bill tattooed on his penis "because I like to keep my money in hand, I like to watch my money grow, and my wife can blow $100 faster than anyone."

In the weeks that followed, a number of people who were in attendance that evening mentioned how vile they found the Pezim performance. The Toronto investment manager Ira Gluskin went so far as to pillory Pezim in his then weekly *Financial Times* column. Gluskin didn't mince words. He said the speech had been revolting, embarrassing, obscene.

"Guys like these give the stock market in Canada a bad name. People come to believe that these highly visible promoters are representative of public companies when, in fact, they are highly unrepresentative. With Pezim, the press is guilty of creating a personality out of a louse."

I wondered about that. A louse. Seemed a bit strong. Gluskin subsequently wrote an apology that covered some of his criticisms, but not the louse part.

Some people dislike what Murray Pezim represents. Some people dislike Murray Pezim period. They are offended by his behaviour, the company he keeps, the foulness of his language. It seems to me that such comment is of no consequence.

The real issue was raised subsequently to Gluskin's column, when the superintendent of brokers alleged that Pezim and his group had played dirty during the Eskay euphoria in August. The allegation of improper repricing of stock options. The allegation of an improper lapse in public disclosure over a temporarily stalled placement of shares and warrants. The allegation, in essence, that Pezim was a stock-market cheat.

If the SOB was right, then Gluskin was right. Pezim was a louse. Or was he?

CHAPTER 11

Swan Song

T hey buried Sam Ciglen on October 15, 1990, at Holy Blossom Memorial Park in Toronto. I had tried to contact Ciglen in the months before his death to talk about the old days, the scam days in the forties, when Toronto was a penny-stock hustle. But when I went to his seedy offices in downtown Toronto, above Winston's Restaurant on Adelaide Street, the receptionist said that Ciglen, in his mid-eighties, had cancer and didn't often make it in to work.

When he died, the Toronto *Sun* ran an obit on the business pages under the headline "Fraud Lawyer Dies." Twenty years earlier, Ciglen had been disbarred and had served nine months of a two-year tax-evasion sentence in Kingston Penitentiary. Ciglen had followed his pen experience with a $1.8-million stock fraud.

I saw Murray Pezim the day they buried Sam Ciglen. It was Pezim who mentioned the promoter's death. He cast his mind back to a post-war Toronto. To the particular day when a broker named Max Guthrie walked into the Pezims' Rogers Road butcher shop and ordered those centre-cut loin chops. To the day Pezim placed his entire savings in the good hands of this man Guthrie, only to watch his whole investment drain through a penny-hope-less company called Duvay Gold Mines, which was run by Sam Ciglen. Ciglen had been a real operator when Pezim first came on the mining scene, in the days when Bay Street was overrun with boiler rooms and the brokers used to hang out at the Savarin Restaurant and pray for the big score.

Pezim and I found ourselves together the day of Ciglen's funeral because we and a couple of hundred other people were assembled at Toronto's Four Seasons Hotel at yet another roast, this time for Ned Goodman. Pezim had flown in from Vancouver to perform his duties as one of the roasters at the black-tie event. When I came upon him he was wandering through the champagne crowd, in a tux, Coke in hand. He seemed out of place, friendless, a man apart. He was, as well, preoccupied by the securities investigation in Vancouver, the one that had him up on charges of insider trading.

That Sam had been buried just hours earlier seemed a fitting harmonic convergence to the story of Murray Pezim. Here he was back in his home town, the place where he had started to hone that grift sense he has. But much of what had once made Toronto home had long since disappeared. The butcher shops were gone. Izzy and Becky were gone. Frances and Rose were gone. The mining promoters, people like Ciglen, had largely drifted away or passed away, replaced by a new kind of hustler, sharpies who would crawl out of the woodwork every so often with some suspect stock – an AIDS disinfectant or bizarre prenatal product.

Earl Glick, Pezim's first partner, was still resident on the Bridle Path, but the two had long ago ceased to be friends. When Pezim decides that he dislikes someone, he dislikes that someone for good.

Izzy Rotterman was still padding around his multi-million-dollar condo in his supple baby-alligator loafers, but he and Pezim ran hot and cold, particularly at times when Rotterman decided he had been burned by Pezim. Rotterman had, in fact, sued Pezim, Art Clemiss, Ned Goodman, Tim Hoare, Peter Brown – the whole lot of them – in January, 1990, alleging a manipulation in Prime shares and alleging, too, that the group had touted Prime shares to the public claiming inside information on the Eskay Creek property. The substance of the allegation was that the supposed touting had hammered Rotterman's own investment, and he and a co-plaintiff wanted $1 million in recompense. Rotterman dropped the suit months before the Goodman roast and wouldn't elaborate on why he had done so. He once complained to me that Pezim will make money for a stranger "while his best friends have their tongues hanging out. The last person that meets Murray is his best friend. Murray has a memory only for today."

In Toronto, that fall of 1990, there was no gathering of long-time Pezim pals. There would be no gathering of family, of Pezim's two daughters, Cheryl and Nanci, who live in Toronto. Cheryl had married for a second time and would soon move to a home in north Toronto, which she would have professionally refurbished, then decorate herself. Nanci had given birth to her third child. Neither daughter saw much of their father, though he had, on occasion, come through for them when they needed him.

It seemed strange to watch the evening's investment brotherhood commingling with a man like Pezim. For many, for those who didn't know him, he was the evening's curiosity, a touch of freak show amid this cluster of a wannabe Toronto establishment.

The regular Goodman troupe had gathered. Tim Hoare, Paul Carroll, Peter Steen, Myron Gottlieb – all the Blackbirds. In an interview before the roast, Paul Carroll explained to me how each of the Blackbirds ranked in his tolerance of Pezim. Goodman and he were the most tolerant. Then Tim Hoare. Then Gottlieb. And finally, Steen, least of all.

Ron Slaght was there, as was his Corona litigation associate

Alan Lenczner, or C.S., for cocksucker, as Pezim affectionately calls him. Peter Cole, then the head of Central Capital, was there, with the television personality Dini Petty. The most notable absence was Peter Brown, who was cycling through the south of France, having attended a meeting of the YPO, the Young Presidents' Organization. And Art Clemiss, who, having announced his retirement, was sailing around Grand Cayman Island.

At Pezim's table were John Ing and several institutional investors who were less than enamoured of Corona. They disliked the multiple-voting shares, the interwoven deals, the labyrinthine corporate structure that had led to the Ned Factor tag that Goodman wanted to shake.

I sat beside Pezim and watched as he pored over his notes for his speech. Pezim the performer, Pezim the Vegas aspirant. A number of people approached, said their hellos. Pezim moaned through the evening. About how he no longer wanted to support Tammy Patrick. About how he couldn't identify the wretched nouvelle-looking cuisine on his plate. He seemed more a cantankerous old woman than the Murray Pezim shtickster the papers had come to love.

For the event, the organizers had put together a parody of *Forbes* magazine called *Factor*, as in Ned Factor. There was also a video show with various Ned tributes, and a voice-over by the Beatles:

> Blackbird singing in the dead of night
> Take these broken wings and learn to fly
> All your life
> You were only waiting for this moment to arise.

Pezim told me once that the Blackbirds had considered enlarging their number to six, the sixth Blackbird being Pezim. It never happened. Never would.

When his turn came, Pezim shuffled to the podium to pay a tribute of sorts to Goodman. He told the crowd, many of whom had watched ABC-TV's *PrimeTime Live* exposé of the Vancouver Stock Exchange a few days before, that the show was pulling together a piece on Goodman, called *Smoke and Mirrors*. He also said, in reference to the securities investigation, that he had retired from the Vancouver scene. "We're opening our new exchange in Scottsdale. Folks, I want to invite you down."

There wasn't a whole lot of humour in Pezim that night, and I wondered whether someone had advised him to launder his comments. The vulgarity of the United Jewish Appeal dinner was still talked about, and a number of his associates told me that the crass manner was what prevented them from spending much time with Murray.

As I watched him up there that night, in front of the crowd, I pondered the rollercoaster that he had ridden for more than forty years. In trying to analyse the man, I had ridden one of my own. He's a good guy. No, he's not. He's an honest man. Perhaps that's not the case. He's compassionate. Hardly. Somewhere on the ride one thing had become very clear. The clownish image served up for the media was all surface. What was on the inside wasn't very funny at all.

Pezim stayed at the Four Seasons that night, and flew back to Vancouver first thing the following morning. The week before the Goodman roast, the VSE's composite index – the monitor of the performance of VSE-listed stocks – fell below the 600 mark, its lowest level ever. It slid even more over the winter months, to under 500. The average stock price hovered around eighty cents. At the height of the Hemlo excitement, it had been three bucks. Peter Brown's securities house, L.O.M. Western, found itself offering few fresh stock offerings of the kind that had made Brown and Pezim rich men.

Over the next few months, Pezim learned that he had been cleared on the insider-trading charges. But the regulators adjudged that he misled the exchange by granting stock options without making material changes known to the public. For this, the Securities Commission barred him from trading for a year. He appealed, though the appeal will not be heard until December, 1991, and probably won't be resolved until the spring of 1992.

Pezim is allowed to play the market in the interim, but he found himself, as he had in the B.X. Development case and in the fight over the Williams mine, in the middle of a muddle that could take a long time to resolve.

He spent most of the winter in Arizona. I called him periodically to see whether he was up or down, supercharged or burned out. He always had a quotable quote at hand.

"Take away my trading privileges? Fuck, the public would burn their building down. Are you kidding? Could you see the mass revolution? Even Gorbachev hasn't got the strength to do that."

He had plans. He was thinking of backing two heavyweight Soviet boxers, Alexander Zolkin and Albert Gugikov, in their hoped-for North American careers. Conversations with Pezim just wouldn't be the same, would be terribly disappointing, were it not for such schemes. Then, too, there was the B.C. Lions football team to promote. There was a fight with Susan over the prenuptial package that gave her $1 million in cash and $2 million in stuff. Susan says the cash never materialized, just as the Lincoln Continental never materialized. They finally settled on a sum that Susan will not disclose, though she did say she had her diamond engagement ring appraised at $70,000. Her $30,000-plus wedding dress had been sold for a couple thou through a second-hand Vancouver dress shop made the news. In 1991, Susan made plans to marry someone other than Murray Pezim.

The most important project Pezim had on the go was the

summer's drilling season in the B.C. interior. As winter became spring, Pezim's companies started to resurface. He was touting a new mining play in the Eskay Creek area – formally called the Rock & Roll Project – a gold-exploration play involving two of his latest companies, Eurus Resources and Thios Resources. There were plenty of other projects under way, stretching north into the less-known Galore Creek area.

All told, Pezim's Prime Equities – Son of Prime, like the second coming of Jesus Christ – had sixty exploration companies on the go in 1991, most of them leftovers from his first Prime foray. In mid-April, he announced he had struck another financing agreement with the Keevils' Teck Corp., giving Teck a fifty-percent interest for taking a company's property into production. Pezim liked working with the Teck people, had done so ever since the deal he struck a decade earlier to finance Hemlo.

Meanwhile, the people at Corona had moved their head offices, and with them Peter Steen, from Toronto to Vancouver, the better to manage the Eskay Creek project itself. Goodman resigned as company chairman, though no-one believed that anything that got done at Corona got done without Goodman's say-so. The sparring for control of Eskay had settled into a working arrangement of sorts, though few felt that the corporate alignments would hold for long. By the summer of 1991, Placer Dome had a forty-four percent interest in Stikine, which had half of Eskay Creek. Corona had the rest of Stikine and all of Calpine, which had the other half of Eskay. But Placer had lots of cash; Corona had little, and further deal-making between the two companies seemed inevitable.

Mining experts say the Eskay ore body will produce, at a conservative estimate, three million ounces of gold. Construction of a road linking the mine site and the Cassiar Highway was expected to begin the summer of 1991. Questions have been raised about problematic ground conditions, and the difficulties that might arise in constructing a mine. The annual sixty-foot snowfall is another obvious hindrance. But no-one was suggesting that Eskay wouldn't happen. A production estimate for finally pulling gold from Eskay is forecast for 1994.

As Pezim pursued his new corporate pursuits, there were persistent rumours on Bay Street that Ned Goodman was about to do away with the multiple-voting share structure of Corona. "The market wants a simple, single voting structure for Corona's gold assets and is weary of the constant financial and corporate gymnastics," said one analyst's report.

Gordon Capital was called in to work on a corporate restructuring aimed at making Corona more appealing to shareholders. But when Corona finally announced its structure proposal, it turned out to be another Goodman voting pyramid with a small number of shareholders controlling the assets of the operating company. The company reverted to its Pez-era name – International Corona.

Though the fight for Hemlo was still a fairly fresh entry in the annals of corporate Canada, both the Williams mine and the David Bell mine had started to age. Annual production had begun to drop. By 1991, though the mines still had fifteen years of production, Corona needed either to acquire or to explore new gold properties to keep it in the top tier of Canadian gold-producers. Which is where Eskay came in.

In late May, an aggressive, many say brilliant, entrepreneur named Peter Munk announced that his American Barrick was proposing a merger with a U.S. gold operator named Newmont, which, had it been successful, would have created the world's second-largest gold-mining house after Minorco, the South African mining giant. Gold-stock watchers started talking about synergies and cost efficiencies and a new world order for gold-miners, one that would include only very large, very powerful mining houses. Such an order would affect a company like Corona, which by 1991 certainly didn't appear to have the stuff of a mining giant. But even if the landscape were to change for the operators, it wouldn't affect a dealer like Pezim. The big mining companies will always need the small man, the prospector, the promoter.

By early summer, Pezim still felt anxious about the regulatory limbo he was in. He started raving about the conspiracy charges he was going to lay hither and yon against his enemies in the Securities Commission. The Vancouver investment community is so peeved by the aggressive manner in which Wade Nesmith, the superintendent of brokers, is prosecuting Howe Street, that the SOB, they say, can be assured he'll have a damned hard time finding employment when his SOB tenure is up in December, 1992.

Nesmith came to the SOB's office in 1987, first as manager of compliance under SOB Neil de Gelder. I once had dinner with the two thirtysomething lawyers when they were still relatively new to their jobs. They had a five-year plan, like some sort of socialist agrarian policy, one that would force the regreening of the Vancouver Stock Exchange. They wanted to make it an internationally competitive venture-capital market, one that would attract funds to British Columbia, one that would be seen as a fair and efficient securities market.

It was the last bit they were having trouble with, the last bit that even today Nesmith has trouble with. It's not that he wants to get rid of all the warts, he explained to me a couple of years later, when Pezim was in the midst of his appeal, it's that he wants to get investors to "see the risks. And to know the game isn't rigged." That, he said, means making changes to the way the game is played. Enforcement, he added, was an inefficient way to regulate. The efficiencies had to come at the front end, through strict listing requirements, an advance sifting of the good from the bad.

There would, I was sure, be gloriously screwball stock promotions romping through the exchange listings when Nesmith departed. Perhaps not as many as when he arrived, but they would be there nonetheless, making the great press copy they've always made, lending a crooked image to the exchange that its advocates have always maintained is undeserved.

Peter Brown once gave me a lecture on this very point. I was heading into the Prime building on West Hastings in Vancouver as he was heading out. He was smoothly attired, as usual, smoking a cigarette, as usual, on his way to the brown Rolls-Royce parked outside. The press, he said, letting the word moisten distastefully in his mouth, walks into a story with a negative attitude. The VSE was not a scam-riddled marketplace and he was pretty damned tired of having it portrayed as such. It was the Toronto Stock Exchange, he said in that unctuous way that he has, that harboured the National Business Systems, the Fidelity Trusts, the Oslers, referring to the owner-pillaged credit-card manufacturer, a defunct trust, and an owner-pillaged brokerage.

This was true. The TSE had made multi-million-dollar mistakes. This was not the VSE's *modus operandi*. Those who knew how to work the VSE well – the creators of crummy little companies touting the latest hair-revival or hair-removal technique – were in it for quick dough, nothing like the magnitude of the disasters Brown cited.

Brown himself, of course, has made size dough on the VSE. When Brown reminded me of how the exchange had raised $8 billion in its history, I found myself wondering just how many millions of that had been made by Brown personally. Much of the money that has come Brown's way has been made off the companies that Pezim has promoted. It is the Pezpromotion that lent credence to Brown's argument that the VSE had done more for the exploration side of the country's mining industry than its eastern counterpart.

In the early summer of 1991 I had a phone call from someone in Pezim's office. Pezim was rounding up people for his salmon tournament, a weekend party for Prime staff, local brokers, and investors, held every August at Sonora Lodge on Sonora Island in B.C. Though Pezim was growing old, was just months away from his seventieth birthday, he was certainly not in retirement mode. He was promoting his sixty stocks. He was in the news for matching, along with unnamed friends and the B.C. Lions, the $100,000 reward on a four-year-old boy gone missing in Victoria. Then he announced that he and other Howe Street types would also be paying the $150,000 fee to hire a U.S. private investigator, Jay J. Armes, to find the boy. "What is money?" asked The Pez of the press. "Get me the kid back. Take it from an old man – life is much more precious."

He phoned to say that *Sports Illustrated* would be devoting twelve pages to a story about him in its August issue. "They shot me in Vegas. They shot me in Arizona," he said of the magazine's photo crew. The piece would be a sports-mining mélange, the way Pez told it. Something told me that if the magazine did run such a story, with the B.C. Lions and Mark Gastineau and Doug Flutie et al., they'd add some Pezgirls to the sports-mining pot.

But one had to wonder how much Pez promotion he had left in him. Nesmith doesn't believe, as some have suggested, that the eventual passing of Pezim will cripple the exchange. "One day he will go," said Nesmith. "The market will continue."

This seems reasonable. The VSE will survive, and it will continue to be what Paul Carroll once described to me as a punter's market. Punting in the British sense of the word. No better than a bet placed with a bookie. No better than the boxing wagers

Pezim placed back in the forties when he was hanging around Jackie Beale's card club in north Toronto. No better than Vegas.

But Pezim will leave a permanent imprint. Because of Hemlo. Because of Eskay. For those who have found him endearing, because of his colossal failures and his propensity for self-destruction. Those who took a drubbing on the same Pez failures will remember him unkindly. Even at that, The Pez was no louse. At least I don't think so.

Pezim once told me that "like all fairy tales there'll be a beautiful ending." He was talking solely about the trading ban. It is too far-fetched to imagine that Pezim's life beyond the stock market will reach a happy conclusion by anyone's standards. There was too much emptiness. Too much void. Someone close to the man once told me that the people who will miss Pezim the most will be his three children, the ones who love him unconditionally, the ones who will have lost their father twice, the first time in the sixties, when they lost him to the market. When that happened Pezim shed his first skin, the one you can catch him in when you watch the old Pezim home movies, the ones where he looks a little goofy, as skinny as a toothpick, happy. Before Murray Pezim became The Pez.

Index

273

INDEX

INDEX

The Pez was set in Monotype Bodoni Book.
Bodoni Book is a Modern typeface designed by Morris Benton
and introduced in 1910 by ATF to provide a type, suited
to lengthy composition, that honours the refined, elegant spirit
of Giambattista Bodoni's 1789 prototype. Chapter titles
and display capitals are set in Benton's turn-of-the-century
Gothic, Franklin Gothic Extra Condensed.

Book design by
James Ireland Design Inc.
Typesetting by MacTrix DTP